# THE PANJAB, NORTH-WEST FRONTIER PROVINCE AND KASHMIR

# THE PANJAB, NORTH-WEST FRONTIER PROVINCE AND KASHMIR

JAMES DOUIE

GYAN

*Published by*

Gyan Publishing House
5, Ansari Road
Daryaganj, New Delhi-110002
Phone: 011-47034999, 9811692060
E-mail: books@gyanbooks.com

*Distribution Network*
gyanbooks.com
India, USA, Canada, UK, Australia, France



ISBN : 978-81-212-3871-7 (PB)
First Published, Cambridge, 1916

2nd Impression 2020

*Printed at:* Gyan Press, Delhi.

# THE PANJAB, NORTH-WEST FRONTIER PROVINCE AND KASHMIR

BY

SIR JAMES DOUIE, M.A., K.C.S.I.

Cambridge:
at the University Press
1916

# EDITOR'S PREFACE

IN his opening chapter Sir James Douie refers to the fact that the area treated in this volume—just one quarter of a million square miles—is comparable to that of Austria-Hungary. The comparison might be extended; for on ethnographical, linguistic and physical grounds, the geographical unit now treated is just as homogeneous in composition as the Dual Monarchy. It is only in the political sense and by force of the ruling classes, temporarily united in one monarch, that the term *Osterreichisch* could be used to include the Poles of Galicia, the Czechs of Bohemia and Moravia, the Szeklers, Saxons and more numerous Rumanians of Transylvania, the Croats, Slovenes and Italians of "Illyria," with the Magyars of the Hungarian plain.

The term *Panjábi* much more nearly, but still imperfectly, covers the people of the Panjáb, the North-West Frontier Province, Kashmír and the associated smaller Native States. The Sikh, Muhammadan and Hindu Jats, the Kashmírís and the Rájputs all belong to the tall, fair, leptorrhine Indo-Aryan main stock of the area, merging on the west and south-west into the Biluch and Pathán Turko-Iranian, and fringed in the hill districts on the north with what have been described as products of the "contact metamorphism" with the Mongoloid tribes of Central Asia. Thus, in spite of the inevitable blurring of boundary lines, the political divisions treated together in this volume, form a fairly clean-cut geographical unit.

Sir James Douie, in this work, is obviously living over again the happy thirty-five years which he devoted to the service of North-West India: his accounts of the physiography, the flora and fauna, the people and the administration are essentially the personal recollections of one who has first studied the details as a District Officer and has afterwards corrected his perspective, stage by stage, from the successively higher view-point of a Commissioner, the Chief Secretary, Financial Commissioner, and finally as Officiating Lieut.-Governor. No one could more appropriately undertake the task of an accurate and well-proportioned thumb-nail sketch of North-West India and, what is equally important to the earnest reader, no author could more obviously delight in his subject.

T. H. H.

ALDERLEY EDGE,
*March 9th*, 1916.

# NOTE BY AUTHOR

My thanks are due to the Government of India for permission to use illustrations contained in official publications. Except where otherwise stated the numerous maps included in the volume are derived from this source. My obligations to provincial and district gazetteers have been endless. Sir Thomas Holdich kindly allowed me to reproduce some of the charts in his excellent book on *India*. The accuracy of the sections on geology and coins may be relied on, as they were written by masters of these subjects, Sir Thomas Holland and Mr R. B. Whitehead, I.C.S. Chapter XVII could not have been written at all without the help afforded by Mr Vincent Smith's *Early History of India*. I have acknowledged my debts to other friends in the "List of Illustrations."

J. M. D.

8 *May* 1916.

# CONTENTS

## TABLES

# LIST OF ILLUSTRATIONS

# CHAPTER I

## AREAS AND BOUNDARIES

**Introductory.**—Of the provinces of India the Panjáb must always have a peculiar interest for Englishmen. Invasions by land from the west have perforce been launched across its great plains. The English were the first invaders who, possessing sea power, were able to outflank the mountain ranges which guard the north and west of India. Hence the Panjáb was the last, and not the first, of their Indian conquests, and the courage and efficiency of the Sikh soldiery, even after the guiding hand of the old Maháraja Ranjít Singh was withdrawn, made it also one of the hardest. The success of the early administration of the province, which a few years after annexation made it possible to use its resources in fighting men to help in the task of putting down the mutiny, has always been a matter of just pride, while the less familiar story of the conquests of peace in the first sixty years of British rule may well arouse similar feelings.

**Fig. 1. Arms of Panjáb.**

**Scope of work.**—A geography of the Panjáb will fitly embrace an account also of the North West Frontier

Province, which in 1901 was severed from it and formed into a separate administration, of the small area recently placed directly under the government of India on the transfer of the capital from Calcutta to Delhi, and of the native states in political dependence on the Panjáb Government. It will also be convenient to include Kashmír and the tribal territory beyond the frontier of British India which is politically controlled from Peshávar. The whole tract covers ten degrees of latitude and eleven of longitude. The furthest point of the Kashmír frontier is in 37° 2′ N., which is much the same as the latitude of Syracuse. In the south-east the Panjáb ends at 27° 4′ N., corresponding roughly to the position of the southernmost of the Canary Islands. Lines drawn west from Peshávar and Lahore would pass to the north of Beirut and Jerusalem respectively. Multán and Cairo are in the same latitude, and so are Delhi and Teneriffe. Kashmír stretches eastwards to longitude 80° 3′ and the westernmost part of Wazíristán is in 69° 2′ E.

**Distribution of Area.**—The area dealt with is roughly 253,000 square miles. This is but two-thirteenths of the area of the Indian Empire, and yet it is less by only 10,000 square miles than that of Austria-Hungary including Bosnia and Herzegovina. The area consists of:

| | | sq. miles |
|---|---|---|
| (1) | The Panjáb .. .. .. .. .. .. | 97,000 |
| (2) | Native States dependent on Panjáb Government .. | 36,500 |
| (3) | Kashmír .. .. .. .. .. .. .. | 81,000 |
| (4) | North West Frontier Province .. .. .. | 13,000 |
| (5) | Tribal territory under the political control of the Chief Commissioner of North West Frontier Province, roughly | 25,500 |

Approximately 136,000 square miles may be classed as highlands and 117,000 as plains, and these may be distributed as follows over the above divisions:

| | | Highlands sq. miles | Plains sq. miles |
|---|---|---|---|
| (1) | Panjáb, British .. .. .. | 11,000 | 86,000 |
| (2) | Panjáb, Native States .. .. | 12,000 | 24,500 |
| (3) | Kashmír .. .. .. .. | 81,000 | — |
| (4) | North West Frontier Province .. | 6,500 | 6,500 |
| (5) | Tribal Territory .. .. .. | 25,500 | — |

On the north the highlands include the Himalayan and sub-Himalayan (Siwálik) tracts to the south and east of the Indus, and north of that river the Muztagh-Karakoram range and the bleak salt plateau beyond that range reaching almost up to the Kuenlun mountains. To the west of the Indus they include those spurs of the Hindu Kush which run into Chitrál and Dir, the Buner and Swát hills, the Safed Koh, the Wazíristán hills, the Sulimán range, and the low hills in the trans-Indus districts of the North West Frontier Province.

**Boundary with China.**—There is a point to the north of Hunza in Kashmír where three great mountain chains, the Muztagh from the south-east, the Hindu Kush from the south-west, and the Sarikol (an offshoot of the Kuenlun) from the north-east, meet. It is also the meeting-place of the Indian, Chinese, and Russian empires and of Afghánistán. Westwards from this the boundary of Kashmír and Chinese Turkestán runs for 350 miles (omitting curves) through a desolate upland lying well to the north of the Muztagh-Karakoram range. Finally in the north-east corner of Kashmír the frontier impinges on the great Central Asian axis of the Kuenlun. From this point it turns southwards and separates Chinese Tibet from the salt Lingzi Thang plains and the Indus valley in Kashmír, and the eastern part of the native state of Bashahr, which physically form a portion of Tibet.

**Boundary with United Provinces.**—The south-east corner of Bashahr is a little to the north of the great Kedárnáth peak in the Central Himálaya and of the source of the Jamna. Here the frontier strikes to the west dividing Bashahr from Teri Garhwál, a native state under the control of the government of the United Provinces. Turning again to the south it runs to the junction of the Tons and Jamna, separating Teri Garhwál from Sirmúr and some of the smaller Simla Hill States. Henceforth the Jamna is with small exceptions the boundary between the Panjáb and the United Provinces.

**Boundary with Afghánistán.**—We must now return to our starting-point at the eastern extremity of the Hindu Kush, and trace the boundary with Afghánistán. The frontier runs west and south-west along the Hindu Kush to the Dorah pass dividing Chitrál from the Afghán province of Wakhan, and streams which drain into the Indus from the head waters of the Oxus. At the Dorah pass it turns sharply to the south, following a great spur which parts the valley of the Chitrál river (British) from that of its Afghán affluent, the Bashgol. Below the junction of the two streams at Arnawai the Chitrál changes its name and becomes the Kunar. Near this point the "Durand" line begins. In 1893 an agreement was made between the Amir Abdurrahman and Sir Mortimer Durand as representative of the British Government determining the frontier line from Chandak in the valley of the Kunar, twelve miles north of Asmar, to the Persian border. Asmar is an Afghán village on the left bank of the Kunar to the south of Arnawai. In 1894 the line was demarcated along the eastern watershed of the Kunar valley to Nawakotal on the confines of Bajaur and the country of the Mohmands.

Thence the frontier, which has not been demarcated, passes through the heart of the Mohmand country to the Kábul river and beyond it to our frontier post in the Khaibar at Landikhána.

From this point the line, still undemarcated, runs

on in a south-westerly direction to the Safed Koh, and then strikes west along it to the Sikarám mountain near the Paiwar Kotal at the head of the Kurram valley. From Sikarám the frontier runs south and south-east crossing the upper waters of the Kurram, and dividing our possessions from the Afghán province of Khost. This line was demarcated in 1894.

At the south of the Kurram valley the frontier sweeps round to the west leaving in the British sphere the valley of the Tochí. Turning again to the south it crosses the upper waters of the Tochí and passes round the back of Wazíristán by the Shawal valley and the plains about Wána to Domandi on the Gomal river, where Afghánistán, Biluchistán, and the North West Frontier Province meet. The Wazíristán boundary was demarcated in 1895.

**Political and Administrative Boundaries.**—The boundary described above defines spheres of influence, and only in the Kurram valley does it coincide with that of the districts for whose orderly administration we hold ourselves responsible. All we ask of Wazírs, Afrídís, or Mohmands is to leave our people at peace; we have no concern with their quarrels or blood feuds, so long as they abide in their mountains or only leave them for the sake of lawful gain. Our administrative boundary, which speaking broadly we took over from the Sikhs, usually runs at the foot of the hills. A glance at the map will show that between Peshávar and Kohát the territory of the independent tribes comes down almost to the Indus. At this point the hills occupied by the Jowákí section of the Afrídí tribe push out a great tongue eastwards. Our military frontier road runs through these hills, and we actually pay the tribesmen of the Kohát pass for our right of way. Another tongue of tribal territory reaches right down to the Indus, and almost severs the Peshávar and Hazára districts. Further north the frontier of Hazára lies well to the east of the Indus.

**Frontier with Biluchistán.**—At Domandí the frontier turns to the east, and following the Gomal river to its junction with the Zhob at Kajúrí Kach forms the boundary of the two British administrations. Henceforth the general direction of the line is determined by the trend of the Sulimán range. It runs south to the Vehoa pass, where the country of the Patháns of the North West Frontier Province ends and that of the Hill and Plain Biluches subject to the Panjáb Government begins. From the Vehoa pass to the Kahá torrent the line is drawn so as to leave Biluch tribes with the Panjáb and Pathán tribes with the Biluchistán Agency. South of the Kahá the division is between Biluch tribes, the Marrís and Bugtís to the west being managed from Quetta, and the Gurchánís and Mazárís, who are largely settled in the plains, being included in Dera Ghází Khán, the trans-Indus district of the Panjáb. At the south-west corner of the Dera Ghází Khán district the Panjáb, Sind, and Biluchistán meet. From this point the short common boundary of the Panjáb and Sind runs east to the Indus.

**The Southern Boundary.**—East of the Indus the frontier runs south-east for about fifty miles parting Sind from the Baháwalpur State, till a point is reached where Sind, Rájputána, and Baháwalpur join. A little further to the east is the southern extremity of Baháwalpur at 70° 8′ E. and 27° 5′ N. From this point a line drawn due east would at a distance of 370 miles pass a few miles to the north of the south end of Gurgaon and a few miles to the south of the border of the Narnaul tract of Patiála. Between Narnaul and the south-east corner of the Baháwalpur State the great Rájputána desert, mainly occupied in this quarter by Bikaner, thrusts northwards a huge wedge reaching almost up to the Sutlej. To the west of the wedge is Baháwalpur and to the east the British district of Hissár. The apex is less than 100 miles from Lahore, while a line drawn due south from that city to latitude 27·5° north would exceed 270 miles in length. The Jaipur State lies to the south and west of Narnaul, while Gurgaon has across its southern frontiers Alwar and Bharatpur, and near the Jamna the Muttra district of the United Provinces.

# CHAPTER II

## MOUNTAINS, HILLS, AND PLAINS

**The Great Northern Rampart.**—The huge mountain rampart which guards the northern frontier of India thrusts out in the north-west a great bastion whose outer walls are the Hindu Kush and the Muztagh-Karakoram ranges. Behind the latter with a general trend from south-east to north-west are the great valley of the Indus to the point near Gilgit where it turns sharply to the south, and a succession of mountain chains and glens making up the Himalayan tract, through which the five rivers of the Panjáb and the Jamna find their way to the plains. To meet trans-Indus extensions of the Himálaya the Hindu Kush pushes out from its main axis great spurs to the south, flanking the valleys which drain into the Indus either directly or through the Kábul river.

**The Himálaya.**—Tibet, which from the point of view of physical geography includes a large and little known area in the Kashmír State to the north of the Karakoram range, is a lofty, desolate, wind swept plateau with a mean elevation of about 15,000 feet. In the part of it situated to the north of the north-west corner of Nipál lies the Manasarowar lake, in the neighbourhood of which three great Indian rivers, the Tsanpo or Brahmapútra, the Sutlej, and the Indus, take their rise. The Indus flows to the north-west for 500 miles and then turns abruptly to the south to seek its distant home in the

Indian Ocean. The Tsanpo has a still longer course of 800 miles eastwards before it too bends southwards to flow through Assam into the Bay of Bengal. Between the points where these two giant rivers change their direction there extends for a distance of 1500 miles the

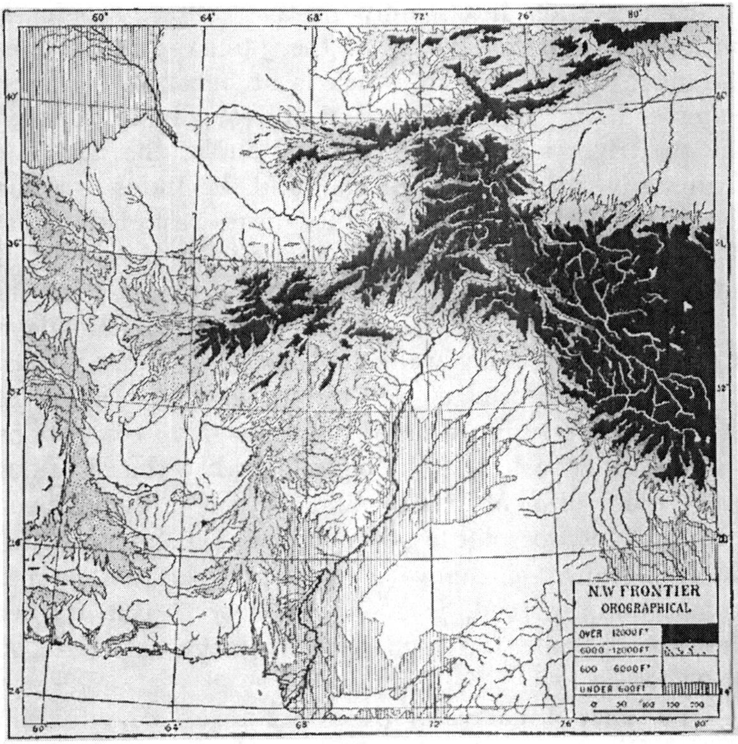


**Fig. 2. Orographical Map.**

vast congeries of mountain ranges known collectively as the "Himálaya" or "Abode of Snow." As a matter of convenience the name is sometimes confined to the mountains east of the Indus, but geologically the hills of Buner and Swát to the north of Pesháwar probably belong to the same system. In Sanskrit literature the

Himálaya is also known as "Himavata," whence the classical Emodus.

**The Kumáon Himálaya.**—The Himálaya may be divided longitudinally into three sections, the eastern or Sikkim, the mid or Kumáon, and the north-western or Ladákh. With the first we are not concerned. The Kumáon section lies mainly in the United Provinces, but it includes the sources of the Jamna, and contains the chain in the Panjáb which is at once the southern watershed of the Sutlej and the great divide between the two river systems of Northern India, the Gangetic draining into the Bay of Bengal, and the Indus carrying the enormous discharge of the north-west Himálaya, the Muztagh-Karakoram, and the Hindu Kush ranges into the Indian Ocean. Simla stands on the south-western end of this watershed, and below it the Himálaya drops rapidly to the Siwálik foot-hills and to the plains. Jakko, the *deodár*-clad hill round which so much of the life of the summer capital of India revolves, attains a height of 8000 feet. The highest peak within a radius of 25 miles of Simla is the Chor, which is over 12,000 feet high, and does not lose its snow cap till May. Hattu, the well-known hill above Narkanda, which is 40 miles from Simla by road, is 1000 feet lower. But further west in Bashahr the higher peaks range from 16,000 to 22,000 feet.

**The Inner Himálaya or Zánskar Range.**—The division of the Himálaya into the three sections named above is convenient for descriptive purposes. But its chief axis runs through all the sections. East of Nipál it strikes into Tibet not very far from the source of the Tsanpo, is soon pierced by the gorge of the Sutlej, and beyond it forms the southern watershed of the huge Indus valley. In the west this great rampart is known as the Zánskar range. For a short distance it is the

Fig. 3. Nanga Parvat.

boundary between the Panjáb and Kashmír, separating two outlying portions of the Kángra district, Lahul and Spití, from Ladákh. In this section the peaks are from 19,000 to 21,000 feet high, and the Baralácha pass on the road from the Kulu valley in Kángra to Leh, the capital of Ladákh, is at an elevation of about 16,500 feet. In Kashmír the Zánskar or Inner Himálaya divides the valley of the Indus from those of the Chenáb and Jhelam. It has no mountain to dispute supremacy with Everest (29,000 feet), or Kinchinjunga in the Eastern Himálaya, but the inferiority is only relative. The twin peaks called Nun and Kun to the east of Srínagar exceed 23,000 feet, and in the extreme north-west the grand mountain mass of Nanga Parvat towers above the Indus to a height of 26,182 feet. The lowest point in the chain is the Zojilá (11,300 feet) on the route from Srínagar, the capital of Kashmír, to Leh on the Indus

The road from Srínagar to Gilgit passes over the Burzil pass at an elevation of 13,500 feet.

The Zojilá is at the top of the beautiful valley of the Sind river, a tributary of the Jhelam. The lofty Zánskar range blocks the inward flow of the monsoon, and once the Zojilá is crossed the aspect of the country entirely changes. The land of forest glades and green pastures is left behind, and a region of naked and desolate grandeur begins.

"The waste of snow....is the frontier of barren Tibet, where sandy wastes replace verdant meadows, and where the wild ridges, jutting up against the sky, are kept bare of vegetation, their strata crumbling under the destructive action of frost and water, leaving bare ribs of gaunt and often fantastic outline....The colouring of the mountains is remarkable throughout Ladákh and nowhere more so than near the Fotulá (a pass on the road to Leh to the south of the Indus gorge)....As we ascend the peaks suggest organ pipes, so vertical are the ridges, so jagged the ascending outlines. And each pipe is painted a different colour.... pale slate green, purple, yellow, grey, orange, and chocolate, each colour corresponding with a layer of the slate, shale, limestone, or trap strata" (Neve's *Picturesque Kashmir*, pp. 108 and 117).

Fig. 4. Burzil Pass.

In all this desolation there are tiny oases where level soil and a supply of river water permit of cultivation and of some tree growth.

**Water divide near Baralácha and Rotang Passes in Kulu.**—We have seen that the Indus and its greatest tributary, the Sutlej, rise beyond the Himálaya in the

Tibetan plateau. The next great water divide is in the neighbourhood of the Barelácha pass and the Rotang pass, 30 miles to the south of it. The route from Simla to Leh runs at a general level of 7000 to 9000 feet along or near the Sutlej-Jamna watershed to Narkanda (8800 feet). Here it leaves the Hindustán-Tibet road and drops rapidly into the Sutlej gorge, where the Lurí bridge is only 2650 feet above sea level. Rising steeply on the other side the Jalaurí pass on the watershed between the Sutlej and the Biás is crossed at an elevation of 10,800 feet. A more gradual descent brings the traveller to the Biás at Lárjí, 3080 feet above sea level. The route then follows the course of the Biás through the beautiful Kulu valley to the Rotang pass (13,326 feet), near which the river rises. The upper part of the valley is flanked on the west by the short, but very lofty Bara Bangáhal range, dividing Kulu from Kángra and the source of the Biás from that of the Ráví. Beyond the Rotang is Lahul, which is divided by a watershed from Spití and the torrents which drain into the Sutlej. On the western side of this watershed are the sources of the Chandra and Bhága, which unite to form the river known in the plains as the Chenáb.

**Mid Himálaya or Pangí Range.**—The Mid Himálayan or Pangí range, striking west from the Rotang pass and the northern end of the Bara Bangáhal chain, passes through the heart of Chamba dividing the valley of the Chenáb (Pangí) from that of the Ráví. After entering Kashmír it crosses the Chenáb near the Kolahoi cone (17,900 feet) and the head waters of the Jhelam. Thence it continues west over Haramukh (16,900 feet), which casts its shadow southwards on the Wular lake, to the valley of the Kishnganga, and probably across it to the mountains which flank the magnificent Kágan glen in Hazára.

Fig. 5. Rotang Pass.

**Outer Himálaya or Dhauladhár-Pír Panjál Range.**—The Outer Himálaya also starts from a point near the Rotang pass, but some way to the south of the offset of the Mid Himalayan chain. Its main axis runs parallel to the latter, and under the name of the Dhauladhár (white ridge) forms the boundary of the Chamba State and Kángra, behind whose headquarters at Dharmsála it stands up like a huge wall. It has a mean elevation

Fig. 6. Mt Haramukh.

of 15,000 feet, but rises as high as 16,000. It passes from Chamba into Bhadarwáh in Kashmír, and crossing the Chenáb is carried on as the Pír Panjál range through the south of that State. With an elevation of only 14,000 or 15,000 feet it is a dwarf as compared with the giants of the Inner Himalayan and Muztagh-Karakoram chains. But it hides them from the dwellers in the Panjáb, and its snowy crest is a very striking picture as seen in the cold weather from the plains of Ráwalpindí, Jhelam, and Gujrát. The Outer Himálaya is continued beyond the gorges of the Jhelam and Kishnganga rivers in Kajnág and the hills of the Hazára district. Near the eastern extremity of the Dhauladhár section of the Outer Himálaya it sends out southwards between Kulu and Mandí a lower offshoot. This is crossed by the Babbu (9480 feet) and Dulchí passes, connecting Kulu with Kángra through Mandí. Geologically the Kulu-Mandí range appears to be continued to the east of the Biás and across the Sutlej over Hattu and the Chor to the hills near Masúrí (Mussoorie), a well-known hill station in the United Provinces. Another offshoot at the western end of the Dhauladhár passes through the beautiful hill station of Dalhousie, and sinks into the low hills to the east of the Ráví, where it leaves Chamba and enters the British district of Gurdáspur.

**River Valleys and Passes in the Himálaya.**—While these principal chains can be traced from south-east to north-west over hundreds of miles it must be remembered that the Himálaya is a mountain mass from 150 to 200 miles broad, that the main axes are linked together by subsidiary cross chains dividing the head waters of great rivers, and flanked by long and lofty ridges running down at various angles to the gorges of these streams and their tributaries. The typical Himalayan river runs in a gorge with mountains dipping down pretty steeply to its sides. The lower slopes are cultivated, but the land is usually stony and uneven, and as a whole the crops are not of a high class. The open valleys of the Jhelam in Kashmír and of the Biás in Kulu are exceptions. Passes in the Himálaya are not defiles between high cliffs, but cross the crest of a ridge at a point where the chain is locally depressed, and snow melts soonest. In the Outer and Mid Himálaya the line of perpetual snow is at about 16,000 feet, but for six months of the year the snow-line comes down 5000 feet lower. In the Inner Himálaya and the Muztagh-Karakoram, to which the monsoon does not penetrate, the air is so dry that less snow falls and the line is a good deal higher.

**Himalayan Scenery.**—Certain things strike any observant traveller in the Himálaya. One is the comparative absence of running or still water, except in the

Fig. 7. R. Jhelam in Kashmír—View towards Mohand Marg.

height of the rainy season, away from the large rivers. The slope is so rapid that ordinary falls of rain run off with great rapidity. The mountain scenery is often magnificent and the forests are beautiful, but the absence of water robs the landscape of a charm which would make it really perfect. Where this too is present, as in the valley of the Biás in Kulu and those of the Jhelam and its tributaries in Kashmír and Hazára, the eye has

Fig. 8. Near Náran in Kágan Glen, Hazára.

its full fruition of content. Another is the silence of the forests. Bird and beast are there, but they are little in evidence. A third feature which can hardly be missed is the contrast between the northern and the southern slopes. The former will often be clothed with forest while the latter is a bare stony slope covered according to season with brown or green grass interspersed with bushes of indigo, barberry, or the hog plum (Prinsepia utilis). The reason is that the northern side enjoys much more shade, snow lies longer, and the supply of moisture is therefore greater. The grazier for the same reason is less tempted to fire the hill side in order to promote the growth of grass, a practice which is fatal to all forest growth. The rich and varied flora of the Himálaya will be referred to later.

**Muztagh-Karakoram Ranges.**—The Muztagh-Karakoram mountains form the northern watershed of the Indus. The range consists of more than one main axis. The name Karakoram is appropriated to the eastern part of the system which originates at E. longitude 79° near the Pangong lake in the Tibetan plateau a little beyond the boundary of Kashmír. Beyond the Karakoram pass (18,550 ft.) is a lofty bleak upland with salt lakes dotted over its surface. Through this inhospitable region and over the Karakoram pass and the Sasser-lá (17,500 ft.) the trade route from Yarkand to Leh runs. The road is only open for three months in the year, and the dangers and hardships are great. In 1898 Dr Bullock Workman and his wife marched along it across the Shyok river, up the valley of the Nubra, and over the Sasser-lá to the Karakoram pass. The scenery is an exaggeration of that described by Dr Neve as seen on the road from the Zoji-lá to Leh. There is a powerful picture of its weird repellent grandeur in the Workmans' book entitled *In the Ice World of Himálaya* (pp. 28–29, 30–32). The poet who had found ideas for a new Paradiso in the Vale of Kashmír might here get suggestions for a new Inferno.

The Karakoram range culminates in the north-west near the Muztagh pass in a group of majestic peaks including K 2 or Mount Godwin Austen (28,265 feet),

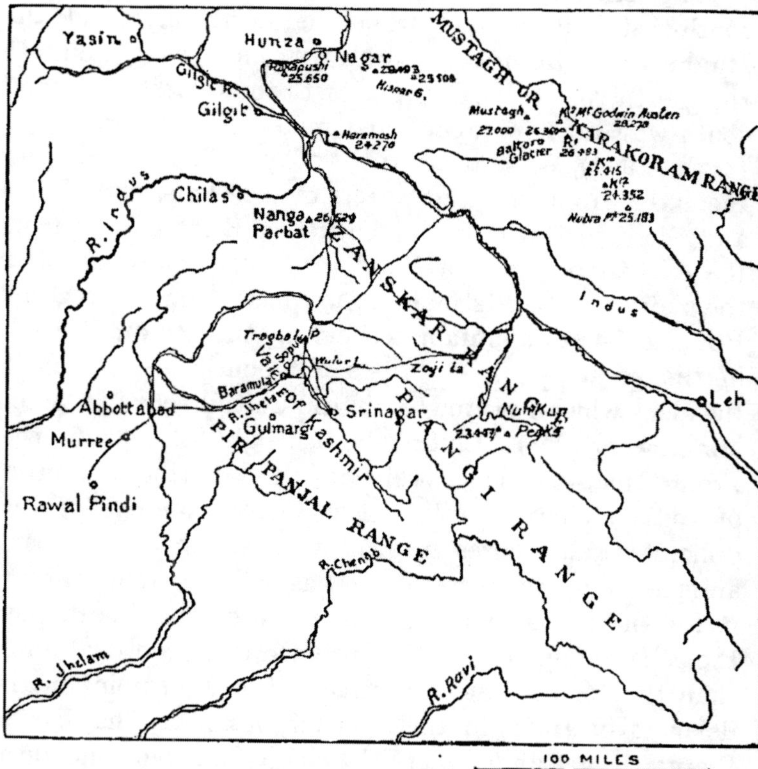


Fig. 9. Muztagh-Karakoram and Himalayan Ranges in Kashmír.

Gasherbrum, and Masherbrum, which tower over and feed the vast Boltoro glacier. The first of these giants is the second largest mountain in the world. The Duke of the Abruzzi ascended it to the height of 24,600 feet, and so established a climbing record. The Muztagh chain carries on the northern bastion to the valley of the Hunza river and the western extremity of the Hindu Kush. It has several peaks exceeding 25,000 feet. The most famous is Rakiposhi which looks down on Hunza from a height of 25,550 feet.

**The Hindu Kush.**—The Muztagh chain from the south-east, the Sarikol from the north-east, and the Hindu Kush from the south-west, meet at a point to the north of Hunza. The last runs westward and south-westward for about 200 miles to the Dorah pass (14,800 feet), separating the valleys which drain into the Indus from the head waters of the Oxus, and Hunza and Gilgit in Kashmír and Chitrál in British India from the Afghán province of Wakhan. The highest point in the main axis, Sad Istragh (24,171 feet), is in this section. But the finest mountain scenery in the Hindu Kush is in the great spurs it thrusts out southwards to flank the glens which feed the Gilgit and Chitrál rivers. Tirach Mír towers above Chitrál to a height of 25,426 feet. From Tibet to the Dorah pass the northern frontier of India is impregnable. It is pierced by one or two difficult trade routes strewn with the bones of pack animals, but no large army has ever marched across it for the invasion of India. West of the Dorah pass the general level of the Hindu Kush is a good deal lower than that of its eastern section. The vital point in the defences of India in this quarter lies near Charikár to the north of Kábul, where the chain thins out, and three practicable passes debouch on the valley of the Kábul river. It is this fact that gives the town of Kábul its great strategic importance. The highest of the three passes, the Kaoshan or Hindu Kush (dead Hindu), crosses the chain at an elevation of 14,340 feet. It took its own name from the fate that befel a Hindu army when attempting to cross it, and has handed it on to the whole range. It is the pass which the armies of Alexander and Bábar used. The historical road for the invasion of India on this side has been by Charikár and the valley of the Kábul river to its junction with the Kunar below Jalálábád, thence up the Kunar valley and over one of the practicable passes which connect its eastern watershed with the Panjkora and Swát river valleys, whence the descent on Pesháwar is easy. This is the route by which Alexander led the wing of the Grecian army which he commanded in person, and the one followed by Bábar in 1518–19. Like Alexander, Bábar fought his way through Bajaur, and crossed the Indus above Attock.

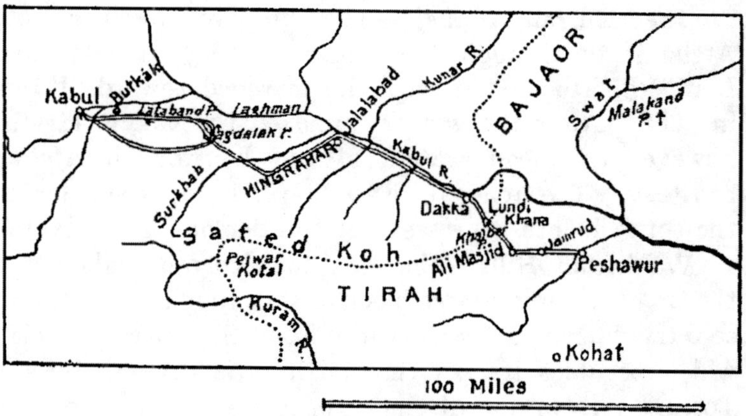


Fig. 10. The Khaibar Road.

**The Khaibar.**—A British force advancing on Kábul from Pesháwar has never marched by the Kunar and Kábul valley route. It has always taken the Khaibar road, which only follows the Kábul river for less than one-third of the 170 miles which separate Pesháwar from the Amir's capital. The military road from Pesháwar to Landikhána lies far to the south of the river, from which it is shut off by difficult and rugged country held by the Mohmands.

**Safed Koh.**—From Landikhána the political boundary runs south-west to the Safed Koh (white mountain) and is continued westwards along that range to the Paiwar Kotal or pass (8450 feet). The Safed Koh forms the watershed of the Kábul and Kurram rivers. It is a fine pine clad chain with a general level of 12,000 feet, and its skyline is rarely free from snow. It culminates in the west near Paiwar Kotal in Sikarám (15,620 feet). To the west of the Peshâwar and Kohát districts is a tangle of hills and valleys formed by outlying spurs of the Safed Koh. This difficult country is in the occupation of Afrídís and Orakzais, who are under our political control.

**The Kurram Valley.**—The line of advance into Afghánistán through the Kurram valley is easy, and Lord Roberts used it when he marched towards Kábul in 1898. After the war we annexed the valley, leaving however the head waters of the Kurram in Afghán territory. The road to Kábul leaves the river far to the south before it crosses our frontier at Paiwar Kotal.

**Wazíristán Hills.**—Between the Kurram valley and the Gomal river is a large block of very rough mountainous country known as Wazíristán from the turbulent clan which occupies it. In the north it is drained by the Tochí. Westwards of the Tochí valley the country rises into lofty mountains. The upper waters of the Tochí and its affluents drain two fine glens known as Birmal and Shawal to the west of the country of the Mahsud Wazírs. The Tochí valley is the direct route from India to Ghazní, and nine centuries ago, when that decayed town was the capital of a powerful kingdom, it must often have heard the tramp of armed men. The loftiest peaks in Wazíristán, Shuidár (11,000 feet) and Pírghal (11,600 feet), overhang Birmal. Further south, Wána, our post in south-west Wazíristán, overlooks from its plateau the Gomal valley.

**The Gomal Pass as a trade route.**—East of Kajúrí Kach the Gomal flows through tribal territory to the Gomal pass from which it debouches into the plains of the Dera Ismail Khán district "The Gomal route is the oldest of all trade routes. Down it there yearly pours a succession of *káfilas* (caravans) led and followed up by thousands of well-armed Pathán traders, called Powindahs, from the plains of Afghánistán to India. The Powindahs mostly belong to the Ghilzai tribes, and are not therefore true Afgháns[1]. Leaving their women and children encamped within British territory on our border, and their arms in the keeping of our frontier political officials, the Powindah makes his way southwards with his camel loads of fruit and silk, bales of camel and goat hair or sheepskin goods, carpets and other merchandise from Kábul and Bokhára, and conveys himself through the length and breadth of the Indian peninsula....He returns yearly to the cool summits of the Afghán hills and the open grassy plains, where his countless flocks of sheep and camels are scattered for the summer grazing" (Holdich's *India*, pp. 80–81).

**Physical features of hilly country between Peshávar and the Gomal river.**—The physical features of the hill country between Peshávar and the Gomal pass may best be described in the words of Sir Thomas Holdich:

"Natural landscape beauty, indeed, may here be measured to a certain extent by altitude. The low ranges of sun-scorched, blackened ridge and furrow formation which form the approaches to the higher altitudes of the Afghán upland, and which are almost as regularly laid out by the hand of nature in some parts of the frontier as are the parallels....of the engineer who is besieging a fortress—these are by no means 'things of beauty,' and it is this class of formation and this form

[1] They are held to be of Turkish origin.

of barren desolation that is most familiar to the frontier officer....Shades of delicate purple and grey will not make up for the absence of the living green of vegetation ....But with higher altitudes a cooler climate and snow-fed soil is found, and as soon as vegetation grasps a root-hold there is the beginning of fine scenery. The upper pine-covered slopes of the Safed Koh are as picturesque as those of the Swiss Alps; they are crowned by peaks whose wonderful altitudes are frozen beyond the possibility of vegetation, and are usually covered with snow wherever snow can lie. In Wazíristán, hidden away in the higher recesses of its great mountains, are many valleys of great natural beauty, where we find the spreading poplar and the ilex in all the robust growth of an indigenous flora....Among the minor valleys Birmal perhaps takes precedence by right of its natural beauty. Here are stretches of park-like scenery where grass-covered slopes are dotted with clumps of *deodár* and pine and intersected with rivulets hidden in banks of fern; soft green glades open out to view from every turn in the folds of the hills, and above them the silent watch towers of Pírghal and Shuidár....look down from their snow-clad heights across the Afghán uplands to the hills beyond Ghazní." (Holdich's *India*, pp. 81–82.)

**The Sulimán Range.**—A well-marked mountain chain runs from the Gomal to the extreme south-west corner of the Dera Ghází Khán district where the borders of Biluchistán, Sind, and the Panjáb meet. It culminates forty miles south of the Gomal in the fine Kaisargarh mountain (11,295 feet), which is a very conspicuous object from the plains of the Deraját. On the side of Kaisargarh there is a shrine called Takht i Sulimán or Throne of Solomon, and this is the name by which Englishmen usually know the mountain, and which has been passed on to the whole range. Proceeding southwards the general elevation of the chain drops steadily. But Fort Munro, the hill station of the Dera Ghází Khán district, 200 miles south of the Takht, still stands 6300 feet above sea level, and it looks across at the fine peak of Ekbhai, which is more than 1000 feet higher. In the south of the Dera Ghází Khán district the general level of the chain is low, and the Giandári hill, though only 4160 feet above the sea, stands out conspicuously. Finally near where the three jurisdictions meet the hills melt into the Kachh Gandáva plain. Sir Thomas Holdich's description of the rugged Pathán hills applies also to the Sulimán range. Kaisargarh is a fine limestone mountain crowned by a forest of the edible *chilgoza* pine. But the ordinary tree growth, where found at all, is of a much humbler kind, consisting of gnarled olives and dwarf palms.

**Passes and torrents in Sulimán Hills.**—The drainage of the western slopes of the Sulimán range finding no exit on that side has had to wear out ways for itself towards the plains which lie between the foot of the hills and the Indus. This is the explanation of the large number of passes, about one hundred, which lead from the plains into the Sulimán hills. The chief from north to south are the Vehoa, the Sangarh, the Khair, the Kahá, the Cháchar, and the Sirí, called from the torrents which flow through them to the plains. There is an easy route through the Cháchar to Biluchistán. But unfortunately the water of the torrent is brackish.

**Sub Himálaya or Siwáliks.**—In its lowest ridges the Himálaya drops to a height of about 5000 feet. But the traveller to any of the summer resorts in the mountains passes through a zone of lower hills interspersed sometimes with valleys or "duns." These consist of Tertiary sandstones, clays, and boulder conglomerates, the débris in fact which the Himálaya has dropped in the course of ages. To this group of hills and valleys the general name of Siwáliks is given. East of the Jhelam it includes the Náhan hills to the north of Ambála, the low hills of Kángra, Hoshyárpur, Gurdáspur, and Jammu, and the Pabbí hills in Gujrát. But it is to the west of the Jhelam that the system has its greatest extension. Practically the whole of the soil of the plains of the Attock, Ráwalpindí, and Jhelam districts consists of disintegrated Siwálik sandstone, and differs widely in appearance and agricultural quality from the alluvium of the true Panjáb plains. The low hills of these districts belong to the same system, but the Salt Range is only in part Siwálik. Altogether Siwálik deposits in the Panjáb cover an area of 13,000 square miles. Beyond the Indus the hills of the Kohát district and a part of the Sulimán range are of Tertiary age.

**The Great Panjáb Plain.**—The passage from the highlands to the plains is as a rule abrupt, and the contrast between the two is extraordinary. This is true without qualification of the tract between the Jamna and the Jhelam. It is equally true of British districts west of the Jhelam and south of the Salt Range and of lines drawn from Kálabágh on the west bank of the Indus southwards to Paniála and thence north-west through the Pezu pass to the Wazíristán hills. In all that vast plain, if we except the insignificant hills in the extreme south-west of the province ending to the north in the historic ridge at Delhi, some hillocks of gneiss near Toshám in Hissár, and the curious little isolated rocks at Kirána, Chiniot, and Sángla near the Chenáb and Jhelam, the only eminences are petty ridges of wind-blown sand and the "*thehs*" or mounds which represent the accumulated débris of ancient village sites. At the end of the Jurassic period and later this great plain was part of a sea bed. Far removed as the Indian ocean now is the height above sea level of the Panjáb plain east of the Jhelam is nowhere above 1000 feet. Delhi and Lahore are both just above the 700 feet line. The hills mentioned above are humble time-worn outliers of the very ancient Aravalli system, to which the hills of Rájputána belong. Kirána and Sángla were already of enormous age, when they were islands washed by the waves of the Tertiary sea. A description of the different parts of the vast Panjáb plain, its great stretches of firm loam, and its tracts of sand and sand hills, which the casual observer might regard as pure desert, will be given in the paragraphs devoted to the different districts.

**The Salt Range.**—The tract west of the Jhelam, and bounded on the south by the Salt Range cis-Indus, and trans-Indus by the lines mentioned above, is of a more varied character. Time worn though the Salt Range has become by the waste of ages, it still rises at Sakesar, near its western extremity, to a height of 5000 feet. The eastern part of the range is mostly in the Jhelam district, and there the highest point is Chail (3700 feet). The hill of Tilla (3242 feet), which is a marked feature of the landscape looking westwards from Jhelam cantonment, is on a spur running north-east from the main chain. The Salt Range is poorly wooded, the dwarf acacia or *phuláhi* (Acacia modesta), the olive, and the *sanattha* shrub (Dodonea viscosa) are the commonest species. But these jagged and arid hills include some not infertile valleys, every inch of which is put under crop by the crowded population. To geologists the range is of special interest, including as it does at one end of the scale Cambrian beds of enormous antiquity and at the other rocks of Tertiary age. Embedded in the Cambrian strata there are great deposits of rock salt at Kheora, where the Mayo mine is situated.

At Kálabágh the Salt Range reappears on the far side of the Indus. Here the salt comes to the surface, and its jagged pinnacles present a remarkable appearance.

**Country north of the Salt Range.**—The country to the north of the Salt Range included in the districts of Jhelam, Ráwalpindí, and Attock is often ravine-bitten and seamed with the white sandy beds of torrents. Generally speaking it is an arid precarious tract, but there are fertile stretches which will be mentioned in the descriptions of the districts. The general height of the plains north of the Salt Range is from 1000 feet to 2000 feet above sea level. The rise between Lahore and Ráwalpindí is just over a thousand feet. Low hills usually form a feature of the landscape, pleasing at a distance or when softened by the evening light, but bare and jagged on a nearer view. The chief hills are the Márgalla range between Hazára and Ráwalpindí, the Ķálachitta and the Khairimurat hills running east and west through Attock and the very dry and broken Narrara hills on the right bank of the Indus in the same district. Between the Márgalla and Kálachitta hills is the Márgalla pass on the main road from Ráwalpindí to the passage of the Indus at Attock, and therefore a position of considerable strategical importance. The Kálachitta (black and white) chain is so called because the north side is formed of nummulitic limestone and the south mainly of a dark purple sandstone. The best tree-growth is therefore on the north side.

**Peshávar, Kohát, and Bannu.**—Across the Indus the Peshávar and Bannu districts are basins ringed with hills and drained respectively by the Kábul and Kurram rivers with their affluents. Between these two basins lies the maze of bare broken hills and valleys which make up the Kohát district. The cantonment of Kohát is 1700 feet above sea level and no hill in the district reaches 5000 feet. Near the Kohát border in the south-west of the Peshâwar district are the Khattak hills, the culmination of which at Ghaibana Sir has a height of 5136 feet, and the military sanitarium of Cherát in the same chain is 600 feet lower. On the east the Maidâni hills part Bannu from Isakhel, the trans-Indus *tahsíl* of Mianwáli, and on the south the Marwat hills divide it from Dera Ismail Khán. Both are humble ranges. The highest point in the Marwat hills is Shekhbudín, a bare and dry limestone rock rising to an elevation of over 4500 feet.

# CHAPTER III

## RIVERS

**The Panjáb Rivers.**—" Panjáb " is a Persian compound word, meaning " five waters," and strictly speaking the word denotes the country between the valley of the Jhelam and that of the Sutlej. The intermediate rivers from west to east are the Chenáb, the Rávi, and the Biás. Their combined waters at last flow into the Panjnad or " five rivers " at the south-west corner of the Multán district, and the volume of water which 44 miles lower down the Panjnad carries into the Indus is equal to the discharge of the latter. The first Aryan settlers knew this part of India as the land of the seven rivers (*sapta sindhavas*), adding to the five mentioned above the Indus and the Sarasvatí. The old Vedic name is more appropriate than Panjáb if we substitute the Jamna for the Sarasvatí or Sarustí, which is now a petty stream.

**River Valleys.**—The cold weather traveller who is carried from Delhi to Ráwalpindí over the great railway bridges at points chosen because there the waters of the rivers are confined by nature, or can be confined by art, within moderate limits, has little idea of what one of these rivers is like in flood time. He sees that, even at such favoured spots, between the low banks there is a stretch of sand far exceeding in width the main channel, where a considerable volume of water is running, and the minor depressions, in which a sluggish and shallow flow may still be found. If, leaving the railway, he crosses a river by some bridge of boats or local ferry, he will find still wider expanses of sand sometimes bare and dry and white, at others moist and dark and covered with dwarf tamarisk. He may notice that, before he

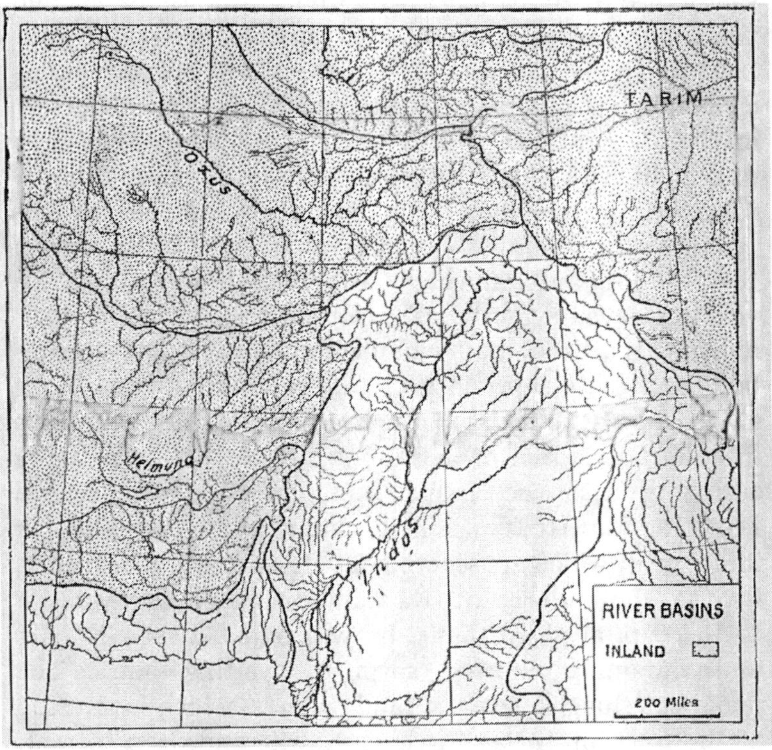


Fig. 11. Panjáb Rivers.

reaches the sand and the tamarisk scrub, he leaves by a gentle or abrupt descent the dry uplands, and passes into a lower, greener, and perhaps to his inexperienced eye more fertile seeming tract. This is the valley, often miles broad, through which the stream has moved in ever-shifting channels in the course of centuries. He finds it hard to realize that, when the summer heats melt the Himalayan snows, and the monsoon currents, striking against the northern mountain walls, are precipitated in torrents of rain, the rush of water to the plains swells the river 20, 30, 40, or even 50 fold. The sandy bed then becomes full from bank to bank, and the silt laden waters spill over into the cultivated lowlands beyond. Accustomed to the stable streams of his own land, he cannot conceive the risks the riverside farmer in the Panjáb runs of having fruitful fields smothered in a night with barren sand, or lands and well and house sucked into the river-bed. So great and sudden are the changes, bad and good, wrought by river action that the loss and gain have to be measured up year by year for revenue purposes. Nor is the visitor likely to imagine that the main channel may in a few seasons become a quite subsidiary or wholly deserted bed. Like all streams, e.g. the Po, which flow from the mountains into a flat terrain, the Panjáb rivers are perpetually silting up their beds, and thus, by their own action, becoming diverted into new channels or into existing minor ones, which are scoured out afresh. If our traveller, leaving the railway at Ráwalpindí, proceeds by *tonga* to the capital of Kashmír, he will find between Kohála and Báramúla another surprise awaiting him. The noble but sluggish river of the lowlands, which he crossed at the town of Jhelam, is here a swift and deep torrent, flowing over a boulder bed, and swirling round water-worn rocks in a gorge hemmed in by mountains. That is the typical state of the Himalayan rivers, though the same Jhelam above Báramúla is an exception, flowing there sluggishly through a very flat valley into a shallow lake.

**The Indus Basin.**—The river Sindh (Sanskrit, Sindhu), more familiar to us under its classical name of the Indus, must have filled with astonishment every invader from the west, and it is not wonderful that they called after it the country that lay beyond. Its basin covers an area of 373,000 square miles. Confining attention to Asia these figures, large though they seem, are far exceeded by those of the Yangtsze-Kiang. The area of which a description is attempted in this book is, with the exception of a strip along the Jamna and the part of Kashmír lying beyond the Muztagh-Karakoram range, all included in the Indus basin. But it does not embrace the whole of it. Part is in Tibet, part in Afghánistán and Biluchistán, and part in Sindh, through which province the Indus flows for 450 miles, or one-quarter of its whole course of 1800 miles. It seems likely that the Jamna valley was not always an exception, or at least that that river once flowed westwards through Rájputána to the Indian ocean. The five great rivers of the Panjáb all drain into the Indus, and the Ghagar with its tributary, the Sarustí, which now, even when in flood, loses itself in the sands of Bikaner, probably once flowed down the old Hakra bed in Baháwalpur either into the Indus or by an independent bed now represented by an old flood channel of the Indus in Sindh, the Hakro or Nara, which passes through the Rann of Kachh.

**The Indus outside British India.**—To the north of the Manasarowar lake in Tibet is Kailás, the Hindu Olympus. On the side of this mountain the Indus is said to rise at a height of 17,000 feet. After a course of 200 miles or more it crosses the south-east boundary of the Kashmír State at an elevation of 13,800 feet. From the Kashmír frontier to Mt Haramosh west of Gilgit it flows steadily to the north-west for 350 miles. After 125 miles Leh, the capital of Ladákh, is reached at a height of 10,500 feet, and here the river is crossed by the trade route to Yarkand. A little below Leh the Indus receives the Zánskar, which drains the south-east of Kashmír. After another 150 miles it flows through the basin, in which Skardo, the principal town in Baltistán, is situated. Above Skardo a large tributary, the Shyok, flows in from the east at an elevation of 8000 feet. The Shyok and its affluent, the Nubra, rise in the giant glaciers to the south-west of the Karakoram pass. After the Skardo basin is left behind the descent is rapid. The river rushes down a tremendous gorge, where it appears to break through the western Himálaya, skirts Haramosh, and at a point twenty-five miles east of Gilgit bends abruptly to the south. Shortly after it is joined from the west by the Gilgit river, and here the bed is about 4000 feet above sea level. Continuing to flow south for another twenty miles it resumes its westernly course to the north of Nanga Parvat and persists in it for 100 miles. Our political post of Chilás lies in this section on the south bank. Fifty or sixty miles west of Chilás the Indus turns finally to the south. From Jálkot, where the Kashmír frontier is left, to Palosí below the Mahaban mountain it flows for a hundred miles through territory over which we only exercise political control. Near Palosí, 812 miles from the source, the river enters British India. In Kashmír the Indus and the Shyok in some places flow placidly over alluvial flats, and at others with a rapid and broken current through narrow gorges. At Skardo their united stream is said, even in winter, to be 500 feet wide and nine or ten feet deep. If one of the deep gorges, as sometimes happens, is choked by a landslip, the flood that follows when the barrier finally bursts may spread devastation hundreds of miles away. To the north of the fertile Chach plain in Attock there is a wide stretch of land along the Indus, which still shows in its stony impoverished soil the effects of the great flood of 1841.

**The Indus in British India.**—After reaching British India the Indus soon becomes the boundary dividing Hazára and Pesháwar, two districts of the North West Frontier Province. Lower down it parts Pesháwar from the Panjáb district of Attock. In this section after a time the hills recede on both sides, and the stream is wide and so shallow that it is fordable in places in the cold weather. There are islands, ferry boats and rafts

Fig. 12. The Indus at Attock.

can ply, and the only danger is from sudden freshets. Ohind, where Alexander crossed, is in this section. A more famous passage is at Attock just below the junction of the Kábul river. Here the heights again approach the Indus on either bank. The volume of water is vastly increased by the union of the Kábul river, which brings down the whole drainage of the southern face of the Hindu Kush. From the north it receives near Jalálábád the Kunar river, and near Charsadda in Pesháwar the

Swát, which with its affluent the Panjkora drains Dír, Bajaur, and Swát. In the cold weather looking northwards from the Attock fort one sees the Kábul or Landai as a blue river quietly mingling with the Indus, and in the angle between them a stretch of white sand. But during floods the junction is the scene of a wild turmoil of waters. At Attock there are a railway bridge, a bridge of boats, and a ferry. The bed of the stream is 2000

**Fig. 13. Indus at Kafirkot, D.I. Khán dt.**

feet over sea level. For ninety miles below Attock the river is confined between bare and broken hills, till it finally emerges into the plains from the gorge above Kálabágh, where the Salt Range impinges on the left bank. Between Attock and Kálabágh the right bank is occupied by Pesháwar and Kohát and the left by Attock and Mianwálí. In this section the Indus is joined by the Haro and Soán torrents, and spanned at Khushálgarh by a railway bridge. This is the only other masonry bridge crossing it in the Panjáb. Elsewhere the passage has to be made by ferry boats or by boat bridges, which are taken down in the rainy season. At Kálabágh the height above sea level is less than 1000 feet. When it passes the western extremity of the Salt Range the river spreads out into a wide lake-like expanse of waters. It has now performed quite half of its long journey. Henceforth it receives no addition from the east till the Panjnad in the south-west corner of the Muzaffargarh district brings to it the whole tribute of the five rivers of the Panjáb. Here, though the Indian ocean is still 500 miles distant, the channel is less than 300 feet above the sea. From the west it receives an important tributary in the Kurram, which, with its affluent the Tochí, rises in Afghánistán. The torrents from the Sulimán Range are mostly used up for irrigation before they reach the Indus, but some of them mingle their waters with it in high floods. Below Kálabágh the Indus is a typical lowland river of great size, with many sandy islands in the bed and a wide valley subject to its inundations. Opposite Dera Ismail Khán the valley is seventeen miles across. As a plains river the Indus runs at first through the Mianwálí district of the Panjáb, then divides Mianwálí from Dera Ismail Khán, and lastly parts Muzaffargarh and the Baháwalpur State from the Panjáb frontier district of Dera Ghází Khán.

**The Jhelam.**—The Jhelam, the most westernly of the five rivers of the Panjáb, is called the Veth in Kashmír and locally in the Panjáb plains the Vehat. These names correspond to the Bihat of the Muhammadan historians and the Hydaspes of the Greeks, and all go back to the Sanskrit Vitasta. Issuing from a deep pool at Vernág to the east of Islámábád in Kashmír it becomes navigable just below that town, and flows north-west in a lazy stream for 102 miles through Srínagar, the summer capital, into the Wular lake, and beyond it to Báramúla. The banks are quite low and often cultivated to the river's edge. But across the flat valley there is on either side a splendid panorama of mountains. From Báramúla the character of the Jhelam suddenly changes, and for the next 70 miles to Kohála, where the traveller crosses by a fine bridge into the Panjáb, it rushes down a deep gorge, whose sides are formed by the Kajnág mountains on the right, and the Pír Panjál on the left, bank. Between Báramúla and Kohála there is a drop from 5000 to 2000 feet. At Domel, the stage before Kohála the Jhelam receives from the north the waters of the Kishnganga, and lower down it is joined by the Kunhár, which drains the Kágan glen in Hazára. A little above Kohála it turns sharply to the south, continuing its character as a mountain stream hemmed in by the hills of Ráwalpindí on the right bank and of the Púnch State on the left. The hills gradually sink lower and lower, but on the left side only disappear a little above the cantonment of Jhelam, where there is a noble railway bridge. From Jhelam onwards the river is of the usual plains' type. After dividing the districts of Jhelam (right bank) and Gujrát (left), it flows through the Sháhpur and Jhang districts, falling finally into the Chenáb at Trimmu, 450 miles from its source. There is a second railway bridge at Haranpur on the Sind Ságar line, and a bridge of boats at Khusháb, in the Sháhpur district. The noblest and most varied scenery in the north-west Himálaya is in the catchment area of the Jhelam. The Kashmír valley and the valleys which drain into the Jhelam from the north, the Liddar, the Loláb, the Sind, and the Kágan glen, display a wealth of beauty unequalled elsewhere. Nor does this river wholly lose its association with beauty in the plains. Its very rich silt gives the lands on its banks the green charm of rich crops and pleasant trees.

**The Chenáb.**—The Chenáb (more properly Chínáb or river of China) is the Asikní of the Vedas and the Akesines of the Greek historians. It is formed by the union of the Chandra and Bhága, both of which rise in Lahul near the Báralácha pass. Having become the Chandrabhága the river flows through Pángí in Chamba and the south-east of Kashmír. Near Kishtwár it breaks through the Pír Panjál range, and thenceforwards receives the drainage of its southern slopes. At Akhnúr it becomes navigable and soon after it enters the Panjáb district of Siálkot. A little later it is joined from the west by the Tawí, the stream above which stands Jammu, the winter capital of Kashmír. The Chenáb parts Siálkot and Gujránwála on the left bank from Gujrát and Sháhpur on the right. At Wazírábád, near the point where Siálkot, Gujrát, and Gujránwála meet, it is crossed by the Alexandra railway bridge. Leaving Sháhpur and Gujránwála behind, the Chenáb flows through Jhang to its junction with the Jhelam at Trimmu. In this section there is a second railway bridge at Chund Bharwána. The united stream runs on under the name of Chenáb to be joined on the north border of the Multán district by the Rávi and on its southern border by the Sutlej. Below its junction with the latter the stream is known as the Panjnad. In the plains the Chenáb cannot be called an attractive river, and its silt is far inferior to that of the Jhelam.

**The Rávi.**—The Rávi was known to the writers of the Vedic hymns as the Parushní, but is called in classical Sanskrit Irávatí, whence the Hydraotes of the Greek historians. It rises near the Rotang pass in Kángra, and flows north-west through the southern part of Chamba. Below the town of Chamba, it runs as a swift slaty-blue mountain stream, and here it is spanned by a fine bridge. Passing on to the north of the hill station of Dalhousie it reaches the Kashmír border, and turning to the south-west flows along it to Basolí where Kashmír, Chamba, and the British district of Gurdáspur meet. At this point it is 2000 feet above the sea level. It now forms the boundary of Kashmír and Gurdáspur, and finally near Madhopur, where the head-works of the Bárí Doáb canal are situated, it passes into the Gurdáspur district. Shortly after it is joined from the north by a large torrent called the Ujh, which rises in the Jammu hills. After

Fig. 14. Fording the River at Lahore.

reaching the Siálkot border the Rávi parts that district first from Gurdáspur and then from Amritsar, and, passing through the west of Lahore, divides Montgomery and Lyallpur, and flowing through the north of Multán joins the Chenáb near the Jhang border. In Multán there is a remarkable straight reach in the channel known as the Sídhnai, which has been utilized for the site of the head-works of a small canal. The Degh, a torrent which rises in the Jammu hills and has a long course through the Siálkot and Gujránwála districts, joins the Rávi when in flood in the north of the Lyallpur district. But its waters will now be diverted into the river higher up in order to safeguard the Upper Chenáb canal. Lahore is on the left bank of the Rávi. It is a mile from the cold weather channel, but in high floods the waters have often come almost up to the Fort. At Lahore the North Western Railway and the Grand Trunk Road are carried over the Rávi by masonry bridges. There is a second railway bridge over the Sídhnai reach in Multán. Though the Rávi, like the Jhelam, has a course of 450 miles, it has a far smaller catchment area, and is really a somewhat insignificant stream. In the cold weather the canal takes such a heavy toll from it that below Mádhopur the supply of water is mainly drawn from the Ujh, and in Montgomery one may cross the bed dryshod for months together. The valley of the Rávi is far narrower than those of the rivers described in the preceding paragraphs, and the floods are most uncertain, but when they occur are of very great value.

**The Biás.**—The Biás (Sanskrit, Vipasa; Greek, Hyphasis) rises near the Rotang pass at a height of about 13,000 feet. Its head-waters are divided from those of the Rávi by the Bara Bangáhal range. It flows for about sixty miles through the beautiful Kulu valley to Lárjí (3000 feet). It has at first a rapid course, but before it reaches Sultánpur (4000 feet), the chief village in Kulu, some thirty miles from the source, it has become, at least in the cold weather, a comparatively peaceful stream fringed with alder thickets. Heavy floods, however, sometimes cover fields and orchards with sand and boulders. There is a bridge at Manálí (6100 feet), a very lovely spot, another below Nagar, and a third at Lárjí. Near Lárjí the river turns to the west down a bold ravine and becomes for a time the boundary between

Kulu and the Mandí State. Near the town of Mandí, where it is bridged, it bends again, and winds in a north-west and westerly direction through low hills in the south of Kángra till it meets the Siwáliks on the Hoshyárpur border. In this reach there is a bridge of boats at Dera Gopípur on the main road from Jalandhar and Hoshyárpur to Dharmsála. Elsewhere in the south of Kángra the traveller can cross without difficulty on

Fig. 15. Biás at Manálí.

a small bed supported on inflated skins. Sweeping round the northern end of the Siwáliks the Biás, having after long parting again approached within about fifteen miles of the Ráví, turns definitely to the south, forming henceforth the dividing line between Hoshyárpur and Kapúrthala (left bank) and Gurdáspur and Amritsar (right). Finally above the Harike ferry at a point where Lahore, Amritsar, Ferozepur, and Kapúrthala nearly meet, it falls into the Sutlej. The North Western

Railway crosses it by a bridge near the Biás station and at the same place there is a bridge of boats for the traffic on the Grand Trunk Road. The chief affluents are the Chakkí, the torrent which travellers to Dharmsála cross by a fine bridge twelve miles from the rail-head at Pathánkot, and the Black Bein in Hoshyárpur and Kapúrthala. The latter is a winding drainage channel, which starts in a swamp in the north of the Hoshyárpur district. The Biás has a total course of 390 miles. Only for about eighty miles or so is it a true river of the plains, and its floods do not spread far.

**The Sutlej.**—The Sutlej is the Shatadru of Vedic hymns and the Zaradros of Greek writers. The peasant of the Panjáb plains knows it as the Nílí or Ghara. After the Indus it is the greatest of Panjáb rivers, and for its source we have to go back to the Manasarowar lakes in Tibet. From thence it flows for 200 miles in a north-westerly direction to the British frontier near Shipkí. A little beyond the Spití river brings it the drainage of the large tract of that name in Kángra and of part of Western Tibet. From Shipkí it runs for forty miles in deep gorges through Kunáwar in the Bashahr State to Chíní, a beautiful spot near the Wangtu bridge, where the Hindustán-Tibet road crosses to the left bank. A little below Chíní the Baspa flows in from the south-east. The fall between the source and Chíní is from 15,000 to 7500 feet. There is magnificent cliff scenery at Rogí in this reach. Forty miles below Chíní the capital of Bashahr, Rámpur, on the south bank, is only 3300 feet above sea level. There is a second bridge at Rámpur, and from about this point the river becomes the boundary of Bashahr and Kulu, the route to which from Simla passes over the Lurí bridge (2650 feet) below Nárkanda. Beyond Lurí the Sutlej runs among low hills through several of the Simla Hill States. It pierces the Siwáliks at the Hoshyárpur border and then turns to the south, maintaining that trend till Rúpar and the head-works of the Sirhind canal are reached. For the next hundred miles to the Biás junction the general direction is west. Above the Harike ferry the Sutlej again turns, and flows steadily, though with many windings, to the south-west till it joins the Chenáb at the south corner of the Multán district. There are railway bridges at Phillaur, Ferozepur, and Adamwáhan. In the plains the Sutlej districts are—on the right bank Hoshyárpur, Jalandhar, Lahore, and Montgomery, and on the left Ambála, Ludhiána and Ferozepur. Below Ferozepur the river divides Montgomery and Multán from Baháwalpur (left bank). The Sutlej has a course of 900 miles, and a large catchment area in the hills. Notwithstanding the heavy toll taken by the Sirhind canal, its floods spread pretty far in Jalandhar and Ludhiána and below the Biás junction many monsoon canals have been dug which inundate a large area in the lowlands of the districts on either bank and of Baháwalpur. The dry bed of the Hakra, which can be traced through Baháwalpur, Bikaner, and Sindh, formerly carried the waters of the Sutlej to the sea.

**The Ghagar and the Sarustí.**—The Ghagar, once a tributary of the Hakra, rises within the Sirmúr State in the hills to the east of Kálka. A few miles south of Kálka it crosses a narrow neck of the Ambála district, and the bridge on the Ambála-Kálka railway is in this section. The rest of its course, till it loses itself in the sands of Bikaner, is chiefly in Patiála and the Karnál and Hissár districts. It is joined by the Umla torrent in Karnál and lower down the Sarustí unites with it in Patiála just beyond the Karnál border. It is hard to believe that the Sarustí of to-day is the famous Sarasvatí of the Vedas, though the little ditch-like channel that bears the name certainly passes beside the sacred sites of Thanesar and Pehowa. A small sandy torrent bearing the same name rises in the low hills in the north-east of the Ambála district, but it is doubtful if its waters, which finally disappear into the ground, ever reach the Thanesar channel. That seems rather to originate in the overflow of a rice swamp in the plains, and in the cold weather the bed is usually dry. In fact, till the Sarustí receives above Pehowa the floods of the Márkanda torrent, it is a most insignificant stream. The Márkanda, when in flood, carries a large volume of water, and below the junction the small channel of the Sarustí cannot carry the tribute received, which spreads out into a shallow lake called the Sainsa *jhíl*. This has been utilized for the supply of the little Sarustí canal, which is intended to do the work formerly effected in a rude way by throwing *bands* or embankments across the bed of the stream, and forcing the water over the surrounding lands. The same wasteful form of irrigation was used on a large scale on the Ghagar and is still practised on its upper reaches. Lower down earthen *bands* have been superceded by a masonry weir at Otu in the Hissár district. The northern and southern Ghagar canals, which irrigate lands in Hissár and Bikaner, take off from this weir.

**Action of Torrents.**—The Ghagar is large enough to exhibit all the three stages which a *cho* or torrent of intermittent flow passes through. Such a stream begins in the hills with a well-defined boulder-strewn bed, which is never dry. Reaching the plains the bed of a *cho* becomes a wide expanse of white sand, hardly below the level of the adjoining country, with a thread of water passing down it in the cold weather. But from time to time in the rainy season the channel is full from bank to bank and the waters spill far and wide over the fields. Sudden spates sometimes sweep away men and cattle before they can get across. If, as in Hoshyárpur, the *chos* flow into a rich plain from hills composed of friable sandstone and largely denuded of tree-growth, they are in their second stage most destructive. After long delay an Act was passed in 1900, which gives the government large powers for the protection of trees in the Siwáliks and the reclamation of torrent beds in the plains. The process of recovery cannot be rapid, but a measure of success has already been attained. It must not be supposed that the action of *chos* in this second stage is uniformly bad. Some carry silt as well as sand, and the very light loam which the great Márkanda *cho* has spread over the country on its banks is worth much more to the farmer than the stiff clay it has overlaid. Many *chos* do not pass into the third stage, when all the sand has been dropped, and the bed shrinks into a narrow ditch-like channel with steep clay banks. The inundations of torrents like the Degh and the Ghagar after this stage is reached convert the soil into a stiff impervious clay, where flood-water will lie for weeks without being absorbed into the soil. In Karnál the wretched and fever-stricken tract between the Ghagar and the Sarustí known as the Nailí is of this character.

**The Jamna.**—The Jamna is the Yamuna of Sanskrit writers. Ptolemy's and Pliny's versions, Diamouna and Jomanes, do not deviate much from the original. It rises in the Kumáon Himálaya, and, where it first meets the frontier of the Simla Hill States, receives from the north a large tributary called the Tons. Henceforth, speaking broadly, the Jamna is the boundary of the Panjáb and the United Provinces. On the Panjáb bank are from north to south the Sirmúr State, Ambála, Karnál, Rohtak, Delhi, and Gurgáon. The river leaves the Panjáb where Gurgáon and the district of Mathra, which belongs to the United Provinces, meet, and finally falls into the Ganges at Allahábád. North of Mathra Delhi is the only important town on its banks. The Jamna is crossed by railway bridges between Delhi and Meerut and between Ambála and Sahåranpur.

**Changes in Rivers.**—Allusion has already been made to the changes which the courses of Panjáb rivers are subject to in the plains. The Indus below Kálabágh once ran through the heart of what is now the Thal desert. We know that in 1245 A.D. Multán was in the Sind Ságar Doáb between the Indus and the united streams of the Jhelam, Chenáb, and Rávi. The Biás had then no connection with the Sutlej, but ran in a bed of its own easily to be traced to-day in the Montgomery and Multán districts, and joined the Indus between Multán and Uch. The Sutlej was still flowing in the Hakra bed. Indeed its junction with the Biás near Harike, which probably led to a complete change in the course of the Biás, seems only to have taken place within the last 150 years[1].

[1] Raverty's "The Mehran of Sind and its Tributaries," in *Journal of Asiatic Society of Bengal*, 1897.

# CHAPTER IV

## GEOLOGY AND MINERAL RESOURCES

**Extent of Geological Record.**—Although the main part of the Panjáb plain is covered by a mantle of comparatively recent alluvium, the provinces described in this book display a more complete record of Indian geological history than any other similar area in the country. The variety is so great that no systematic or sufficient description could be attempted in a short chapter, and it is not possible, therefore, to do more in these few pages than give brief sketches of the patches of unusual interest.

**Aravallí System.**—In the southern and south-eastern districts of the Panjáb there are exposures of highly folded and metamorphosed rocks which belong to the most ancient formations in India. These occupy the northern end of the Aravallí hills, which form but a relic of what must have been at one time a great mountain range, stretching roughly south-south-west through Rájputána into the Bombay Presidency. The northern ribs of the Aravallí series disappear beneath alluvial cover in the Delhi district, but the rocks still underlie the plains to the west and north-west, their presence being revealed by the small promontories that peep through the alluvium near the Chenáb river, standing up as small hills near Chiniot in the Sháhpur, Jhang, and Lyallpur districts.

The Salt Range in the Jhelam and Sháhpur districts, with a western continuation in the Mianwálí district to and beyond the Indus, is the most interesting part of the Panjáb to the geologist. It contains notable records of three distinct eras in geological history. In association with the well-known beds of rock-salt, which are being extensively mined at Kheora, occur the most ancient fossiliferous formations known in India, corresponding in age with the middle and lower part of the Cambrian system of Europe. These very ancient strata immediately overlie the red marls and associated rock-salt beds, and it is possible that they have been thrust over bodily to occupy this position, as we have no parallel elsewhere for the occurrence of great masses of salt in formation older than the Cambrian.

The second fragment of geological history preserved in the Salt Range is very much younger, beginning with rocks which were formed in the later part of the Carboniferous period. The most remarkable feature in this fragment is a boulder-bed, resting unconformably on the Cambrian strata and including boulders of various shapes and sizes, which are often faceted and striated in a way indicative of glacial action. Several of the boulders belong to rocks of a peculiar and unmistakable character, such as are found *in situ* on the western flanks of the Aravallí Range, some 750 miles to the south. The glacial conditions which gave rise to these boulder-beds were presumably contemporaneous with those that produced the somewhat similar formation lying at the base of the great coal-bearing system in the Indian peninsula. The glacial boulder-bed thus offers indirect evidence as to the age of the Indian coal-measures, for immediately above this bed in the Salt Range there occur sandstones containing fossils which have affinities with the Upper Carboniferous formations of Australia, and on these sandstones again there lie alternations of shales and limestones containing an abundance of fossils that are characteristic of the Permo-Carboniferous rocks of Russia. These are succeeded by an apparently conformable succession of beds of still younger age, culminating in a series of shales, sandstones, and limestones of unmistakably Triassic age.

There is then an interruption in the record, and the next younger series preserved occurs in the western part of the Salt Range as well as in the hills beyond the Indus. This formation is of Upper Jurassic age, corresponding to the well-known beds of marine origin preserved in Cutch. Then follows again a gap in the record, and the next most interesting series of formations found in the Salt Range become of great importance from the economic as well as from the purely scientific point of view; these are the formations of Tertiary age.

The oldest of the Tertiary strata include a prominent limestone containing Nummulitic fossils, which are characteristic of these Lower Tertiary beds throughout the world. Here, as in many parts of North-Western India, the Nummulitic limestones are associated with coal which has been largely worked. The country between the Salt Range plateau and the hilly region away to the north is covered by a great stretch of comparatively young Tertiary formations, which were laid down in fresh water after the sea had been driven back finally from this region. The incoming of fresh-water conditions was inaugurated by the formation of beds which are regarded as equivalent in age to those known as the Upper Nari in Sind and Eastern Baluchistán, but the still later deposits, belonging to the well-known Siwálik series, are famous on account of the great variety and large size of many of the vertebrate fossil remains which they have yielded. In these beds to the north of the Salt Range there have been found remains of Dinotherium, forms related to the ancestors of the giraffe and various other mammals, some of them, like the Sivatherium, Mastodon, and Stegodon, being animals of great size. On the northern side of the Salt Range three fairly well-defined divisions of the Siwálik series have been recognised, each being conspicuously fossiliferous—a feature that is comparatively rare in the Siwálik hills further to the south-east, where these rocks were first studied. The Siwálik series of the Salt Range are thus so well developed that this area might be conveniently regarded as the type succession for the purpose of correlating isolated fragmentary occurrences of the same general series in northern and western India. To give an idea as to the age of these rocks, it will be sufficient to mention that the middle division of the series corresponds roughly to the well-known deposits of Pikermi and Samos.

**Kashmír** deserves special mention, as it is a veritable paradise for the geologist. Of the variety of problems that it presents one might mention the petrological questions connected with the intrusion of the great masses of granite, and their relation to the slates and associated metamorphic rocks. Of fossiliferous systems there is a fine display of material ranging in age from Silurian to Upper Trias, and additional interest is added by the long-continued volcanic eruptions of the "Panjál trap." Students of recent phenomena have at their disposal interesting problems in physiography, including a grand display of glaciers, and the extensive deposits of so-called *karewas*, which appear to have been formed in drowned valleys, where the normal fluviatile conditions are modified by those characteristic of lakes. The occurrence of sapphires in Zánskar gives the State also an interest to the mineralogist and connoisseur of gem-stones.

Of this kaleidoscopic assemblage of questions the ones of most immediate interest are connected with the Silurian-Trias succession in the Kashmír valley, for here we have a connecting-link between the marine formations of the Salt Range area and those which are preserved in greater perfection in Spití and other parts of the Tibetan highlands, stretching away to the south-east at the back of the great range of crystalline snow-covered peaks.

In this interesting part of Kashmír the most important feature to Indian geologists is the occurrence of plant remains belonging to genera identical with those that occur in the lower part of the great coal-bearing formation of Peninsular India, known as the Gondwána system. Until these discoveries were made in Kashmír about ten years ago the age of the base of the Gondwánas was estimated only on indirect evidence, partly due to the assumption that glacial conditions in the Salt Range and those at the base of the Gondwánas were contemporaneous, and partly due to analogy with the coal measures of Australia and South Africa. In Kashmír the characteristic plant remains of the Lower Gondwánas are found associated with marine fossils in great abundance, and these permit of a correlation of the strata with the upper part of the Carboniferous system of the European standard stratigraphical scale.

Kashmír seems to have been near the estuary of one of the great rivers that formerly flowed over the ancient continent of *Gondwánaland* (when India and South Africa formed parts of one continental mass) into the great Eurasian Ocean known as *Tethys*. As the deposits formed in this great ocean give us the principal part of our data for forming a standard stratigraphical scale, the plants which were carried out to sea become witnesses of the kind of flora that flourished during the main Indian coal period; they thus enable us with great precision to fix the position of the fresh-water Gondwánas in comparison with the marine succession.

**Spití.**—With a brief reference to one more interesting patch among the geological records of this remarkable region, space will force us to pass on to consideration of minerals of economic value. The line of snow-covered peaks, composed mainly of crystalline rocks and forming a core to the Himálaya in a way analogous to the granitic core of the Alps, occupies what was once apparently the northern shore of Gondwánaland, and to the north of it there stretched the great ocean of Tethys, covering the central parts of Asia and Europe, one of its shrunken relics being the present Mediterranean Sea. The bed of this ocean throughout many geological ages underwent gradual depression and received the sediments brought down by the rivers from the continent which stretched away to the south. The sedimentary deposits thus formed near the shore-line or further out in deep water attained a thickness of well over 20,000 feet, and have been studied in the *tahsíl* of Spití, on the northern border of Kumáon, and again on the eastern Tibetan plateau to the north of Darjeeling. A reference to the formations preserved in Spití may be regarded as typical of the geological history and the conditions under which these formations were produced.

**Succession of Fossiliferous Beds.**—In age the fossiliferous beds range from Cambrian right through to the Tertiary epoch; between these extremes no single period was passed without leaving its records in some part of the great east-to-west Tibetan basin. At the base of the whole succession there lies a series of schists which have been largely metamorphosed, and on these rest the oldest of the fossiliferous series, which, on account of their occurring in the region of snow, has been named the *Haimanta system.* The upper part of the Haimanta system has been found to contain the characteristic trilobites of the Cambrian period of Europe. Over this system lie beds which have yielded in succession Ordovician and Silurian fossils, forming altogether a compact division which has been distinguished locally as the *Muth system*. Then follows the so-called *Kanáwar system*, which introduces Devonian conditions, followed by fossils characteristic of the well-known mountain limestone of Europe.

Then occurs a break in the succession which varies in magnitude in different localities, but appears to correspond to great changes in the physical geography which widely affect the Indian region. This break corresponds roughly to the upper part of the Carboniferous system of Europe, and has been suggested as a datum line for distinguishing in India an older group of fossiliferous systems below (formed in an area that has been distinguished by the name *Dravidian*), from the younger group above, which has been distinguished by the name *Aryan*.

During the periods that followed this interruption the bed of the great Eurasian Ocean seems to have subsided persistently though intermittently. As the various sediments accumulated the exact position of the shore-line must have changed to some extent to give rise to the conditions favourable for the formation at one time of limestone, at another of shale and at other times of sandy deposits. The whole column of beds, however, seems to have gone on accumulating without any folding movements, and they are consequently now found lying apparently in perfect conformity stage upon stage, from those that are Permian in age at the base, right through the Mesozoic group, till the time when Tertiary conditions were inaugurated and the earth movements began which ultimately drove back the ocean and raised the bed, with its accumulated load of sediments into the great folds that now form the Himalayan Range. This great mass of Aryan strata includes an enormous number of fossil remains, giving probably a more complete record of the gradual changes that came over the marine fauna of Tethys than any other area of the kind known. One must pass over the great number of interesting features still left unmentioned, including the grand architecture of the Sub-Himálaya and the diversity of formations in different parts of the Frontier Province ; for the rest of the available space must be devoted to a brief reference to the minerals of value.

**Rock-salt,** which occurs in abundance, is possibly the most important mineral in this area. The deposits most largely worked are those which occur in the well-known Salt Range, covering parts of the districts of Jhelam, Sháhpur, and Mianwálí. Near the village of Kheora the main seam, which is being worked in the Mayo mines, has an aggregate thickness of 550 feet, of which five seams, with a total thickness of 275 feet, consist of salt pure enough to be placed on the table with no more preparation than mere pulverising. The associated beds are impregnated with earth, and in places there occur thin layers of potash and magnesian salts. In this area salt quarrying was practised for an unknown period before the time of Akbar, and was continued in a primitive fashion until it came under the control of the British Government with the occupation of the Panjáb in 1849. In 1872 systematic mining operations were planned, and the general line of work has been continued ever since, with an annual output of roughly 100,000 tons.

Open quarries for salt are developed a short distance to the east-north-east of Kálabágh on the Indus, and similar open work is practised near Kohát in the North

West Frontier Province, where the quantity of salt may be regarded as practically inexhaustible. At Bahádur Khel the salt lies at the base of the Tertiary series, and can be traced for a distance of about eight miles with an exposed thickness of over 1000 feet, sometimes standing up as hills of solid salt above the general level of the plains. In this area the production is naturally limited by want of transport and the small local demand, the total output from the quarries being about 16,000 tons per annum. A small quantity of salt (generally about 4000 tons a year), is raised also from open quarries in the Mandí State, where the rock-salt beds, distinctly impure and earthy, lie near the junction between Tertiary formations and the older unfossiliferous groups.

**Coal** occurs at numerous places in association with the Nummulitic limestones of Lower Tertiary age, in the Panjáb, in the North West Frontier Province, and in the Jammu division of Kashmír. The largest output has been obtained from the Salt Range, where mines have been opened up on behalf of the North Western Railway. The mines at Dandot in the Jhelam district have considerable fluctuations in output, which, however, for many years ranged near 50,000 tons. These mines, having been worked at a financial loss, were finally abandoned by the Railway Company in 1911, but a certain amount of work is still being continued by local contractors. At Bháganwála, 19 miles further east, in the adjoining district of Sháhpur, coal was also worked for many years for the North Western State Railway, but the maximum output in any one year never exceeded 14,000 tons, and in 1900, owing to the poor quality of material obtained, the collieries were closed down. Recently, small outcrop workings have been developed in the same formation further west on the southern scarp of the Salt Range at Tejuwála in the Sháhpur district.

**Gold** to a small amount is washed from the gravel of the Indus and some other rivers by native workers, and large concessions have been granted for systematic dredging, but these enterprises have not yet reached the commercially paying stage.

**Other Metals.**—Prospecting has been carried on at irregular intervals in Kulu and along the corresponding belt of schistose rocks further west in Kashmír and Chitrál. The copper ores occur as sulphides along certain bands in the chloritic and micaceous schists, similar in composition and probably in age to those worked further east in Kumáon, in Nipál, and in Sikkim. In Lahul near the Shigrí glacier there is a lode containing **antimony** sulphide with ores of **zinc** and **lead**, which would almost certainly be opened up and developed but for the difficulty of access and cost of transport to the only valuable markets.

**Petroleum** springs occur among the Tertiary formations of the Panjáb and Biluchistán, and a few thousand gallons of oil are raised annually Prospecting operations have been carried on vigorously during the past two or three years, but no large supplies have so far been proved. The principal oil-supplies of Burma and Assam have been obtained from rocks of Miocene age, like those of Persia and the Caspian region, but the most promising "shows" in North West India have been in the older Nummulitic formations, and the oil is thus regarded by some experts as the residue of the material which has migrated from the Miocene beds that probably at one time covered the Nummulitic formations, but have since been removed by the erosive action of the atmosphere.

**Alum** is manufactured from the pyritous shales of the Mianwálí district, the annual output being generally about 200 to 300 tons. Similar shales containing pyrites are known to occur in other parts of this area, and possibly the industry might be considerably extended, as the annual requirements of India, judged by the import returns, exceed ten times the native production of alum.

**Borax** is produced in Ladákh and larger quantities are imported across the frontier from Tibet. In the early summer one frequently meets herds of sheep being driven southwards across the Himalayan passes, each sheep carrying a couple of small saddle-bags laden with borax or salt, which is bartered in the Panjáb bazars for Indian and foreign stores for the winter requirements of the snow-blocked valleys beyond the frontier.

**Sapphires.**—The sapphires of Zánskar have been worked at intervals since the discovery of the deposit in 1881, and some of the finest stones in the gem market have been obtained from this locality, where work is, however, difficult on account of the great altitude and the difficulty of access from the plains.

**Limestone.**—Large deposits of Nummulitic limestone are found in the older Tertiary formations of North-West India. It yields a pure lime and is used in large quantities for building purposes. The constant association of these limestones with shale beds, and their frequent association with coal, naturally suggest their employment for the manufacture of cement; and special concessions have recently been given by the Panjáb Government with a view of encouraging the development of the industry. The nodular impure limestone, known generally by the name of *kankar*, contains sufficient clay to give it hydraulic characters when burnt, and much cement is thus manufactured. The varying composition of *kankar* naturally results in a product of irregular character, and consequently cement so made can replace Portland cement only for certain purposes.

**Slate** is quarried in various places for purely local use. In the Kángra valley material of very high quality is obtained and consequently secures a wide distribution, limited, however, by competition with cheaply made tiles.

**Gypsum** occurs in large quantities in association with the rock-salt of the Salt Range, but the local demand is small. There are also beds of potash and magnesian salts in the same area, but their value and quantity have not been thoroughly proved.

January—February.

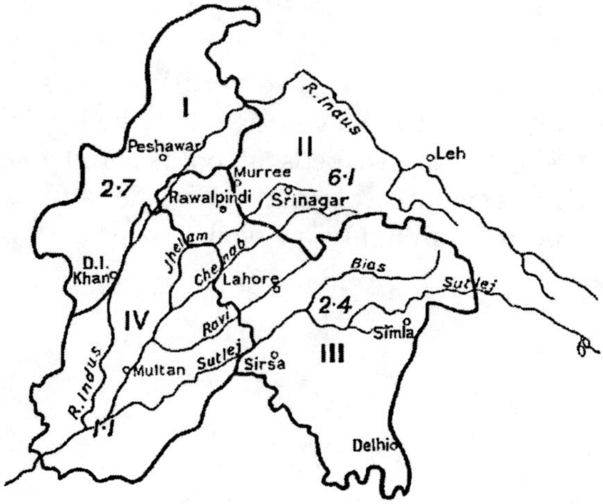


March to May.

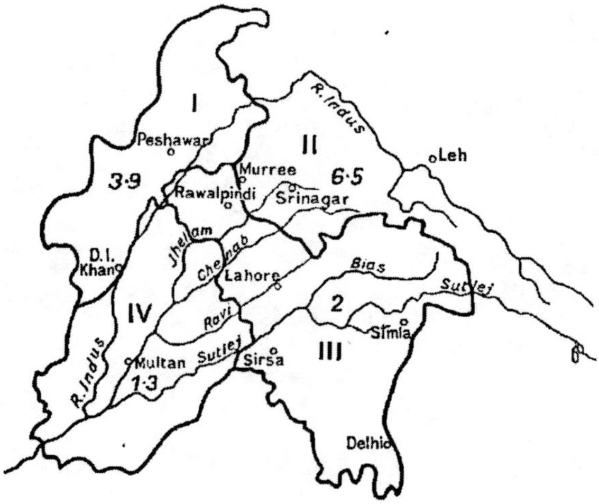


*Normal Rainfall.*

I. N.W.F. Province. II. Kashmír.

III. Panjáb E. and N. IV. Panjáb S.W.

Fig. 16. Rainfall of different Seasons.

June to September.

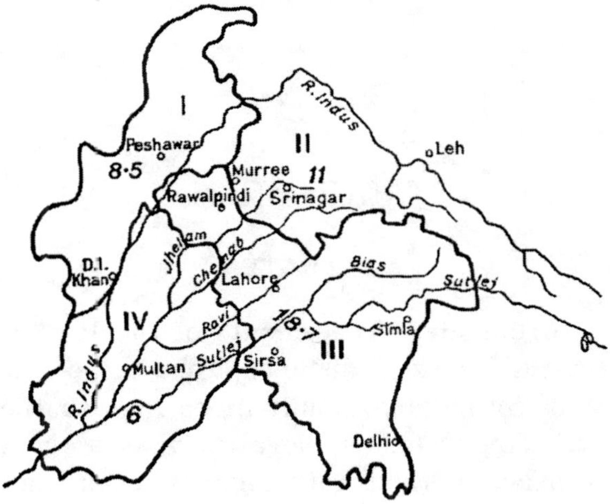


October to December.

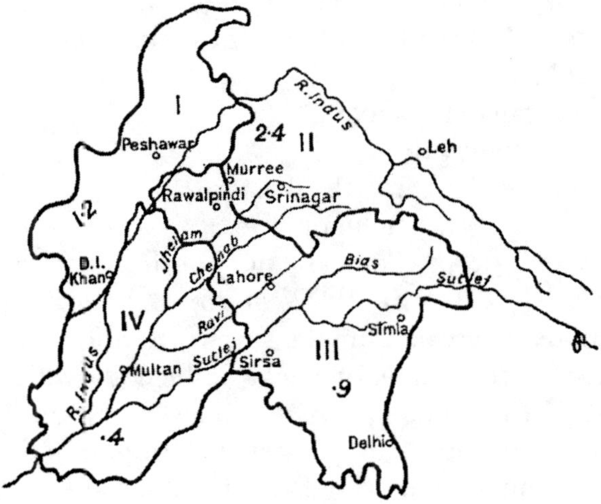


*Normal Rainfall.*

| | | | |
|---|---|---|---|
| I. | N.W.F. Province. | II. | Kashmír. |
| III. | Panjáb E. and N. | IV. | Panjáb S.W. |

Fig. 16 (*cont.*). Rainfall of different Seasons.

## CHAPTER V

### CLIMATE

**Types of Climate.**—The climate of the Panjáb plains is determined by their distance from the sea and the existence of formidable mountain barriers to the north and west. The factor of elevation makes the climate of the Himalayan tracts very different from that of the plains. Still more striking is the contrast between the Indian Himalayan climate and the Central Asian Trans-Himalayan climate of Spití, Lahul, and Ladákh.

**Zones.**—A broad division into six zones may be recognised :

A 1. Trans-Himalayan.

B 2. Himalayan.

C. Plains
   3. North Western.
   4. Submontane.
   5. Central and South Eastern.
   6. South Western.

**Trans-Himalayan Climate.**—Spití, Lahul, and Ladákh are outside the meteorological influences which affect the rest of the Indian Empire. The lofty ranges of the Himálaya interpose an almost insurmountable barrier between them and the clouds of the monsoon. The rainfall is extraordinarily small, and, considering the elevation of the inhabited parts, 10,000 to 14,000 feet, the snowfall there is not heavy. The air is intensely dry and clear, and the daily and seasonal range of temperature is extreme. Leh, the capital of Ladákh (11,500 feet), has an average rainfall (including snow) of about 3 inches. The mean temperature is 43° Fahr., varying from 19° in January to 64° in July. But these figures give no idea of the rigours of the severe but healthy climate. The daily range is from 25 to 30 degrees, or double what we are accustomed to in England. Once 17° below zero was

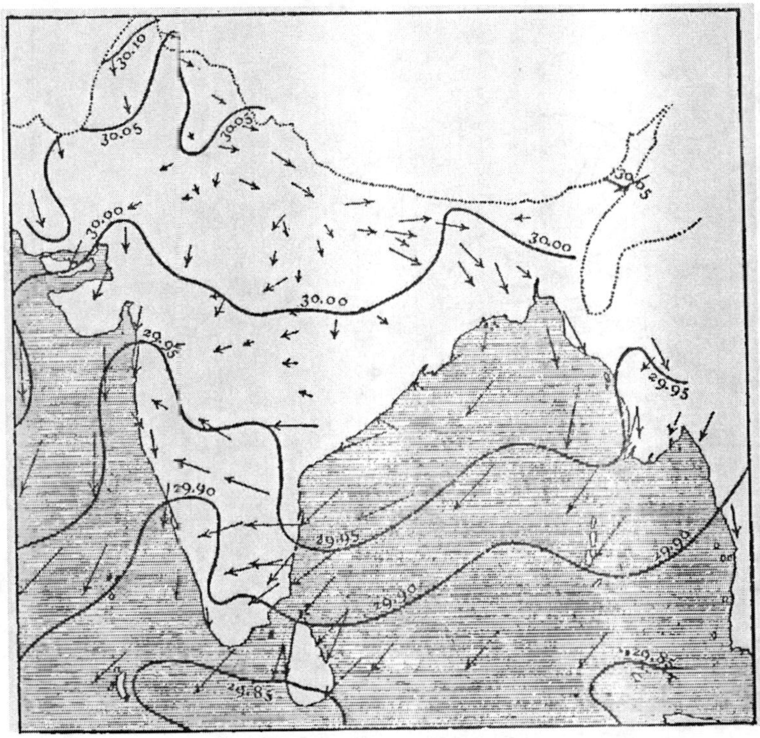


Fig. 17. Average Barometric and Wind Chart for January.

recorded. In the rare dry clear atmosphere the power of the solar rays is extraordinary. "Rocks exposed to the sun may be too hot to lay the hand upon at the same time that it is freezing in the shade."

**The Indian Zones—Meteorological factors.**—The distribution of pressure in India, determined mainly by changes of temperature, and itself determining the direction of the winds and the character of the weather, is shown graphically in figures 17 and 18. The winter or north-east monsoon does not penetrate into the Panjáb, where light westernly and northernly winds

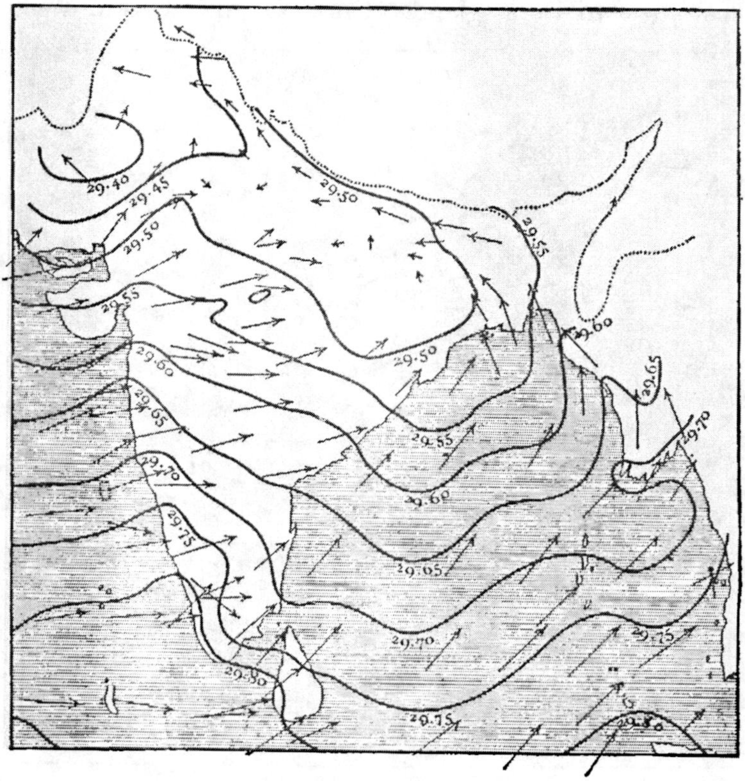


**Fig. 18. Average Barometric and Wind Chart for July.**

prevail during the cold season. What rain is received is due to land storms originating beyond the western frontier. The branch of the summer or south-west monsoon which chiefly affects the Panjáb is that which blows up the Bay of Bengal. The rain-clouds striking the Eastern Himálaya are deflected to the west and forced up the

Gangetic plain by south-westernly winds. The lower ranges of the Panjáb Himálaya receive in this way very heavy downpours. The rain extends into the plains, but exhausts itself and dies away pretty rapidly to the south and west. The Bombay branch of the monsoon mostly spends itself on the Gháts and in the Deccan. But a part of it penetrates from time to time to the south-east Panjáb, and, if it is sucked into the Bay current, the result is widespread rain.

**Himalayan Zone.**—The impressions which English people get of the climate of the Himálaya, or in Indian phrase "the Hills," are derived mainly from stations like Simla and Murree perched at a height of from 6500 to 7500 feet on the outer ranges. The data of meteorologists are mainly taken from the same localities. Places between 8000 and 10,000 feet in height and further from the plains enjoy a finer climate, being both cooler and drier in summer. But they are less accessible, and weakly persons would find the greater rarity of the air trying.

In the first fortnight of April the plains become disagreeably warm, and it is well to take European children to the Hills. The Panjáb Government moves to Simla in the first fortnight of May. By that time Simla is pretty warm in the middle of the day, but the nights are pleasant. The mean temperature of the 24 hours in May and June is 65° or 66°, the mean maximum and minimum being 78° and 59°. Thunderstorms with or without hail are not uncommon in April, May, and June. In a normal year the monsoon clouds drift up in the end of June, and the next three months are "the Rains." Usually it does not rain either all day or every day, but sometimes for weeks together Simla is smothered in a blanket of grey mist. Normally the rain comes in bursts with longer or shorter breaks between. About the third week of September the rains often cease quite suddenly, the end being usually proclaimed by a thunder-storm. Next morning one wakes to a new heaven and a new earth, a perfectly cloudless sky, and clean, crisp, cool air. This ideal weather lasts for the next three months. Even in December the days are made pleasant by bright sunshine, and the range of temperature is much less than in the plains. In the end of December or beginning of January the night thermometer often falls lower at Ambála and Ráwalpindí than at Simla and Murree. After Christmas the weather becomes broken, and in January and February falls of snow occur. It is a disagreeable time, and English residents are glad to descend to the plains. In March also the weather is often unsettled. The really heavy falls of snow occur at levels much higher than Simla. These remarks apply *mutatis mutandis* to Dharmsála, Dalhousie, and Murree. Owing to its position right under a lofty mountain wall Dharmsála is a far wetter place than Simla. Murree gets its monsoon later, and the summer rainfall is a good deal lighter. In winter it has more snow, being nearer the source of origin of the storms. Himalayan valleys at an elevation of 5000 feet, such as the Vale of Kashmír, have a pleasant climate. The mean temperature of Srínagar (5255 feet) varies from 33° in January to 75° in July, when it is unpleasantly hot, and Europeans often move to Gulmarg. Kashmír has a heavy snowfall even in the Jhelam valley. Below 4000 feet, especially in confined river valleys the Himalayan climate is often disagreeably hot and stuffy.

**Climate of the Plains.**—The course of the seasons is the same in the plains. The jaded resident finds relief when the rains cease in the end of September. The days are still warm, but the skies are clear, the air dry, and the nights cool. November is rainless and in every way a pleasant month. The clouds begin to gather before Christmas, but rain often holds off till January. Pleasant though the early months of the cold weather are, they lay traps for the unwary. In October and November the daily range of temperature is very large, exceeding 30°, and the fall at sunset very sudden. Care is needed to avoid a chill and the fever that follows. Clear and dry though the air is, the blue of the skies is pale owing to a light dust haze in the upper atmosphere. For the same reason the Himalayan snows except after rain are veiled from dwellers in the plains at a distance of 30 miles from the foot-hills. The air in these months before the winter rains is wonderfully still. In the three months after Christmas the Panjáb is the pathway of a series of small storms from the west, preceded by close weather and occurring usually at intervals of a few weeks. After a day or two of wet weather the sky clears, and the storm is followed by a great drop in the temperature. The traveller who shivers after a January rainstorm finds it hard to believe that the Panjáb plain is a part of the hottest region of the Old World which stretches from the Sahára to Delhi. If he had to spend the period from May to July there he would have small doubts on the subject. The heat begins to be unpleasant in April, when hot westernly winds prevail. An occasional thunderstorm with hail relieves the strain for a little. The warmest period of the year is May and June. But the intense dry heat is healthier and to many less trying than the mugginess of the rainy season. The dust-storms which used to be common have become rarer and lighter with the spread of canal irrigation in the western Panjáb. The rains ought to break at Delhi in the end of June and at Lahore ten days or a fortnight later. There is often a long break when the climate is particularly trying. The nights are terribly hot. The outer air is then less stifling than that of the house, and there is the chance of a little comparative coolness shortly before dawn. Many therefore prefer to sleep on the roof or in the verandah. September, when the rains slacken, is a muggy, unpleasant, and unhealthy month. But in the latter half of it cooler nights give promise of a better time.

**Special features of Plain Zones.**—The submontane zone has the most equable and the pleasantest climate in the plains. It has a rainfall of from 30 to 40 inches, five-sevenths or more of which belongs to the monsoon period (June—September) The north-western area has a longer and colder winter and spring. In the end of December and in January the keen dry cold is distinctly trying. The figures in Statement I, for Ráwalpindí and Pesháwar, are not very characteristic of the zone as a whole. The average of the rainfall figures, 13 inches for Pesháwar and 32 for Ráwalpindí, would give a truer result. The monsoon rains come later and are much less abundant than in the submontane zone. Their influence is very feeble in the western and south-western part of the area. On the other hand the winter rains are heavier than in any other part of the province. Delhi and Lahore represent the extreme conditions of the central and south-eastern plains. The latter is really on the edge of the dry south-western area. The eastern districts of the zone have a shorter and less severe cold weather than the western, an earlier and heavier monsoon, but scantier winter rains. The total rainfall varies from 16 to 30 inches. The south-western zone, with a rainfall of from 5 to 15 inches, is the driest part of India proper except northern Sindh and western Rájputána. Neither monsoon current affects it much. At Multán there are only about fifteen days in the whole year on which any rain falls.

# CHAPTER VI

## HERBS, SHRUBS, AND TREES

**Affinities of Panjáb Flora.**—It is hopeless to describe except in the broadest outline the flora of a tract covering an area of 250,000 square miles and ranging in altitude from a few hundred feet to a height 10,000 feet above the limit of flowering plants. The nature of the vegetation of any tract depends on rainfall and temperature, and only secondarily on soil. A desert is a tract with a dry substratum and dry air, great heat during some part of the year, and bright sunshine. The soil may be loam or sand, and as regards vegetation a sandy desert is the worst owing to the rapid drying up of the subsoil after rain. In the third of the maps appended to Schimper's *Plant Geography* by far the greater part of the area dealt with in this book is shown as part of the vast desert extending from the Sahára to Manchuria. Seeing that the monsoon penetrates into the province and that it is traversed by large snow-fed rivers the Panjáb, except in parts of the extreme western and south-western districts, is not a desert like the Sahára or Gobí, and Schimper recognised this by marking most of the area as semi-desert. Still the flora outside the Hills and the sub-montane tract is predominantly of the desert type, being xerophilous or drought-resisting. The adaptations which enable plants to survive in a tract deficient in moisture are of various kinds. The roots may be greatly developed to enable them to tap the subsoil moisture, the leaves may be reduced in size, converted into thorns, or entirely dispensed with, in order to check rapid evaporation, they may be covered with silky or felted hairs, a modification which produces the same result, or their internal tissue may be succulent or mucilaginous. In the plants of the Panjáb plains there is no difficulty in recognising these features of a drought-resisting flora. Schimper's map shows in the north-east of the area a wedge thrust in between the plains' desert and the dry elevated alpine desert cut off from the influence of the monsoon by the lofty barrier of the Inner Himálaya. This consists of two parts, monsoon forest, corresponding roughly with the Himalayan area Cis Rávi above the 5000 feet contour, and dry woodland of a semi-tropical stamp, consisting of the adjoining foot-hills and sub-montane tract. This wedge is in fact treated as part of the zone, which in the map (after Drude) prefixed to Willis' *Manual and Dictionary of the Flowering Plants and Ferns*, is called Indo-Malayan, and which embraces the Malayan Archipelago and part of North Australia, Burma, and practically the whole of India except the Panjáb, Sindh, and Rájputána. In Drude's map the three countries last mentioned are included in a large zone called "the Mediterranean and Orient." This is a very broad classification, and in tracing the relationships of the Panjáb flora it is better to treat the desert area of North Africa, which in Tripoli and Egypt extends to the coast, apart from the Mediterranean zone. It is a familiar fact that, as we ascend lofty mountains like those of the Himálaya, we pass through belts or regions of vegetation of different types. The air steadily becomes rarer and therefore colder, especially at night, and at the higher levels there is a marked reduction in the rainfall. When the alpine region, which in the Himálaya may be taken as beginning at 11,000 feet, is reached, the plants have as a rule bigger roots, shorter stems, smaller leaves, but often larger and more brilliantly coloured flowers. These are adaptations of a drought-resisting kind.

**Regions.**—In this sketch it will suffice to divide the tract into six regions:

Plains 1. Panjáb dry plain.
2. Salt Range and North West Plateau, from the frontier to Pabbí Hills.
3. Submontane Hills on east bank of Jhelam.

Hills 4. Sub-Himálaya, 2000–5000 feet.
5. Temperate Himálaya, 5000–11,000 feet.
6. Alpine Himálaya, 11,000–16,000 feet.

Of course a flora does not fit itself into compartments, and the changes of type are gradual.

**Panjáb Dry Plain.**—The affinities of the flora of the Panjáb plains south of the Salt Range and the submontane tract are, especially in the west, with the desert areas of Persia, Arabia, and North Africa, though the spread of canal irrigation is modifying somewhat the character of the vegetation. The soil and climate are unsuited to the growth of large trees, but adapted to scrub jungle of a drought-resisting type, which at one time covered very large areas from the Jamna to the Jhelam. The soil on which this sparse scrub grew is a good strong loam, but the rainfall was too scanty and the water-level too deep to admit of much cultivation outside the valleys of the rivers till the labours of canal engineers carried their waters to the uplands. East of the Sutlej the Bikaner desert thrusts northwards a great wedge of sandy land which occupies a large area in Baháwalpur, Hissár, Ferozepur, and Patiála. Soil of this description is free of forest growth, and the monsoon rainfall in this part of the province is sufficient to encourage an easy, but very precarious, cultivation of autumn millets and pulses. The great Thal desert to the south of the Salt Range between the valleys of the Jhelam and the Indus has a similar soil, but the scantiness of the rainfall has confined cultivation within much narrower limits. Between the Sutlej and the Jhelam the uplands between the river valleys are known locally as Bárs. The largest of the truly indigenous trees of the Panjáb plains are the *farásh* (Tamarix articulata) and the thorny *kíkar* (Acacia Arabica). The latter yields excellent wood for agricultural implements, and fortunately it grows well in sour soils. Smaller thorny acacias are the *nímbar* or *raunj* (Acacia leucophloea) and the *khair* (Acacia senegal). The dwarf tamarisk, *pilchí* or *jhao* (Tamarix dioica), grows freely in moist sandy soils near rivers. The scrub jungle consists mostly of *jand* (Prosopis spicigera), a near relation of the Acacias, *jál* or *van* (Salvadora oleoides), and the coral-flowered *karíl* or leafless caper (Capparis aphylla). All these show their desert affinities, the *jand* by its long root and its thorns, the *jál* by its small leathery leaves, and the *karíl* by the fact that it has managed to dispense with leaves altogether. The *jand* is a useful little tree, and wherever it grows the natural qualities of the soil are good. The sweetish fruit of the *jál*, known as *pílu*, is liked by the people, and in famines they will even eat the berries of the leafless caper. Other characteristic plants of the Panjáb plains are under Leguminosae, the *khip* (Crotalaria burhia), two Farsetias (*faríd kí búti*), and the *jawása* or camel thorn (Alhagi camelorum), practically leafless, but with very long and stout spines; under Capparidaceae several Cleomes, species of Corchorus (Tiliaceae), under Zygophyllaceae three Mediterranean genera, Tribulus, Zygophyllum, and Fagonia, under Solanaceae several Solanums and Withanias, and various salsolaceous Chenopods known as *lána*.

In the sandier tracts the *ak* (Calotropis procera, N.O. Asclepiadaceae), the *harmal* (Peganum harmala, N.O. Rutaceae), and the colocynth gourd (Citrullus colocynthis, N.O. Cucurbitaceae), which, owing to the size of its roots, manages to flourish in the sands of African and Indian deserts, grow abundantly. Common weeds of cultivation are Fumaria parviflora, a near relation of the English fumitory, Silene conoidea, and two Spergulas

Fig. 19. Banian or Bor trees.

(Caryophyllaceae), and Sisymbrium Irio (Cruciferae). A curious little Orchid, Zeuxine sulcata, is found growing among the grass on canal banks. The American yellow poppy, Argemone Mexicana, a noxious weed, has unfortunately established itself widely in the Panjáb plain. Two trees of the order Leguminosae, the *shisham* or *tálí* (Dalbergia Sissoo) and the *siris* (Albizzia lebbek), are commonly planted on Panjáb roads. The true home of the former is in river beds in the low hills or in ravines below the hills. But it is a favourite tree on roads and near wells throughout the province, and deservedly so, for it yields excellent timber. The *siris* on the other hand is an untidy useless tree. The *kikar* might be planted as a roadside tree to a greater extent. Several species of figs, especially the *pípal* (Ficus religiosa) and *bor* or banian (Ficus Indica) are popular trees.

**Salt Range and North-West Plains.**—Our second region may be taken as extending from the Pabbí hills on the east of the Jhelam in Gujrát to our administrative boundary beyond the Indus, its southern limit being the Salt Range. Here the flora is of a distinctly Mediterranean type. Poppies are as familiar in Ráwalpindí as they are in England or Italy, and Hypecoum procumbens, a curious Italian plant of the same order, is found in Attock. The abundance of Crucifers is also a Mediterranean feature. Eruca sativa, the oil-seed known as *táramíra* or *jamián*, which sows itself freely in waste land and may be found growing even on railway tracks in the Ráwalpindí division, is an Italian and Spanish weed. Malcolmia strigosa, which spreads a reddish carpet over the ground, and Malcolmia Africana are common Crucifers near Ráwalpindí. The latter is a Mediterranean species. The Salt Range genera Diplotaxis and Moricandia are Italian, and the peculiar Notoceras Canariensis found in Attock is also a native of the Canary Islands. Another order, Boraginaceae, which is very prominent in the Mediterranean region, is also important in the North-West Panjáb, though the showier plants of the order are wanting. One curious Borage, Arnebia Griffithii, seems to be purely Asiatic. It has five brown spots on its petals, which fade and disappear in the noonday sunshine. These are supposed to be drops of sweat which fell from Muhammad's forehead, hence the plant is called *paighambarí phúl* or the prophet's flower. Among Composites Calendulas and Carthamus oxyacantha or the *pohlí*, a near relation of the Carthamus which yields the saffron dye, are abundant. Both are common Mediterranean genera. Silybum Marianum, a handsome thistle with large leaves mottled with white, extends from Britain to Ráwalpindí. Interesting species are Tulipa stellata and Tulipa chrysantha. The latter is a Salt Range plant, as is the crocus-like Merendera Persica, and the yellow Iris Aitchisoni. A curious plant found in the same hills is the cactus-like Boucerosia (N.O. Asclepiadaceae), recalling to botanists the more familiar Stapelias of the same order. Another leafless Asclepiad, Periploca aphylla, which extends westwards to Arabia and Nubia and southwards to Sindh, is, like Boucerosia, a typical xerophyte adapted to a very dry soil and atmosphere. The thorny Acacias, A. eburnea and A. modesta (vern. *phuláhí*), of the low bare hills of the N.W. Panjáb are also drought-resisting plants.

**Submontane Region.**—The Submontane region consists of a broad belt below the Siwáliks extending from the Jamna nearly to the Jhelam, and may be said to include the districts of Ambála, Karnál (part), Hoshyárpur, Kángra (part), Hazára (part), Jalandhar, Gurdáspur, Siálkot, Gujrát (part). In its flora there is a strong infusion of Indo-Malayan elements. An interesting member of it is the Butea frondosa, a small tree of the order Leguminosae. It is known by several names, *dhák, chichra, paláh,* and *palás*. Putting out its large orange-red flowers in April it ushers in the hot weather. It has a wide range from Ceylon to Bengal, where it has given its name to the town of Dacca and the battlefield of Plassy (Palási). From Bengal it extends all the way to Hazára. There can be no doubt that a large part of the submontane region was once *dhák* forest. Tracts in the north of Karnál—Chachra, in Jalandhar—Dardhák, and in Gujrát—Palábí, have taken their names from this tree. It coppices very freely, furnishes excellent firewood and good timber for the wooden frames on which the masonry cylinders of wells are reared, it exudes a valuable gum, its flowers yield a dye, and the dry leaves are eaten by buffaloes. A tree commonly planted near wells and villages in the submontane tract is the *dhrek* (Melia azedarach, N.O. Meliaceae), which is found as far west as Persia and is often called by English people the Persian lilac. The *bahera* (Terminalia belerica, N.O. Combretaceae), a much larger tree, is Indo-Malayan. Common shrubs are the *marwan* (Vitex negundo, N.O. Verbenaceae), Plumbago Zeylanica (Plumbaginaceae), the *bánsa* or *bhekar* (Adhatoda vasica, N.O. Acanthaceae). The last is Indo-Malayan. Among herbs Cassias, which do not occur in Europe, are common. The curious cactus-like Euphorbia Royleana grows abundantly and is used for making hedges.

**Sub-Himálaya.**—A large part of the Sub-Himalayan region belongs to the Siwáliks. The climate is fairly moist and subject to less extremes of heat and cold than the regions described above. A strong infusion of Indo-Malayan types is found and a noticeable feature is the large number of flowering trees and shrubs. Such beautiful flowering trees as the *simal* or silk-cotton tree (Bombax Malabaricum, N.O. Malvaceae), the *amaltás* (Cassia fistula), Albizzia mollis and Albizzia stipulata, Erythrina suberosa, Bauhinia purpurea and Bauhinia variegata, all belonging to the order Leguminosae, are unknown in Europe, but common in the Indo-Malayan region. This is true also of Oroxylum Indicum (N.O. Bignoniaceae) with its remarkable long sword-like capsules, and of the *kamíla* (Mallotus Philippinensis), which abounds in the low hills, but may escape the traveller's notice as its flowers have no charm of form or colour. He will in spring hardly fail to observe another Indo-Malayan tree, the *dháwi* (Woodfordia floribunda, N.O. Lythraceae) with its bright red flowers. Shrubs with conspicuous flowers are also common, among which may be noted species of Clematis, Capparis spinosa, Kydia calycina, Mimosa rubicaulis, Hamiltonia suaveolens, Caryopteris Wallichiana, and Nerium Oleander. The latter grows freely in sandy torrent beds. Rhus cotinus, which reddens the hillsides in May, is a native also of Syria, Italy, and Southern France. Other trees to be noticed are a wild pear (Pyrus pashia), the olive (Olea cuspidata), the *khair* (Acacia catechu) useful to tanners, the *tun* (Cedrela toona), whose wood is often used for furniture, the *dháman* (Grewia oppositifolia, N.O. Tiliaceae), and several species of fig. The most valuable products however of the forests of the lower hills are the *chír* or *chíl* pine (Pinus longifolia), and a giant grass, the bamboo (Dendrocalamus strictus), which attains a height of from 20 to 40 feet. Shrubs which grow freely on stony hills are the *sanattha* or *mendru* (Dodonaea viscosa, N.O. Sapindaceae), which is a valuable protection against denudation, as goats pass it by, the *garna*, which is a species of Carissa, and Plectranthus rugosus. Climbers are common. The great Hiptage madablota (N.O. Malpighiaceae), the Bauhinia Vahlii or elephant creeper, and some species of the parasitic Loranthus, deserve mention, also Acacia caesia, Pueraria tuberosa, Vallaris Heynei, Porana paniculata, and several vines, especially Vitis lanata with its large rusty leaves. Characteristic herbs are the sweet-scented Viola patrinii, the slender milkwort, Polygala Abyssinica, a handsome pea, Vigna vexillata, a borage, Trichodesma Indicum, a balsam, Impatiens balsamina, familiar in English gardens, the beautiful delicate little blue Evolvulus alsinoides, the showy purple convolvulus, Ipomaea hederacea, and a curious lily, Gloriosa superba.

**Temperate Himálaya.**—The richest part of the temperate Himalayan flora is probably in the 7500–10,000 zone. Above 10,000 feet sup-alpine conditions begin, and at 12,000 feet tree growth becomes very scanty and the flora is distinctly alpine. The *chír* pine so common in sub-Himalayan forests extends up to 6500 feet. At this height

Fig. 20. Deodárs and Hill Temple.

and 1000 feet lower the *ban* oak (Quercus incana), grey on the lower side of the leaf, which is so common at Simla, abounds. Where the *chíl* stops, the *kail* or blue pine (Pinus excelsa), after the *deodár* the most valuable product of Himalayan forests, begins. Its zone may be taken as from 7000 to 9000 feet. To the same zone belong the *kelu* or *deodár* (Cedrus Libani), the glossy leaved *mohru* oak (Quercus dilatata), whose wood is used for making charcoal, and two small trees of the Heath order, Rhododendron arborea and Pieris ovalifolia. The former in April and May lightens up with its bright red flowers the sombre Simla forests. The *kharshu* or rusty-leaved oak (Quercus semecarpifolia) affects a colder climate than its more beautiful glossy-leaved relation, and may almost be considered sub-alpine. It is common on Hattu, and the oaks there present a forlorn appearance after rain with funereal mosses dripping with moisture hanging from their trunks. The firs, Picea morinda, with its grey tassels, and Abies Pindrow with its dark green yew-like foliage, succeed the blue pine. Picea may be said to range from 8000 to 10,000 feet, and the upper limit of Abies is from 1000 to 2000 feet higher. These splendid trees are unfortunately of small commercial value. The yew, Taxus baccata, is found associated with them. Between 5000 and 8000 feet, besides the oaks and other broad-leaved trees already noticed, two relations of the dogwood, Cornus capitata and Cornus macrophylla, a large poplar, Populus ciliata, a pear, Pyrus lanata, a holly, Ilex dipyrena, an elm and its near relation, Celtis australis, and species of Rhus and Euonymus, may be mentioned. Cornus capitata is a small tree, but it attracts notice because the heads of flowers surrounded by bracts of a pale yellow colour have a curious likeness to a rose, and the fruit is in semblance not unlike a strawberry. Above 8000 feet several species of maple abound. The *chinár* or Platanus orientalis, found as far west as Sicily, grows to splendid proportions by the quiet waterways of the Vale of Kashmír. The undergrowth in temperate Himalayan forests consists largely of barberries, Desmodiums, Indigoferas, roses, brambles, Spiraeas, Viburnums, honeysuckles with their near relation, Leycesteria formosa,

Fig. 21. Firs in Himálaya.

which has been introduced into English shrubberies. The great vine, Vitis Himalayana, whose leaves turn red in autumn, climbs up many of the trees. Of the flowers it is impossible to give any adequate account. The flora is distinctly Mediterranean in type; the orders in Collett's *Flora Simlensis* which are not represented in the Italian flora contain hardly more than 5 per cent. of the total genera. The plants included in some of these

Fig. 22. Chinárs.

non-Mediterranean orders are very beautiful, for example, the Begonias, the Amphicomes (Bignoniaceae), Chirita bifolia and Platystemma violoides (Gesneraceae), and Hedychium (Scitamineae). More important members of the flora are species of Clematis, including the beautiful white Clematis montana, anemones, larkspurs, columbine, monkshoods, St John's worts, geraniums, balsams, species of Astragalus, Potentillas, Asters, ragworts, species of

Cynoglossum, gentians and Swertias, Androsaces and primroses, Wulfenia and louseworts, species of Strobilanthes, Salvias and Nepetas, orchids, irises, Ophiopogon, Smilax, Alliums, lilies, and Solomon's seal. Snake plants (Arisaema) and their relation Sauromatum guttatum of the order Araceae are very common in the woods. The striped spathe in some species of Arisaema bears

Fig. 23. Rhododendron campanulatum.

a curious resemblance to the head of a cobra uplifted to strike. Orchids decrease as one proceeds westwards, but irises are much more common in Kashmír than in the Simla hills. The Kashmír fritillaries include the beautiful Crown Imperial.

**Alpine Himálaya.**—In the Alpine Himálaya the scanty tree-growth is represented by willows, junipers, and birches. After 12,000 or 12,500 feet it practically disappears. A dwarf shrub, Juniperus recurva, is found clothing hill-sides a good way above the two trees of the same genus. Other alpine shrubs which may be noticed are two rhododendrons, which grow on cliffs at an elevation of 10,000 to 14,000 feet, R. campanulatum and R. lepidotum, Gaultheria nummularioides with its black-purple berry, and Cassiope fastigiata, all belonging to the order Ericaceae. The herbs include beautiful primulas, saxifrages, and gentians, and in the bellflower order species of Codonopsis and Cyananthus. Among Composites may be mentioned the tansies, Saussureas, and the fine Erigeron multiradiatus common in the forest above Narkanda. In the bleak uplands beyond the Himálaya tree-growth is very scanty, but in favoured localities willows and the pencil cedar, Juniperus pseudo-sabina, are found. The people depend for fuel largely on a hoary bush of the Chenopod order, Eurotia ceratoides. In places a profusion of the red Tibetan roses, Rosa Webbiana, lightens up the otherwise dreary scene.

# CHAPTER VII

## FORESTS

**Rights of State in Waste.**—Under Indian rule the State claimed full power of disposing of the waste, and, even where an exclusive right in the soil was not maintained, some valuable trees, e.g. the *deodár* in the Himálaya, were treated as the property of the Rája. Under the tenure prevailing in the hills the soil is the Rája's, but the people have a permanent tenant right in any land brought under cultivation with his permission. In Kulu the British Government asserted its ownership of the waste. In the south-western Panjáb, where the scattered hamlets had no real boundaries, ample waste was allotted to each estate, and the remainder was claimed as State property.

**Kinds of Forest.**—The lands in the Panjáb over which authority, varying through many degrees from full ownership unburdened with rights of user down to a power of control exercised in the interests of the surrounding village communities, may be roughly divided into

(*a*) Mountain forests ;

(*b*) Hill forests ;

(*c*) Scrub and grass *Jangal* in the Plains.

The first are forests of *deodár*, blue pine, fir, and oak in the Himálaya above the level of 5000 feet. The hill forests occupy the lower spurs, the Siwáliks in Hoshyárpur, etc., and the low dry hills of the north-west. A strong growth of *chír* pine (Pinus longifolia) is often found in the Himálaya between 3000 and 5000 feet. Below 3000 feet is scrub forest, the only really valuable product being bamboo. The hills in the north-western districts of the Panjáb and N.W.F. Province, when nature is allowed to have its way, are covered with low scrub including in some parts a dwarf palm (Nannorhops Ritchieana), useful for mat making, and with a taller, but scantier growth of *phuláhí* (Acacia modesta) and wild olive. What remains of the scrub and grass *jangal* of the plains is to be found chiefly in the Bár tracts between the Sutlej and the Jhelam. Much of it has disappeared, or is about to disappear, with the advance of canal irrigation. Dry though the climate is the Bár was in good seasons a famous grazing area. The scrub consisted mainly of *jand* (Prosopis spicigera), *jál* (Salvadora oleoides), the *karíl* (Capparis aphylla) and the *farásh* (Tamarix articulata).

**Management and Income of Forests.**—The Forest Department of the Panjáb has existed since 1864, when the first Conservator was appointed. In 1911–12 it managed 8359 square miles in the Panjáb consisting of:

| | | | |
|---|---|---|---|
| Reserved Forests | 1844 | square | miles |
| Protected ,, | 5203 | ,, | ,, |
| Unclassed ,, | 1312 | ,, | ,, |

It was also in charge of 235 square miles of reserved forest in the Hazára district of the N.W.F. Province, and of 364 miles of fine mountain forest in the native State of Bashahr. In addition a few reserved forests have been made over as grazing areas to the Military Department, and Deputy Commissioners are in charge of a very large area of unclassed forest.

No forest can be declared " reserved " or " protected " unless it is owned in whole or in part by the State. It is enough if the trees or some of them are the property of the Government. In order to safeguard all private rights a special forest settlement must be made before a forest can be declared to be " reserved." In the case of a protected forest it is enough if Government is satisfied that the rights of the State and of private persons have been recorded at a land revenue settlement. After deducting income belonging to the year 1909-10 realized in 1910-11, the average income of the two years ending 1911-12 was £81,805 (Rs. 1,227,082) and the average expenditure £50,954 (Rs. 764,309).

**Sources of Income.**—In the mountain forests the chief source of income is the *deodár*, which is valuable both for railway sleepers and as building timber. The blue pine is also of commercial value. *Deodár*, blue pine, and some *chír* are floated down the rivers to depots in the plains. Firwood is inferior to cedar and pine, and the great fir forests are too remote for profitable working at present. There are fine mountain forests in Chitrál, on the Safed Koh, and in Western Wazíristán, but these have so far not even been fully explored. The value of the hill forests may be increased by the success which has attended the experimental extraction of turpentine from the resin of the *chír* pine. The bamboo forests of Kángra are profitable. At present an attempt is being made to acclimatize several species of Eucalyptus in the low hills. The scrub *jangal* in the plains yields good fuel. As the area is constantly shrinking it is fortunate that the railways have ceased to depend on this source of supply, coal having to a great extent taken the place of wood. To prevent shortage of fuel considerable areas in the tracts commanded by the new canals are being reserved for irrigated forests. A forest of this class covering an area of 37 square miles and irrigated from the Upper Bárí Doáb Canal has long existed at Changa Manga in the Lahore district.

**Forests in Kashmír.**—The extensive and valuable Kashmír forests are mountain and hill forests, the former, which cover much the larger area yielding, *deodár*, blue pine, and firs, and the latter *chír* pine. The total area exceeds 2600 square miles.

# CHAPTER VIII

## BEASTS, BIRDS, FISHES, AND INSECTS

**Fauna.**—With the spread of cultivation and drainage the Panjáb plains have ceased to be to anything like the old extent the haunt of wild beasts and wild fowl. The lion has long been extinct and the tiger has practically disappeared. Leopards are to be found in low hills, and sometimes stray into the plains. Wolves are seen occasionally, and jackals are very common. The black buck (Antilope cerricapra) can still be shot in many places. The graceful little *chinkára* or ravine deer (Gazella Bennetti) is found in sandy tracts, and the hogdeer or *párha* (Cervus porcinus) near rivers. The *nílgai* (Boselaphus tragocamelus) is less common. Monkeys abound in the hills and in canal-irrigated tracts in the Eastern districts, where their sacred character protects them from destruction, though they do much damage to crops Peafowl are to be seen in certain tracts, especially in the eastern Panjáb. They should not be shot where the people are Hindus or anywhere near a Hindu shrine. The great and lesser bustards and several kinds of sand grouse are to be found in sandy districts. The grey partridge is everywhere, and the black can be got near the rivers. The *sísí* and the *chikor* are the partridges of the hills, which are also the home of fine varieties of pheasants including the *mondl.* Quail frequent the ripening fields in April and late in September. Duck of various kinds abound where there are *jhíls*, and snipe are to be got in marshy ground. The green parrots, crows, and vultures are familiar sights. Both the sharp-nosed (Garialis Gangetica, vern. *ghariál*) and the blunt-nosed (Crocodilus palustris, vern. *magar*) crocodiles haunt the rivers. The fish are tasteless; the *rohu* and *mahseer* are the best. Poisonous snakes are the *karait*, the *cobra*, and Russell's viper. The first is sometimes an intruder into houses. Lizards and mongooses are less unwelcome visitors. White ants attack timber and ruin books, and mosquitoes and sand-flies add to the unpleasant features of the hot weather. The best known insect pest is the locust, but visitations on a large scale are rare. Of late years much more damage has been done by an insect which harbours in the cotton bolls.

**Game of the Mountains.**—If sport in the plains has ceased to be first rate, it is otherwise in the hills. Some areas and the heights at which the game is to be found are noted below:

(*a*) Goats and goat-antelopes:

1. Ibex (Capra Sibirica) 10,000–14,000 ft. Kashmír, Lahul, Bashahr.
2. Márkhor (Capra Falconeri). Kashmír, Astor, Gilgit, Sulimán hills.
3. Thár (Hemitragus jemlaicus), 9000–14,000 ft. Kashmír, Chamba.
4. Gural (Cemas goral), 3000–8000 ft. Kashmír, Chamba, Simla hills, Bashahr.
5. Serow (Nemorhaedus bubalinus), 6000–12,000 ft. From Kashmír eastwards.

(*b*) Sheep:

1. Bharal (Ovis nahura), 10,000–12,000 ft. and over. Ladákh, Bashahr.
2. Argalí (Ovis Ammon). Ladákh.
3. Uriál (Ovis Vignei) Salt Range, Sulimán hills.

Fig. 24. Big game in Ladákh.

KEY: 1, 3, 7, 9, Chiru or Tibetan Antelope. 2, Argalí or Ovis Ammon. 4, 6, 8, Bharal or Ovis nahura. 5, Yák or Bos grunniens. 10, 11, 12, Uriál or Ovis Vignei. 13, Bear skin.

(*c*) Antelopes:

1. Chiru or Tibetan Antelope (Pantholops hodgsoni). Ladákh.

(*d*) Oxen—Yák (Bos grunniens). Ladákh. The domesticated *yák* is invaluable as a beast of burden in the Trans-Himalayan tract The royal fly whisk or *chaurí* is made from pure white yák tails.

Fig. 25. Yáks.

(*e*) Stag:

1. Bárasingha (Cervus Duvanceli). Foot of Himálaya in Kashmír.

(*f*) Bears:

1. Red or Brown (Ursus Arctos), 10,000–13,000 ft. Kashmír, Chamba, Bashahr, etc.

2. Black (Ursus torquatus), 6000–12,000 ft. Same regions, but at lower elevations. The small bear of the southern Sulimán hills known as *mam* is now considered a variety of the black bear.

(*g*) Leopards:

1. Snow Leopard (Felis Uncia), 9000–15,000 ft. Kashmír, Chamba, Bashahr.
2. Ordinary Leopard (Felis Pardus). Lower hills.

## Shooting in Hills

**Shooting in Hills.**—The finest shooting in the north-west Himálaya is probably to be got in Ladákh and Baltistán, but the trip is somewhat expensive and requires more time than may be available. In many areas licenses have to be obtained, and the conditions limit the number of certain animals, and the size of heads, that may be shot. For example, the permit in Chamba may allow the shooting of two red bear and two *thár*, and when these have been got the sportsman must turn his attention to black bear and *gural*. Any one contemplating a shooting expedition in the Himálaya should get from one who has the necessary experience very complete instructions as to weapons, tents, clothing, stores, etc.

## Sport in the Plains

(*a*) **Black Buck Shooting.**—To get a good idea of what shooting in the plains is like Major Glasford's *Rifle and Romance in the Indian Jungle* may be consulted. As regards larger game the favourite sport is black buck shooting. A high velocity cordite rifle is dangerous to the country people, and some rifle firing black powder should be used. It is well to reach the home of the herd soon after sunrise while it is still in the open, and not among the crops. There will usually be one old buck in each herd. He himself is not watchful, but his does are, and the herd gallops off with great leaps at the first scent of danger, the does leading and their lord and master bringing up the rear. If by dint of careful and patient stalking you get to some point of vantage, say 100 yards from the big buck, it is worth while to shoot. Even if the bullet finds its mark the quarry may gallop 50 yards before it drops. Good heads vary from 20″ to 24″ or even more.

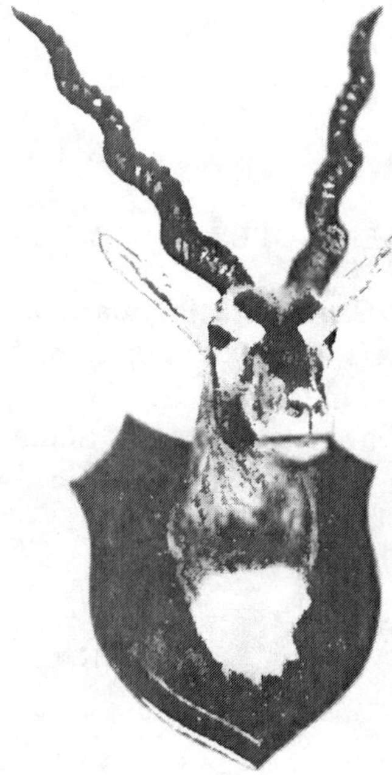

Fig. 26. Black buck.

(*b*) **Small game in Plains.**—The cold weather shooting begins with the advent of the quail in the end of September and ends when they reappear among the ripening wheat in April. The duck arrive from the Central Asian lakes in November and duck and snipe shooting lasts till February in districts where there are *jhíls* and swampy land. For a decent shot 30 couple of snipe is a fair bag. To get duck the *jhíl* should be visited at dawn and again in the evening, and it is well to post several guns in favourable positions in the probable line of flight. 40 or 50 birds would be a good morning's bag. In drier tracts the bag will consist of partridges and a hare or two, or, if the country is sandy, some sand-grouse and perhaps a bustard.

# CHAPTER IX

## THE PEOPLE: NUMBERS, RACES, AND LANGUAGES

**Growth of Population.**—It is probable that in the 64 years since annexation the population of the Panjáb has increased by from 40 to 50 per cent. The first reliable census was taken in 1881. The figures for the four decennial enumerations are:

| Year | Panjáb | | | N.W.F. Province | Kashmír |
|---|---|---|---|---|---|
| | British | Native States | Total | | |
| 1881 | 17,274,597 | 3,861,683 | 21,136,280 | 1,543,726 | |
| 1891 | 19,009,368 | 4,263,280 | 23,272,648 | 1,857,504 | 2,543,952 |
| 1901 | 20,330,337 | 4,424,398 | 24,754,735 | 2,041,534 | 2,905,578 |
| 1911 | 19,974,956 | 4,212,974 | 24,187,730 | 2,196,933 | 3,158,126 |

**Incidence of Population in Panjáb.**—The estimated numbers of independent tribes dwelling within the British sphere of influence is 1,600,000 The incidence of the population on the total area of the Panjáb including native States is 177 per square mile, which may be compared with 189 in France and 287 in the British Isles. As the map shows, the density is reduced by the large area of semi-desert country in the south-west and by the mountainous tract in the north-east. The distribution of the population is the exact opposite of that which prevails in Great Britain. There are only 174 towns as compared with 44,400 villages, and nearly nine-tenths of the people are to be found in the latter. Some of the so-called towns are extremely small, and

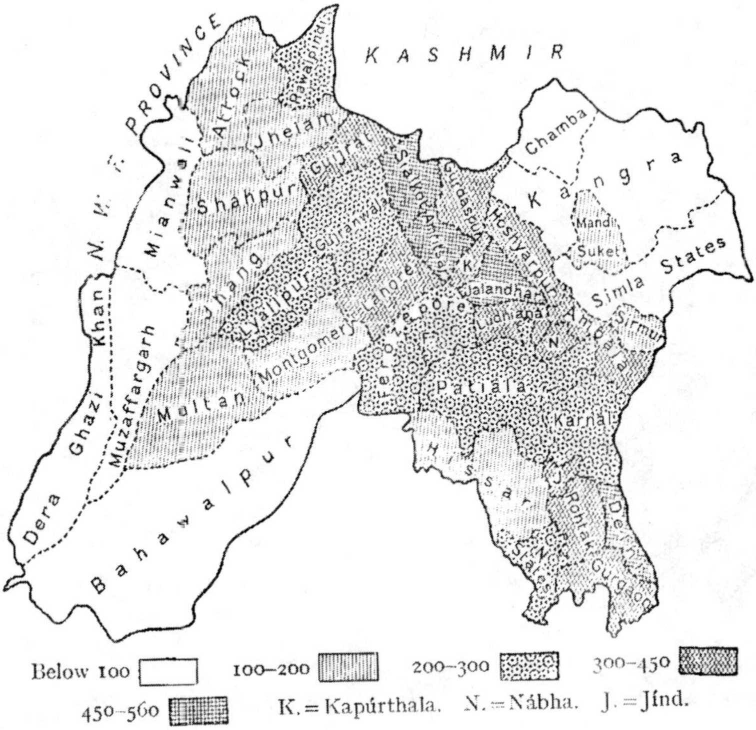


Fig. 27. Map showing density of population.

the average population per town is but 14,800 souls. There are no large towns in the European sense. The biggest, Delhi and Lahore, returned respectively 232,837 and 228,687 persons.

**Growth stopped by Plague.**—The growth of the population between 1881 and 1891 amounted to 10 p.c. Plague, which has smitten the Panjáb more severely than any other province, appeared in 1896, and its effect was seen in the lower rate of expansion between 1891 and 1901. Notwithstanding great extensions of irrigation and cultivation in the Rechna Doáb the numbers declined

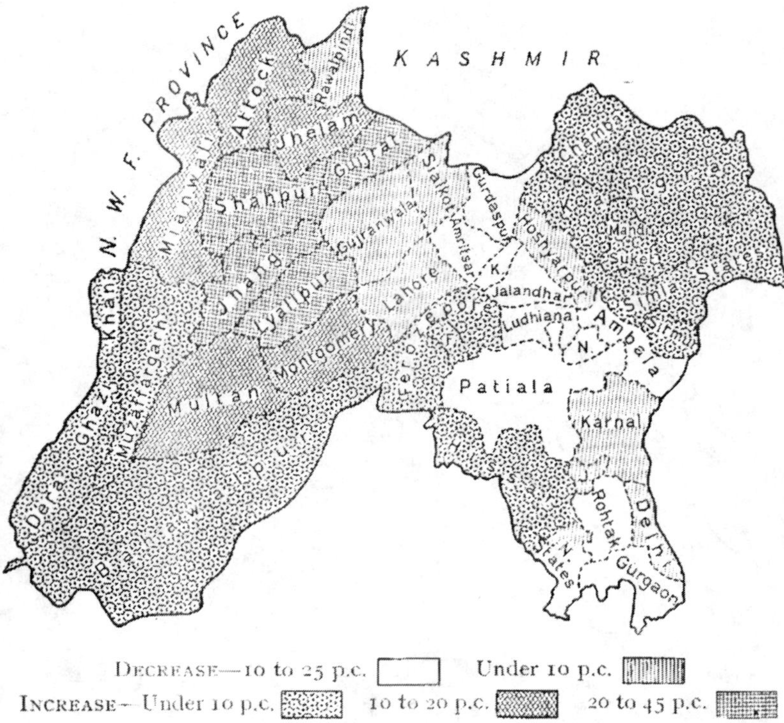


**Fig. 28. Map showing increase and decrease of population.**

by 2 p.c. between 1901 and 1911. In the ten years from 1901 to 1910 in the British districts alone over two million people died of plague and the death-rate was raised to 12 p.c. above the normal. It actually exceeded the birth-rate by 2 p.c. Of the total deaths in the decade nearly one in four was due to plague.

The part which has suffered most is the rich submontane tract east of the Chenáb, Lahore and Gujránwála, and some of the south-eastern districts. A glance at the map will show how large the loss of population has been there. It is by no means entirely due to plague. The submontane districts were almost over-populated, and many of their people have emigrated as colonists, tenants, and labourers to the waste tracts brought under cultivation by the excavation of the Lower Chenáb and Jhelam canals. The districts which have received very marked additions of population from this cause are Jhang (21 p.c.), Sháhpur (30 p.c.), and Lyallpur (45 p.c.). Deaths from plague have greatly increased the deficiency of females, which has always been a noteworthy feature. In 1911 the proportion had very nearly fallen to four females for every five males.

**Increase and Incidence in N.W.F. Province.**—The incidence of the population in the area covered by the five districts of the N.W.F. Province is 164 per square mile. The district figures are given in the map in the margin. The increase between 1901 and 1911 in these districts was $7\frac{1}{2}$ p.c. There have been no severe outbreaks of plague like those which have decimated the population of some of the Panjáb districts.

Fig. 29. Map showing density of population in N.W.F. Province.

General figures for the territory of the Mahárája of Kashmír are meaningless. In the huge Indus valley the incidence is only 4 persons per sq. mile. In Jammu and Kashmír it is 138. The map taken from the Census

Report gives the details. The increase in the decade was on paper $8\frac{1}{2}$ p.c., distributed between $5\frac{1}{4}$ in Jammu, 12 in Kashmír, and 14 in the Indus valley. A great part of the increase in the last must be put down to better enumeration.

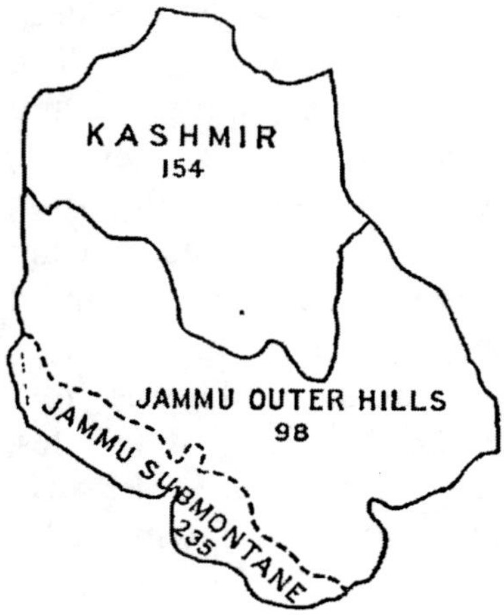


Fig. 30. Map showing density of population in Kashmír.

**Health and duration of life.**—The climate of the Panjáb plains has produced a vigorous, but not a long-lived, race. The mean age of the whole population in the British districts is only 25. The normal birth-rate of the Panjáb is about 41 per 1000, which exceeds the English rate in the proportion of 5 to 3. In 1910 the recorded birth-rate in the N.W.F. Province was 38 per 1000. Till plague appeared the Panjáb death-rate averaged 32 or 33 per 1000, or more than double that of England. The infantile mortality is enormous, and one out of every four or five children fails to survive its first year. The death-rate in the N.W.F. Province was 27 per 1000 in 1910. In the ten years ending 1910 plague pushed up the average death-rate in the Panjáb to $43\frac{1}{2}$ per 1000. Even now malarial fever is a far worse foe than plague. The average annual deaths in the ten years ending 1910 were:

| | |
|---|---|
| Fevers .. .. .. | 450,376 |
| Plague .. .. .. | 202,522 |
| Other diseases .. | 231,473 |
| Total.. .. | 884,371 |

Fever is very rife in October and November, and these are the most unhealthy months in the year, March and April being the best. The variations under fevers and plague from year to year are enormous. In 1907 the latter claimed 608,685 victims, and the provincial death-rate reached the appalling figure of 61 per 1000 Next year the plague mortality dropped to 30,708, but there were 697,058 deaths from fever. There is unfortunately no reason to believe that plague has spent its force or that the people as a whole will in the near future generally accept the protective measures of inoculation and evacuation. Vaccination, the prejudice against which has largely disappeared, has robbed the small-pox goddess of many offerings As a general cause of mortality the effect of cholera in the Panjáb is now insignificant. But it is still to be feared in the Kashmír valley, especially in the picturesque but filthy summer capital. Syphilis is very common in the hill country in the north-east of the province. Blindness and leprosy are both markedly on the decrease. Both infirmities are common in Kashmír, especially the former. The rigours of the climate in a large part of the State force the people to live day and night for the seven winter months almost entirely in dark and smoky huts, and it is small wonder that their eyesight is ruined.

**Occupations.**—The Panjáb is preeminently an agricultural country, and the same is true in an almost greater degree of the N.W.F. Province and Kashmír. The typical holding is that of the small landowner tilling from 3 to 10 acres with his own hands with or without help from village menials. The tenant class is increasing, but there are still three owners to two tenants. Together they make up 50 p.c. of the population of the Panjáb, and 5 p.c. is added for farm labourers. Altogether, according to the census returns 58 p.c. of the population depends for its support on the soil, 20·5 on industries, chiefly the handicrafts of the weaver, potter, leather worker, carpenter, and blacksmith, 9·4 on trade, 2·5 on professions, and 9·6 on other sources of livelihood.

**Measures taken to protect agriculturists.**—In a country owned so largely by small farmers, the first task of the Government must be to secure their welfare and contentment. Before plague laid its grasp on the rich central districts it was feared that they were becoming congested, and the canal colonization schemes referred to in a later chapter were largely designed to relieve them. But there is a much subtler foe to whose insidious attacks small owners are liable, the temptation to abuse their credit till their acres are loaded with mortgages and finally lost. So threatening had this economic disease for years appeared that at last in 1900 the Panjáb Alienation of Land Act was passed, which forbade sales by people of agricultural tribes to other classes without the sanction of the district officer, and greatly restricted the power of mortgaging. The same restrictions are in force in the N.W.F. Province. The Act is popular with those for whose benefit it was devised, and has effected its object of checking land alienation and probably to some extent discouraged extravagance. It has been supplemented by a still more valuable measure, the Cooperative Credit Societies Act. The growth of these societies in the Panjáb has been very remarkable, a notable contrast to the very slow advance of the similar movement in England. In 1913–14 there were 3261 village banks with 155,250 members and a working capital of 133¾ *lakhs* or £885,149, besides 38 central banks with a capital of 42¾ *lakhs* or about £285,000. Village banks held deposits amounting to nearly 37 *lakhs*, more than half of which was received from non-members, and lent out 71½ *lakhs* in the year to their members.

**Tribal Composition.**—Table I based on the Census returns shows the percentages of the total population belonging to the chief tribes. The classification into "land-holding, etc." is a rough one

Fig. 31. Jat Sikh Officers (father and son).

**Jats.**—The Panjáb is *par excellence* the home of the Jats. Everywhere in the plains, except in the extreme north-west corner of the province, they form a large element in the population. In the east they are Hindus, in the centre Sikhs and Muhammadans, and in the west Muhammadans. The Jat is a typical son of the soil, strong and sturdy, hardworking and brave, a fine soldier and an excellent farmer, but slow-witted and grasping. The Sikh Jat finds an honourable outlet for his overflowing energy in the army and in the service of the Crown beyond the bounds of India. When he misses that he sometimes takes to dacoity. Unfortunately he is often given to strong drink, and, when his passions or his greed are aroused, can be exceedingly brutal. Jat in the Western Panjáb is applied to a large number of tribes, whose ethnical affinities are somewhat dubious.

**Rájputs.**—Rájputs are found in considerable numbers all over the province except in a few of the western and south-western districts. As farmers they are much hampered by caste rules which forbid the employment of their women in the fields, and the prohibition of widow remarriage is a severe handicap. They are generally classed as poor cultivators, and this is usually, but by no means universally, a true description. The Dogra Rájputs of the low hills are good soldiers. They are numerous in Kángra and in the Jammu province of Kashmír.

**Brahmans.**—The Brahmans of the eastern plains and north-eastern hills are mostly agriculturists, and the Muhiál Brahman of the north-western districts is a landowner and a soldier. In the hills the Brahman is often a shopkeeper. The priestly Brahman is found everywhere, but his spiritual authority has always been far less in the Panjáb than in most parts of India.

**Biluches.**—When the frontier was separated off the Biluch district of Dera Ghází Khán with its strong tribal organization under chiefs or *tumandárs* was left in the Panjáb. The Biluches are a frank, manly, truthful race, free from fanaticism and ready as a rule to follow their chiefs. They are fine horsemen. Unfortunately it is difficult to get them to enlist.

**Patháns.**—Both politically and numerically the Patháns are the predominant tribe in the N.W.F. Province, and are of importance in parts of the Panjáb districts of Attock and Mianwálí. The Pathán is a democrat and often a fanatic, more under the influence of *mullahs* than of the *maliks* or headmen of his tribe. He has not the frank straightforward nature of the Biluch, is untiring in pursuit of revenge, and is not free from cruelty. But, when he has eaten the *Sarkár's* salt, he is a very brave and dashing soldier, and he is a faithful host to anyone whom he has admitted under his roof.

**Awáns.**—The home of the Awán in the Panjáb is the Salt Range and the parts of Attock and Mianwálí, lying to the north of it, and this tract of country is known as the Awánkárí. In the N.W.F. Province they are, after the Patháns, by far the largest tribe, and are specially numerous in Pesháwar and Hazára.

**Shekhs.**—Of the Shekhs about half are Kureshís, Sadíkís, and Ansárís of foreign origin and high social standing. The rest are new converts to Islám, often of the sweeper caste originally.

**Saiyyids.**—Saiyyids are unsatisfactory landowners, and are kept going by the offerings of their followers. They are mostly Shias. It is not necessary to believe that they are all descended from the Prophet's son-in-law, Ali. A native proverb with pardonable exaggeration says: "The first year I was a weaver (Juláha), the next year a Shekh. This year, if prices rise, I shall be a Saiyyid."

**Trading Castes.**—Aroras are the traders of the S.W. Panjáb and of the N.W.F. Province. They share the Central Panjáb with the Khatrís, who predominate in the north-western districts. The Khatrí of the Ráwalpindí division is often a landowner and a first-class fighting man. Some of our strongest Indian civil officials have been Aroras. In the Delhi division the place of the Arora and Khatrí is taken by the Bania, and in Kángra by the Súd or the Brahman. Khojas and Paráchas are Muhammadan traders.

**Artizans and Menials.**—Among artizans and menials Sunárs (goldsmiths), Rájes (masons), Lohárs (blacksmiths), and Tarkháns (carpenters) take the first rank.

**Impure Castes.**—The vast majority of the impure castes, the "untouchables" of the Hindu religion, are scavengers and workers in leather. The sweeper who embraces Islám becomes a Musallí. The Sikh Mazhbís, who are the descendants of sweeper converts, have done excellent service in our Pioneer regiments. The Hindu of the Panjáb in his avoidance of "untouchables" has never gone to the absurd lengths of the high caste Madrásí, and the tendency is towards a relaxation of existing restrictions.

**Mendicants.**—Men of religion living on charity, wandering *fakírs*, are common sights, and beggars are met with in the cities, who sometimes exhibit their deformities with unnecessary insistence.

**Kashmíris.**—According to the census return the number of Kashmírí Musulmáns, who make up 60 p.c. of the inhabitants of the Jhelam valley, was 765,442. They are no doubt mostly descendants of various Hindu castes, perhaps in the main of Hill Brahmans, but Islám has wiped out all tribal distinctions. Sir Walter Lawrence wrote of them: "The Kashmírí is unchanged in spite of the splendid Moghal, the brutal Afghán, and the bully Sikh. Warriors and statesmen came and went; but there was no egress, and no wish....in normal times to leave their homes. The outside world was far, and from all accounts inferior to the pleasant valley....So the Kashmíris lived their self-centred life, conceited, clever, and conservative."

The Hindu Kashmírí Pandits numbered 55,276.

**Tribes of Jammu.**—Agricultural Brahmans are numerous in the Jammu province. Thakkars and Meghs are important elements of the population of the outer hills. The former are no doubt by origin Rájputs, but

Fig. 32. Blind Beggar.

they have cast off many Rájput customs. The Meghs are engaged in weaving and agriculture, and are regarded as more or less impure by the higher castes.

**Gújars.**—Gújars in the Mahárája's territories are almost always graziers. In 1911 they numbered 328,003.

**Dard Tribes of Astor and Gilgit.**—The people of Astor and Gilgit are Dards speaking Shina and professing Islám. Sir Aurel Stein wrote of them: "The Dard race which inhabits the valleys N. of (the Inner Himálaya) as far as the Hindu Kush is separated from the Kashmírí population by language as well as by physical characteristics....There is little in the Dard to enlist the sympathies of the casual observer. He lacks the intelligence, humour, and fine physique of the Kashmírí, and, though undoubtedly far braver than the latter, has none of the independent spirit and manly

Fig. 33. Dards.

bearing which draw us towards the Patháń despite all his failings. But I can never see a Dard without thinking of the thousands of years of struggle they have carried on with the harsh climate and the barren soil of their mountains[1]."

**Kanjútís.**—The origin of the Kanjútís of Hunza is uncertain, and so are the relationships of their language.

[1] *Sand Buried Ruins of Khotan*, pp. 14—15.

**Mongoloid Population of Ladákh.**—The population of Ladákh and Báltistán is Mongoloid, but the Báltís (72,439) have accepted Islám and polygamy, while the Ladákhís have adhered to Buddhism and polyandry.

**Ethnological theories.**—In *The People of India* the late Sir Herbert Risley maintained that the inhabitants of Rájputána, nearly the whole of the Panjáb, and a

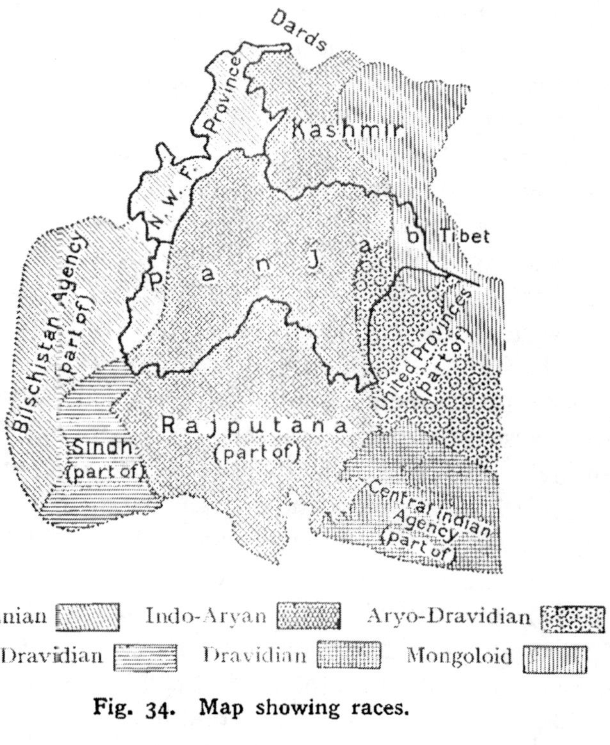


**Fig. 34. Map showing races.**

large part of Kashmír, whatever their caste or social status, belonged with few exceptions to a single racial type, which he called Indo-Aryan. The Biluches of Dera Ghází Khán and the Patháns of the N.W.F. Province formed part of another group which he called Turko-Iranian. The people of a strip of territory on the west of the Jamna he held to be of the same type as the bulk of the inhabitants of the United Provinces, and this type he called Aryo-Dravidian. Finally the races occupying the hills in the north-east and the adjoining part of Kashmír were of Mongol extraction, a fact which no one will dispute. Of the Indo-Aryan type Sir Herbert Risley wrote: "The stature is mostly tall, complexion fair, eyes dark, hair on face plentiful, head long, nose narrow and prominent, but not specially long." He believed that the Panjáb was occupied by Aryans, who came into the country from the west or north-west with their wives and children, and had no need to contract marriages with the earlier inhabitants. The Aryo-Dravidians of the United Provinces resulted from a second invasion or invasions, in which the Aryan warriors came alone and had to intermarry with the daughters of the land, belonging to the race which forms the staple of the population of Central India and Madras. This theory was based on measurements of heads and noses, and it seems probable that deductions drawn from these physical characters are of more value than any evidence based on the use of a common speech. But it is hard to reconcile the theory with the facts of history even in the imperfect shape in which they have come down to us, or to believe that Sakas, Yuechí, and White Huns (see historical section) have left no traces of their blood in the province. If such there are, they may perhaps be found in some of the tribes on both sides of the Salt Range, such as Gakkhars, Janjúas, Awáns, Tiwánas, Ghebas, and Johdras, who are fine horsemen and expert tent-peggers, not "tall heavy men without any natural aptitude for horsemanship," as Sir Herbert Risley described his typical Panjábí (p. 59 of his book).

**Languages.**—In the area dealt with in this book no less than eleven languages are spoken, and the dialects are very numerous. It is only possible to tabulate the languages and indicate on the map the localities

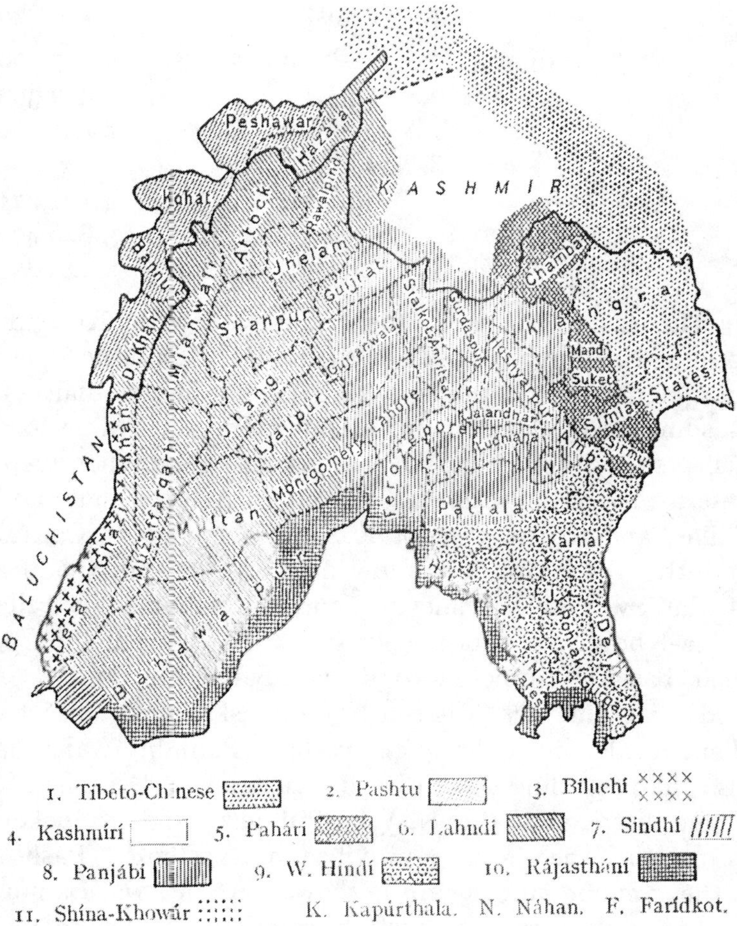


Fig. 35. Map showing distribution of languages.

in which they are spoken. For the Panjáb the figures of the recent census are:

A 1. Tibeto-Chinese .. .. .. .. 41,607

B. Aryan:

| | | | | |
|---|---|---|---|---|
| (*a*) Iranian: | 2. | Pashtu .. | .. | 67,174 |
| | 3. | Biluchí .. | .. | 70,675 |
| | 4. | Kohistání | .. | 26 |
| (*b*) Indian: | 5. | Kashmírí | .. | 7,190 |
| | 6. | Pahárí .. | .. | 993,363 |
| | 7. | Lahndí .. | .. | 4,253,566 |
| | 8. | Sindhí .. | .. | 24 |
| | 9 | Panjábí .. | .. | 14,111,215 |
| | 10. | Western Hindí | | 3,826,467 |
| | 11. | Rájasthání | .. | 725,850 |

The eastern part of the Indus valley in Kashmír forming the provinces of Ladákh and Báltistán is occupied by a Mongol population speaking Tibeto-Chinese dialects. Kashmírí is the language of Kashmír Proper, and various dialects of the Shina-Khowár group comprehensively described as Kohistání are spoken in Astor, Gilgit, and Chilás, and to the west of Kashmír territory in Chitrál and the Kohistán or mountainous country at the top of the Swát river valley. Though Kashmírí and the Shina-Khowár tongues belong to the Aryan group, their basis is supposed to be non-Sanskritic, and it is held that there is a strong non-Sanskritic or Pisácha element also in Lahndí or western Panjábí, which is also the prevailing speech in the Hazára and Dera Ismail Khán districts of the N.W.F. Province, and is spoken in part of the Jammu province of Kashmír. Pashtu is the common language in Pesháwar, Kohát, and Bannu, and is spoken on the western frontiers of Hazára and Dera Ismail Khán, and in the independent tribal territory in the west between the districts of the N.W.F. Province and the Durand Line and immediately adjoining the Pesháwar district on the north. Rájasthání is a collective name for the dialects of Rájputána, which overflow into the Panjáb, occupying a strip along the southern frontier from Baháwalpur to Gurgáon. The infiltration of English words and phrases into the languages of the province is a useful process and as inevitable as was the enrichment of the old English speech by Norman-French. But for the present the results are apt to sound grotesque, when the traveller, who expects a train to start at the appointed time, is told: "*tren late hai, lekin singal down hogaya*" (the train is late, but the signal has been lowered), or the criticism is passed on a popular officer: "*bahut affable hai, lekin hand shake nahín kartá*" (very affable, but doesn't shake hands).

# CHAPTER X

## THE PEOPLE (*continued*): RELIGIONS

**Religions in N.W.F. Province.**—In the N.W.F. Province an overwhelming majority of the population professes Islám. In 1911 there were 2,039,994 Musalmáns as compared with 119,942 Hindus, 30,345 Sikhs, and 6585 Christians.

**Religions in Kashmír.**—In Kashmír the preponderance of Muhammadans is not so overwhelming. The figures are:

| | |
|---|---|
| Muhammadans .. .. | 2,398,320 |
| Hindus .. .. .. | 690,390 |
| Buddhists .. .. .. | 36,512 |
| Sikhs .. .. .. | 31,553 |

The Hindus belong mostly to the Jammu province, where nearly half of the population professes that faith. The people of Kashmír, Báltistán, Astor and Gilgit, Chilás and Hunza Nagár, are Musalmáns. The Ladákhís are Buddhists.

**Religions in Panjáb.**—The distribution by religions of the population of the Panjáb and its native States in 1911 was:

| | | | |
|---|---|---|---|
| Muhammadans .. .. .. | 12,275,477 | or | 51 p.c. |
| Hindus .. .. .. .. | 8,773,621 | or | 36 p.c. |
| Sikhs .. .. .. .. | 2,883,729 | or | 12 p.c. |
| Others, chiefly Christian (199,751) | 254,923 | or | 1 p.c. |

The strength of the Muhammadans is in the districts west of the Biás and the Sutlej below its junction with the Biás. 83 p.c. of the subjects of the Nawáb of Bahá-walpur are also Muhammadans. In all this western region there are few Hindus apart from the shopkeepers and traders. On the other hand the hill country in the

MUHAMMADAN Above 80 p.c. 60–80 p.c.

HINDU. Above 90 p.c. 75–90 p.3. 50–75 p.c.

SIKH. 20—43 p.c.

**Fig. 36. Map showing distribution of religions.**

north-east is purely Hindu, except on the borders of Tibet, where the scanty population professes Buddhism. While Hinduism is the predominant faith in the south-east, quite a fourth of the people there are Musalmáns. Sikhs nowhere form a majority. The districts in the eastern part of the Central Plains where they constitute more than one-fifth of the population are indicated in the map. In six districts, Lahore, Montgomery, Gujránwála, Lyallpur, Hoshyárpur, and Ambála the proportion is between 10 and 20 p.c.

Fig. 37. Raghunáth Temple, Jammu.

**Growth and Decline in numbers.**—There was a slight rise in the number of Muhammadans between 1901 and 1911. Their losses in the central districts, where the plague scourge has been heaviest, were counterbalanced by gains in the western tract, where its effect has been slight. On the other hand the decrease under Hindus amounts to nearly 15 p.c. The birth-rate is lower and the death-rate higher among Hindus than among Musalmáns, and their losses by plague in the central and some of the south-eastern districts have been very heavy. A change of sentiment on the part of the Sikh community has led to many persons recording themselves as Sikhs who were formerly content to be regarded as Hindus. It must be remembered that one out of four of the recorded

Fig. 38. Golden Temple, Amritsar.

Hindus belongs to impure castes, who even in the Panjáb pollute food and water by their touch and are excluded from the larger temples. Since 1901 a considerable number of Chúhras or Sweepers have been converted to Islám and Christianity.

**Sikhs.**—Notwithstanding heavy losses by plague Sikhs have increased by 37 p.c. A great access of zeal has led to many more Sikhs becoming *Kesdháris*. *Sajhdháris* or

*Múnas,* who form over one-fifth of the whole Sikh community, were in 1901 classed as Hindus. They are followers of Bába Nának, cut their hair, and often smoke. When a man has taken the "*pahul,*" which is the sign of his becoming a *Kesdhárí* or follower of Guru Govind, he must give up the *hukka* and leave his hair unshorn. The future of Sikhism is with the *Kesdháris.*

Fig. 39. Mosque in Lahore City.

**Muhammadans.**—In the eastern districts the conversions to Islám were political, and Hindu and Muhammadan Rájputs live peaceably together in the same village. The Musalmáns have their mosque for the worship of Allah, but were, and are still, not quite sure that it is prudent wholly to neglect the godlings. The conversion of the western Panjáb was the result largely of missionary effort. *Pírí murídí* is a great institution there. Every man should be the "*muríd*" or pupil of some holy man or *pír*, who combines the functions in the Roman Catholic Church of spiritual director in this world and the saint in heaven. The *pír* may be the custodian of some little saint's tomb in a village, or of some great shrine like that of Baba Faríd at Pákpattan, or Baháwal Hakk at Multán, or Taunsa Sharif in Dera Ghází Khán, or Golra in Ráwalpindí. His own holiness may be more official than personal. About 1400 A.D. the Kashmírís were offered by their Sultán Sikandar the choice between conversion and exile, and chose the easier alternative. Like the western Panjábís they are above all things saint-worshippers. The ejaculations used to stimulate effort show this. The embankment builder in the south-western Panjáb invokes the holy breath of Baháwal Hakk, and the Kashmírí boatman's cry "Yá Pír, dast gír," "Oh Saint, lend me a hand," is an appeal to their national saint.

**Effect of Education.**—The Musalmáns of the western Panjáb have a great dislike to Sikhs, dating from the period of the political predominance of the latter. So far the result of education has been to accentuate religious differences and animosities. Both Sikhs and Musalmáns are gradually dropping ideas and observances retained in their daily life after they ceased to call themselves Hindus. On the other hand, within the Hindu fold laxity is now the rule rather than the exception, and the neglect of the old ritual and restrictions is by no means confined to the small but influential reforming minority which calls itself Árya Samáj.

**Christians.**—The number of Christians increased threefold between 1901 and 1911. The Presbyterian missionaries have been especially successful in attracting large numbers of outcastes into the Christian Church.

**Hinduism in the Panjáb.**—Hinduism has always been, and to-day is more than ever, a very elastic term. The

Census Superintendent, himself a high caste Hindu, wrote: "The definition which would cover the Hindu of the modern times is that he should be born of parents not belonging to some recognised religion other than Hinduism, marry within the same limits, believe in God, respect the cow, and cremate the dead." There is room in its ample folds for the Árya Samájist, who rejects

**Fig. 40. God and Goddess, Chamba.**

idol worship and is divesting himself of caste prejudices and marriage restrictions, and the most orthodox Sanátan dharmist, who carries out the whole elaborate daily ritual of the Brahmanical religion, and submits to all its complicated rules; for the ordinary Hindu trader, who is equally orthodox by profession, but whose ordinary religious exercises are confined to bathing in the morning; for the villager of the eastern districts, who often has the name of Parameshvar or the Supreme Lord on his lips, but who really worships the godlings, Gúgá Pír, Sarwar or Sultán Pír, Sítla (the small-pox goddess), and others, whose little shrines we see round the village

Fig. 41. A Kulu godling and his attendants.

site; and for the childish idolaters of Kulu, who carry their local deities about to visit each other at fairs, and would see nothing absurd in locking them all up in a dungeon if rain held off too long.

# CHAPTER XI

## THE PEOPLE (*continued*): EDUCATION

**Educational progress.**—According to the census returns of 1911 there are not four persons per 100 in the province who are "literate" in the sense of being able to read and write a letter. The proportion of literacy among Hindus and Sikhs is three times as great as among Muhammadans. In 1911–12 one boy in six of school-going age was at school or college and one girl in 37. This may seem a meagre result of sixty years of work, for the Government and Christian missionaries, who have had an honourable connection with the educational history of the province, began their efforts soon after annexation, and a Director of Public Instruction was appointed as long ago as 1856. But a country of small peasant farmers is not a very hopeful educational field, and the rural population was for long indifferent or hostile. If an ex-soldier of the *Khálsa* had expressed his feelings, he would have used words like those of the "Old Pindárí" in Lyall's poem, while the Muhammadan farmer, had he been capable of expressing his hostility, might have argued that the teaching his son could get in a village school would help him not at all in his daily work. Things are better now. We have improved our scheme of teaching, and of late raised the pay of the teachers, which is, however, still hardly adequate. Till a better class of teachers can be secured for primary schools, the best educational theories will not bear fruit in practice. The old indifference is weakening, and the most hopeful sign is the increasing interest taken in towns in female education, a matter of the first importance for the future of the country.

**Present position.**—The present position is as follows:—The Government has made itself directly or indirectly responsible for the education of the province. At the headquarters of each district there is a high school for boys controlled by the Education Department. In each district there are Government middle schools, Anglo-vernacular or Vernacular, and primary schools, managed by the Municipal Committees and District Boards. Each middle school has a primary, and each high school a primary and a middle, department. For the convenience of pupils who cannot attend school while living at home hostels are attached to many middle and high schools. Fees are very moderate. In middle schools, where the income covers 56 p.c. of the expenditure, they range from R. 1 (16 pence) monthly in the lowest class in which they are levied to Rs. 4 (5 shillings) in the highest class. In rural primary schools the children of agriculturists are exempt because they pay local rate, and others, when not exempt on the score of poverty, pay nominal fees. Besides the Government schools there are aided schools of the above classes usually of a sectarian character, and these, if they satisfy the standards laid down, receive grants. There is a decreasing, but still considerable, class of private schools, which make no attempt to satisfy the conditions attached to these grants. The *mullah* in the mosque teaches children passages of the Kurân by rote, or the shopkeeper's son is taught in a Mahájaní school native arithmetic and the curious script in which accounts are kept. A boys' school of a special kind is the Panjáb Chiefs' College at Lahore, intended for the sons of princes and men of high social position.

**Technical Schools.**—In an agricultural country like the Panjáb there is not at present any large field for technical schools. The best are the Mayo School of Art and the Railway Technical School at Lahore. The latter is successful because its pupils can readily find employment in the railway workshops. Mr Kipling,

**Fig. 42. A School in the time preceding annexation.**
(*From a picture book said to have been prepared for the Mahárája Dalip Singh.*)

the father of the poet, when principal of the former, did much for art teaching, and the present principal, Bhai Rám Singh, is a true artist. The Government Engineering School has recently been remodelled and removed to Rasúl, where the head-works of the Lower Jhelam canal are situated.

**Female Education.**—Female education is still a tender plant, but of late growth has been vigorous. The Victoria

May School in Lahore founded in 1908 has developed into the Queen Mary College, which provides an excellent education for girls of what may be called the upper middle class. There is a separate class for married ladies. Hitherto they have only been reached by the teaching given in their own homes by missionary ladies, whose useful work is now being imitated by the Hindu community in Lahore. There is an excellent Hindu Girls' Boarding School in Jalandhar. The Sikhs and the body of reformers known as the Dev Samáj have good girls' schools at Ferozepore. The best mission schools are the Kinnaird High School at Lahore and the Alexandra School at Amritsar. The North India School of Medicine for Women at Ludhiána, also a missionary institution, does admirable work. In the case of elementary schools the difficulty of getting qualified teachers is even greater than as regards boys' schools.

**Education of European Children.**—There are special arrangements for the education of European and Anglo-Indian children. In this department the Roman Catholics have been active and successful. The best schools are the Lawrence Asylum at Sanáwar, Bishop Cotton's School, Auckland House, and St Bede's at Simla, St Denys', the Lawrence Asylum, and the Convent School at Murree.

**The Panjáb University.**—The Panjáb University was constituted in 1882, but the Government Arts College and Oriental College, the Medical College and the Law School at Lahore, which are affiliated with it, are of older date. The University is an examining body like London University. Besides the two Arts Colleges under Government management mentioned above there are nine private Arts Colleges aided by Government grants and affiliated to the University. Four of these are in Lahore, two, the Dayanand Anglo-Vedic and the Diál Singh Colleges, are Hindu institutions, one, the Islámia College, is Muhammadan, the fourth is the popular and efficient Forman Christian College. Four out of five art students read in Lahore. Of the Arts colleges outside Lahore the most important is the St Stephen's College at Delhi. The Khálsa School and College at Amritsar is a Sikh institution. The Veterinary College at Lahore is the best of its kind in India, and the Agricultural College at Lyallpur is a well-equipped institution, which at present attracts few pupils, but may play a very useful rôle in the future. There is little force in the reproach that we built up a superstructure of higher education before laying a broad foundation of primary education. There is more in the charge that the higher educational food we have offered has not been well adapted to the intellectual digestions of the recipients.

**Education in N.W.F. Province, Native States, and Kashmír.**—The Panjáb Native States and Kashmír are much more backward as regards education than the British Province. As is natural in a tract in which the population is overwhelmingly Musalmán by religion and farming by trade the N.W.F. Province lags behind the Panjáb. Six colleges in the States and the N.W.F. Province are affiliated to the Panjáb University.

# CHAPTER XII

## ROADS AND RAILWAYS

**Roads.**—The alignment of good roads in the plains of the Panjáb is easy, and the deposits of calcareous nodules or *kankar* often found near the surface furnish good metalling material. In the west the rainfall is so scanty and in many parts wheeled traffic so rare that it is often wise to leave the roads unmetalled. There are in the Panjáb over 2000 miles of metalled, and above 20,000 miles of unmetalled roads. The greatest highway in the world, the Grand Trunk, which starts from Calcutta and ends at Peshávar, passes through the province from Delhi in the south-east to Attock in the extreme north-west corner, and there crosses the Indus and enters the N.W.F. Province. The greater part of the section from Karnál to Lahore had been completed some years before the Mutiny, that from Lahore to Peshávar was finished in 1863–64. A great loop road connects our arsenal at Ferozepore with the Grand Trunk Road at Lahore and Ludhiána. The fine metalled roads from Ambála to Kálka, and Kálka to Simla have lost much of their importance since the railway was brought to the hill capital. Beyond Simla the Kálka-Simla road is carried on for 150 miles to the Shipkí Pass on the borders of Tibet, being maintained as a very excellent hill road adapted to mule carriage. A fine tonga road partly in the plains and partly in the hills joins Murree with Ráwalpindí.

From Murree it drops into the Jhelam valley crossing the river and entering Kashmír at Kohála. It is carried up the gorge of the Jhelam to Báramúla and thence through the Kashmír valley to Srínagar. A motor-car can be driven all the way from Ráwalpindí to Srínagar. In the N.W.F. Province a great metalled road connects Pesháwar, Kohát, Bannu, and Dera Ismail Khán.

Fig. 43. Poplar lined road to Srínagar.

**Railways. Main Lines.**—It is just over fifty years since the first railway, a short line joining Lahore and Amritsar, was opened in 1862. Three years later Lahore was linked up with Multán and the small steamers which then plied on the Indus. Amritsar was connected with Delhi in 1870, and Lahore with Pesháwar in 1883. The line from Peshávar to Lahore, and branching thence to Karáchí and Delhi may be considered the Trunk Line. The railway service has been enormously developed in the past thirty years. In 1912 there were over 4000

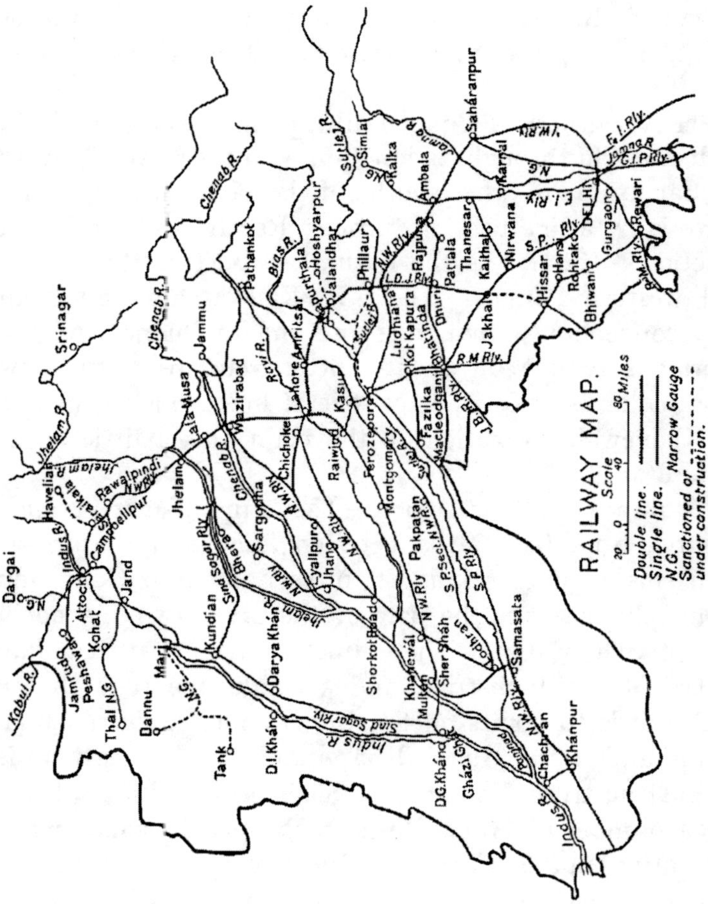


Fig. 44. Map showing railways.

miles of open lines. There are now three routes from Delhi to Lahore:

(*a*) The N.W. Railway *via* Meerut and Saháranpur

(on east of Jamna), and Ambála, Ludhiána, Jalandhar, Amritsar ;

(*b*) The Southern Panjáb Railway *via* Jínd, Rohtak, Bhatinda, and Ferozepore ;

(*c*) The Delhi-Ambála-Kálka branch of the East Indian Railway from Delhi through Karnál to Ambála, and thence by the N.W. Railway. This is the shortest route.

The Southern Panjáb Railway also connects Delhi with Karáchí through its junction with the N.W. Railway at Samasata to the south of Baháwalpur. Another route is by a line passing through Rewárí and the Merta junction Karáchí is the natural seaport of the central and western Panjáb. The S.P Railway now gives an easy connection with Ferozepore and Ludhiána, and the enormous export of wheat, cotton, etc. from the new canal colonies is carried by several lines which converge at Khanewál, a junction on the main line, a little north of Multán.

**Railways. Minor Lines.**—The Sind Ságar branch starting from Lála Musa between Lahore and Amritsar with smaller lines taking off further north at Golra and Campbellpur serves the part of the province lying north of the Salt Range. These lines converge at Kundian in the Mianwálí district, and a single line runs thence southwards to points on the Indus opposite Dera Ismail Khán and Dera Ghází Khán, and turning eastwards rejoins the trunk line at Sher Sháh near Multán. There are a number of branch lines in the plains, some owned by native States. Strategically a very important one is that which crossing the Indus by the Khushálgarh bridge unites Ráwalpindí with Kohát. The only hill railway is that from Kálka to Simla. A second is now under construction which, when completed, will connect Ráwalpindí with Srínagar. All these lines with the exception of the branch of the E.I. Railway mentioned above are worked by the staff of the N W. State Railway, whose manager controls inside and outside the Panjáb some 5000 miles of open line. The interest earned in 1912 was 4½ p.c., a good return when it is considered that the parts of the system to the north of the Salt Range and the Sind Ságar railway were built primarily for strategic reasons.

# CHAPTER XIII

## CANALS

**Importance of Canals.**—One need have no hesitation in placing among the greatest achievements of British rule in the Panjáb the magnificent system of irrigation canals which it has given to the province. Its great alluvial plain traversed by large rivers drawing an unfailing supply of water from the Himalayan snows affords an ideal field for the labours of the canal engineer. The vastness of the arid areas which without irrigation yield no crops at all or only cheap millets and pulses makes his works of inestimable benefit to the people and a source of revenue to the State.

**Canals before annexation.**—In the west of the province we found in existence small inundation canals dug by the people with some help from their rulers. These only ran during the monsoon season, when the rivers were swollen. In 1626 Sháhjahán's Persian engineer, Ali Mardán Khán, brought to Delhi the water of the canal dug by Firoz Sháh as a monsoon channel and made perennial by Akbar. But during the paralysis of the central power in the eighteenth century the channels became silted up. The same able engineer dug a canal from the Rávi near Mádhopur to water the royal gardens at Lahore. What remained of this work at annexation was known as the Haslí.

**Extent of Canal Irrigation.**—In 1911–12, when the deficiency of the rainfall made the demand for water keen, the canals of the Panjáb and the N.W.F. Province irrigated 8½ millions of acres. The figures are:

*Panjáb*

| | | Acres | Interest earned % |
|---|---|---|---|
| A. | Permanent Canals | | |
| | 1. Western Jamna .. | 775,450 | 7¾ |
| | 2. Sirhind .. .. | 1,609,458 | 8 |
| | 3. Upper Bárí Doáb .. | 1,156,808 | 11½ |
| | 4. Lower Chenáb .. | 2,334,090 | 34 |
| | 5. Lower Jhelam .. | 801,649 | 10½ |
| B. | Monsoon Canals .. .. | 1,654,437 | |
| | Total | 8,331,892 | |

*N.W. Frontier Province*

| | Acres | Interest earned % |
|---|---|---|
| Lower Swát River .. .. | 157,650 | 9¾ |
| Two minor Canals .. .. | 67,510 | |
| Total | 225,160 | |

On the Sirhind Canal, on which the demand fluctuates greatly with the character of the season, the area was twice the normal. The three canals of the Triple Project will, when fully developed, add 1,871,000 acres to the irrigated area of the Panjáb, and the Upper Swát Canal will increase that of the N.W.F. Province by 381,000 acres. The canals will therefore in a year of drought be able to water over ten millions of acres without taking account of possible extensions if a second canal should be drawn from the Sutlej. The money spent from imperial funds on Panjáb canals has exceeded twelve millions sterling, and no money has ever been better spent. In 1910–11, when the area irrigated was a good deal less than in 1911–12, the value of the crops raised by the use of canal water was estimated at about 207 millions of rupees or nearly £14,000,000. It is only possible to note very briefly the steps by which this remarkable result has been achieved.

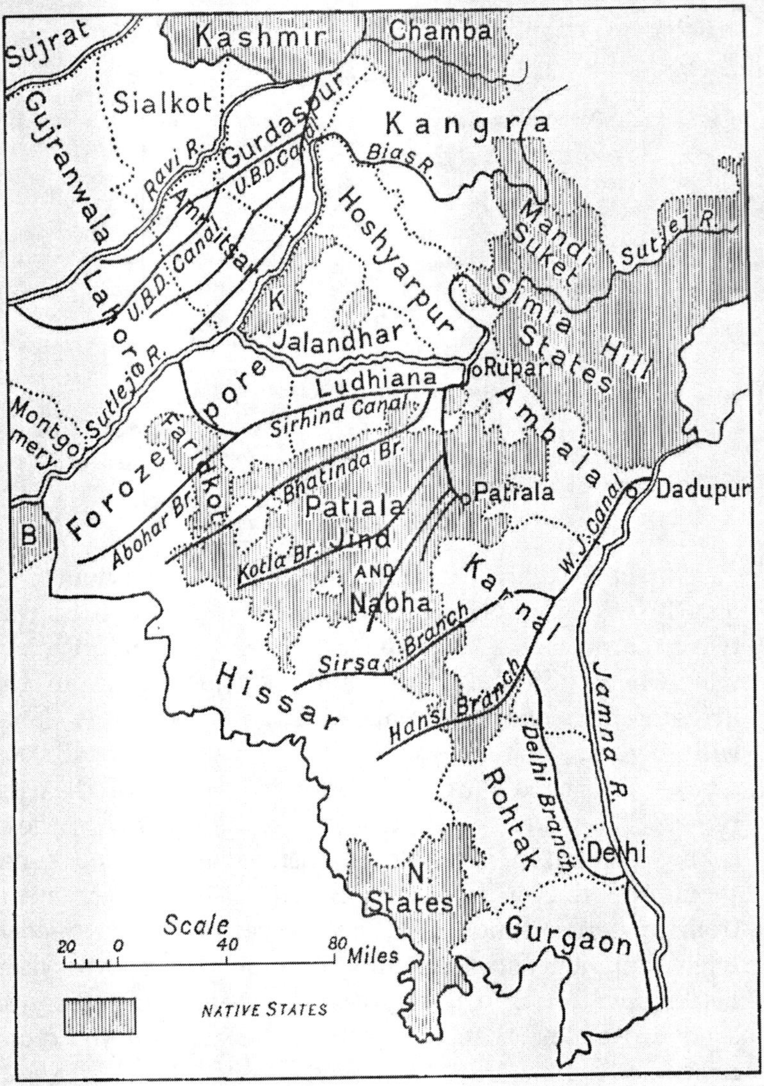


Fig. 45. Map—Older Canals.

**Western Jamna Canal.**—Soon after the assumption of authority at Delhi in 1803 the question of the old Canal from the Jamna was taken up. The Delhi Branch was reopened in 1819, and the Hánsí Branch six years later. In the famine year 1837–38 nearly 400,000 acres were irrigated. For more than half a century that figure represented the irrigating capacity of the canal. The English engineers in the main retained the faulty Moghal alignment, and waterlogging of the worst description developed. The effect on the health of the people was appalling. After long delay the canal was remodelled. The result has been most satisfactory in every way. In the last decade of the nineteenth century the Sirsa Branch and the Nardak Distributary were added, to carry water to parts of the Karnál and Hissár districts where any failure of the monsoon resulted in widespread loss of crops. If a scheme to increase the supply can be carried out, further extension in tracts now very liable to famine will become possible. In the six years ending 1910–11 the interest earned exceeded 8 p.c.

**Upper Bárí Doáb Canal.**—The headworks of the Upper Bárí Doáb Canal are above Mádhopur near the point where the Rávi leaves the hills. The work was started soon after annexation, but only finished in 1859. Irrigation has grown from 90,000 acres in 1860–61 to 533,000 in 1880–81, 861,000 in 1900–1, and 1,157,000 in 1911–12. The later history of the canal consists mainly of great extensions in the arid Lahore district, and the irrigation there is now three-fifths of the whole. In parts of Amritsar, and markedly near the city, waterlogging has become a grave evil, but remedial measures have now been undertaken. The interest earned on the capital expenditure in the six years ending 1910–11 averaged 11½ p.c.

**Sirhind Canal.**—A quarter of a century passed after

the Upper Bárí Doáb Canal began working before the water of the Sutlej was used for irrigation. The Sirhind Canal weir is at Rupar where the river emerges from the Siwáliks. Patiála, Jínd, and Nábha contributed to the cost, and own three of the five branches. But the two British branches are entitled to nearly two-thirds of the water, which is utilized in the Ludhiána and Ferozepore districts and in the Farídkot State. The soil of the tract commanded is for the most part a light sandy loam, and in years of good rainfall it repays dry cultivation. The result is that the area watered fluctuates largely. But in the six years ending 1910–11 the interest earned averaged 7 p.c., and the power of expansion in a bad year is a great boon to the peasantry.

**Canal extensions in Western Panjáb.**—In the last quarter of a century the chief task of the Canal Department in the Panjáb has been the extension of irrigation to the Rechna and Jech Doábs and the lower part of the Bárí Doáb. All three contained large areas of waste belonging to the State, mostly good soil, but incapable of cultivation owing to the scanty rainfall. Colonization has therefore been an important part of all the later canal projects. The operations have embraced the excavation of five canals.

**Lower Chenáb Canal.**—The Lower Chenáb Canal is one of the greatest irrigation works in the world, the area commanded being $3\frac{1}{3}$ million acres, the average discharge four or five times that of the Thames at Teddington, and the average irrigated area $2\frac{1}{4}$ million acres. There are three main branches, the Rakh, the Jhang, and the Gugera. The supply is secured by a great weir built across the Chenáb river at Khánkí in the Gujránwála district, and the irrigation is chiefly in the Gujránwála, Lyallpur, and Jhang districts. In the four years ending 1911–12 the average interest earned was 28 p.c., and in future the rate should rarely fall below 30 p.c. The capital expenditure has been a little over £2,000,000. The interest charges were cleared about five years after the starting of irrigation, and the capital has already been repaid to the State twice over.

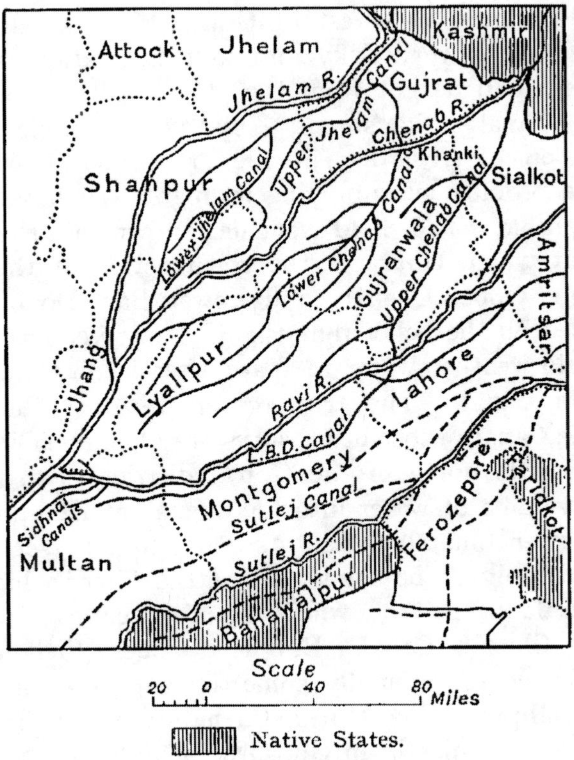


Fig. 46. Map—Canals.

**Lower Jhelam Canal.**—The Lower Jhelam Canal, which waters the tract between the Jhelam and Chenáb in the Sháhpur and Jhang districts, is a smaller and less profitable work. The culturable commanded area is about one million acres. The head-works are at Rasúl in the Gujrát district. Irrigation began in 1901. In the four years ending 1911–12 the average area watered was 748,000 acres and the interest earned exceeded 10 p.c.

**Triple Project—Upper Jhelam and Upper Chenáb Canals and Lower Bárí Doáb Canal.**—The Lower Chenáb Canal takes the whole available supply of the Chenáb river. But it does not command a large area in the Rechna Doáb lying in the west of Gujránwála, in which rain cultivation is very risky and well cultivation is costly. No help can be got from the Rávi, as the Upper Bárí Doáb Canal exhausts its supply. Desirable as the extension of irrigation in the areas mentioned above is, the problem of supplying it might well have seemed insuperable. The bold scheme known as the Triple Project which embraces the construction of the Upper Jhelam, Upper Chenáb, and Lower Bárí Doáb Canals, is based on the belief that the Jhelam river has even in the cold weather water to spare after feeding the Lower Jhelam Canal. The true *raison d'être* of the Upper Jhelam Canal, whose head-works are at Mangla in Kashmír a little north of the Gujrát district, is to throw a large volume of water into the Chenáb at Khánkí, where the Lower Chenáb Canal takes off, and so set free an equal supply to be taken out of the Chenáb higher up at Merála in Siálkot, where are the head-works of the Upper Chenáb Canal. But the Upper Jhelam Canal will also water annually some 345,000 acres in Gujrát and Sháhpur. The Upper Chenáb Canal will irrigate 648,000 acres mostly in Gujránwála, and will be carried across the Rávi by an aqueduct at Balloke in the south of Lahore. Henceforth the canal is known as the Lower Bárí Doáb, which will water 882,000 acres, mostly owned by the State, in the Montgomery and Multán districts. On the other two canals the area of Government land is not large. The Triple Project is approaching completion, and irrigation from the Upper Chenáb

Canal has begun. The engineering difficulties have been great, and the forecast does not promise such large gains as even the Lower Jhelam Canal. But a return of 7½ p.c. is expected.

**Monsoon or Inundation Canals.**—The numerous monsoon or inundation canals, which take off from the Indus, Jhelam, Chenáb, Rávi, and Sutlej, though individually petty works, perform an important office in the thirsty south-western districts. By their aid a *kharíf* crop can be raised without working the wells in the hot weather, and with luck the fallow can be well soaked in autumn, and put under wheat and other spring crops. For the maturing of these crops a prudent cultivator should not trust to the scanty cold weather rainfall, but should irrigate them from a well. The Sidhnai has a weir, but may be included in this class, for there is no assured supply at its head in the Rávi in the winter. In 1910–11 the inundation canals managed by the State watered 1,800,000 acres. There are a number of private canals in Ferozepore, Sháhpur, and the hill district of Kángra. In Ferozepore the district authorities take a share in the management.

**Colonization of Canal Lands.**—The colonization of huge areas of State lands has been an important part of new canal schemes in the west of the Panjáb. When the Lower Chenáb Canal was started the population of the vast Bár tract which it commands consisted of a few nomad cattle owners and cattle thieves. It was a point of honour to combine the two professions. Large bodies of colonists were brought from the crowded districts of the central Panjáb. The allotments to peasants usually consisted of 55 acres, a big holding for a man who possibly owned only four or five acres in his native district. There were larger allotments known as yeoman and capitalist grants, but the peasants are the only class who have turned out quite satisfactory farmers. Colonization began in 1892 and was practically complete by 1904, when over 1,800,000 acres had been allotted. To save the peasants from the evils which an unrestricted right of transfer was then bringing on the heads of many small farmers in the Panjáb it was decided only to give them permanent inalienable tenant right. The Panjáb Alienation of Land Act, No. XIII of 1900, has supplied a remedy generally applicable, and the peasant grantees are now being allowed to acquire ownership on very easy terms. The greater part of the colony is in the new Lyallpur district, which had in 1911 a population of 857,511 souls.

On the Lower Jhelam Canal the area of colonized land exceeds 400,000 acres. A feature of colonization on that canal is that half the area is held on condition of keeping up one or more brood mares, the object being to secure a good class of remounts. Succession to these grants is governed by primogeniture. On the Lower Bárí Doáb Canal a very large area is now being colonized.

**Canals of the N.W.F. Province.**—Hemmed in as the N.W.F. Province is between the Indus and the Hills, its canals are insignificant as compared with the great irrigation works of the Panjáb. The only ones of any importance are in the Pesháwar Valley. These draw their supplies from the Kábul, Bára, and Swát rivers, but the works supplied by the first two streams only command small areas. The Lower Swát Canal was begun in 1876, but the tribesmen were hostile and the diggers had to sleep in fortified enclosures. The work was not opened till 1885. A reef in the river has made it possible to dispense with a permanent weir. The country is not an ideal one for irrigation, being much cut up by ravines. But a large area has been brought under command, and the irrigation has more than once exceeded 170,000 acres. In 1911–12 it was 157,650 acres, and the interest earned was $9\frac{3}{4}$ p.c. The Upper Swát Canal, which was opened in April 1914, was a

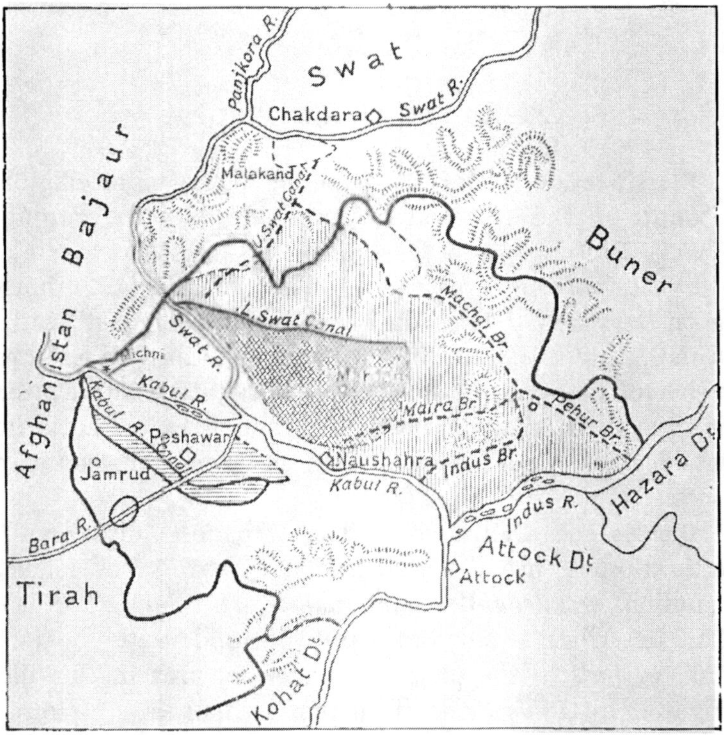


Areas commanded by { Kábul River Canal. / L. Swát Canal. / U. Swát Canal. }

Fig. 47. Map of Canals of Peshâwar district.

more ambitious project, involving the tunnelling at the Málakand of 11,000 feet of solid rock. The commanded area is nearly 450,000 acres, including 40,000 beyond our administrative frontier. The estimated cost is Rs. 18,240,000 or over £1,200,000 and the annual irrigation expected is 381,562 acres.

# CHAPTER XIV

## AGRICULTURE AND CROPS

**Classification by Zones.**—In order to give an intelligible account of the huge area embraced by the Panjáb, N.W.F. Province, and Kashmír it is necessary to make a division of the area into zones. Classification must be on very broad lines based on differences of altitude, rainfall, and soil, leading to corresponding differences in the cultivation and the crops. For statistical purposes districts must be taken as a whole, though a more accurate classification would divide some of them between two zones.

**Classes of Cultivation.**—The broadest division of cultivation is into irrigated and unirrigated, the former including well (*cháhí*), canal (*nahrí*), and *ábi*. The last term describes a small amount of land watered from tanks or *jhíls* in the plains and a larger area in the hills irrigated by *kuhls* or small artificial channels. "Unirrigated" embraces cultivation dependent on rain (*báráni*) or on flooding or percolation from rivers (*sailáb*). (See Table II.)

**Harvests.**—There are two harvests, the autumn or *kharíf*, and the spring or *rabí*. The autumn crops are mostly sown in June and July and reaped from September to December. Cotton is often sown in March. Cane planted in March and cut in January and February is counted as a *kharíf* crop. The spring crops are sown from the latter part of September to the end of December.

They are reaped in March and April. Roughly in the Panjáb three-fifths of the crops belong to the spring harvest. In the N.W.F. Province the proportion is somewhat higher. In Kashmír the autumn crop is by far the more important.

**Implements of Husbandry and Wells.**—The implements of husbandry are simple but effective in a land where as a rule there is no advantage in stirring up the soil

Fig. 48 Persian Wheel Well and Ekka.

very deep. With his primitive plough (*hal*) and a wooden clodcrusher (*sohága*) the peasant can produce a tilth for a crop like cane which it would be hard to match in England. There are two kinds of wells, the *charsa* or rope and bucket well and the *harat* or Persian wheel.

**Rotations.**—The commonest rotation in ordinary loam soils is to put in a spring and autumn crop in succession and then let the land lie fallow for a year. Unless a good deal of manure is available this is the course to follow, even in the case of irrigated land. Some poor hard soils are only fit for crops of coarse rice sown after the embanked fields have been filled in the monsoon by drainage from surrounding waste. Other lands are cropped only in the autumn because the winter rainfall is very scanty. Flooded lands are often sown only for the spring harvest.

Fig. 49. A drove of goats—Lahore.

**Cattle, Sheep, and Goats.**—In 1909 there were in the British districts of the Panjáb $4\frac{1}{4}$ million bullocks and 625,000 male buffaloes available to draw 2,169,000 ploughs and 288,000 carts, thresh the corn, and work a quarter of a million wells, besides sugar, oil, and flour mills. The cattle of the hills, N.W. Panjáb, and riverain tracts are undersized, but in the uplands of the Central Panjáb and S.E. districts fine oxen are used. The horned cattle share 18 millions of pasture land, much extremely poor, with 4 million sheep and $5\frac{1}{2}$ million goats. Hence the enormous area devoted to fodder crops.

**Zones.**—Six zones can be distinguished, but, as no district is wholly confined to the mountain zone, it must for statistical purposes be united to the submontane zone :

| | | |
|---|---|---|
| (*a*) | Mountain above 5000 feet | Panjáb—Kángra, Simla, Native States in Hills, Ambála, Hoshyárpur. |
| (*b*) | Submontane | N.W.F. Province. Hazára, Kashmír—whole |
| (*c*) | North Central Plain | Panjáb—Gujrát, Siálkot, Gurdáspur, Amritsar, Jalandhar, Ludhiána, Kapúrthala, Malerkotla, Powádh tract in Phulkian States. |
| (*d*) | North-West Area | Panjáb—Ráwalpindí, Jhelam, Attock, Mianwálí.<br>N.W.F.P.—Pesháwar, Kohát, Bannu. |
| (*e*) | South-Western Plains | Panjáb—Gujránwála, Lahore, Sháhpur, Jhang, Lyallpur, Montgomery, Multán, Muzaffargarh, Dera Ghází Khán, Baháwalpur.<br>N.W.F.P.—Dera Ismail Khán. |
| (*f*) | South-Eastern Area | Panjáb—Karnál, Rohtak, Gurgáon, Hissár, Ferozepore, Farídkot, Jangal tract in Phulkian States, Native States territory adjoining Gurgáon and Rohtak. |

**Mountain and Submontane Zones.**—In the Mountain Zone the fields are often very minute, consisting of narrow terraces supported by stone revetments built up the slopes of hills. That anyone should be ready to spend time and labour on such unpromising material is a sign of pressure of population on the soil, which is a marked feature of some hill tracts.

Fig. 50. A steep bit of hill cultivation, Hazára.

Below 8000 feet the great crop is maize. Potatoes have been introduced near our hill stations. The chief pulse of the mountain zone is *kulath* (Dolichos biflorus), eaten by the very poor. Wheat ascends to 8000 or 9000 feet, and at the higher levels is reaped in August. Barley is grown at much greater heights. Buckwheat (*úgal*, *trúmba, dráwí*), amaranth (*chauldái, ganhár, sariára*), and a tall chenopod (*bathu*) are grown in the mountain zone. Buckwheat is common on poor stony lands.

The only comparatively flat land is on the banks above river beds, which are devoted to rice cultivation, the water being conducted to the embanked fields by an elaborate system of little canals or *kuhls*. This is

Fig. 51. Preparing rice field in the Hills.

the only irrigation in the mountains, and is much valued. The Submontane Zone has a rainfall of from 30 to 40 inches. Well irrigation is little used and the dry crops are generally secure. Wheat and maize are the great staples, but gram and *charí*, i.e. *jowár* grown for fodder, are also important. Some further information about Kashmír agriculture will be found in a later chapter. For full details about classes of cultivation and crops in all the zones Tables II, III and IV should be consulted.

**North Central Panjáb Plain.**—The best soils and the finest tillage are to be found in the North Central Zone. Gujrát has been included in it, though it has also affinities in the north with the North-West area, and in the south with the South-Western plain. The rainfall varies from 25 to 35 inches. One-third of the cultivated area is protected by wells, and the well cultivation is of a very high class in Ludhiána and Jalandhar, where heavily manured maize is followed by a fine crop of wheat, and cane is commonly grown. In parts of Siálkot and Gujrát the well cultivation is of a different type, the area served per well being large and the object being to protect a big acreage of wheat in the spring harvest. The chief crops in this zone are wheat and *chari*. The latter is included under "Other Fodder" in Tables III and IV.

**North-Western Area.**—The plateau north of the Salt Range has a very clean light white sandy loam soil requiring little ploughing and no weeding. It is often very shallow, and this is one reason for the great preference for cold weather crops. *Kharíf* crops are more liable to be burned up. Generally speaking the rainfall is from 15 to 25 inches, the proportion falling in the winter and spring being larger than elsewhere. There is, except in Pesháwar and Bannu, where the conditions involve a considerable divergence from the type of this zone, practically no canal irrigation. The well irrigation is unimportant and in most parts consists of a few acres round each well intensively cultivated with market-gardening crops. The dry crops are generally very precarious. In Mianwálí the Indus valley is a fine tract, but the harvests fluctuate greatly with the extent of the floods. The Thal in Mianwálí to the south of the Sind Ságar railway is really a part of the next zone.

**The South-Western Plains.**—This zone contains nine districts. With the exception of the three on the north border of the zone they have a rainfall of from 5 to 10 inches. Of these six arid districts, only one, Montgomery, has any dry cultivation worth mentioning. In the zone as a whole three-fourths of the cultivation is protected by canals or wells, or by both. In the lowlands near the great rivers cultivation depends on the floods brought to the land direct or through small canals which carry water to parts which the natural overflow would not reach. In the uplands vast areas formerly untouched by the plough have been brought under tillage by the help of perennial canals, and the process of reclamation is still going on. The Thal is a large sandy desert which becomes more and more worthless for cultivation as one proceeds southwards. In the north the people have found out of late years that this unpromising sand can not only yield poor *kharíf* crops, but is worth sowing with gram in the spring harvest. The expense is small, and a lucky season means large profits. In Dera Ghází Khán a large area of "*pat*" below the hills is dependent for cultivation on torrents. The favourite crop in the embanked fields into which the water is diverted is *jowár*.

**The South-Eastern Plains.**—In the south-eastern Panjáb except in Hissár and the native territory on the border of Rájputána, the rainfall is from 20 to 30 inches. In Hissár it amounts to some 15 inches. These are averages; the variations in total amount and distribution over the months of the year are very great. In good seasons the area under dry crops is very large, but the fluctuations in the sown acreage are extraordinary, and the matured is often far below the sown area. The great crops are gram and mixtures of wheat or barley with gram in the spring, and *bájra* in the autumn, harvest. Well cultivation is not of much importance generally, though some of it in the Jamna riverain is excellent. The irrigated cultivation depends mainly on the Western Jamna and Sirhind canals, and the great canal crops are wheat and cotton. This is the zone in which famine conditions are still most to be feared.

In the Panjáb as a whole about one-third of the cultivated area is yearly put under wheat, which with *bájra* and maize is the staple food of the people. A large surplus of wheat and oil-seeds is available for export.

Fig. 52. Carved doorway.

# CHAPTER XV

## HANDICRAFTS AND MANUFACTURES

**Handicrafts.**—The chief handicrafts of the province are those of the weaver, the shoemaker, the carpenter, the potter, and the worker in brass and copper. The figures of the 1911 census for each craft including dependents were: weavers 883,000; shoemakers 540,000; carpenters 381,000; potters and brickmakers 349,000; metalworkers 240,000. The figures for weavers include a few working in factories. The hand-spun cotton-cloth is a coarse strong fabric known as "*khaddar*" with a single warp and weft. "*Khes*" is a better article with a double warp and weft. "*Súsí*" is a smooth cloth with coloured stripes used for women's trousers. A superior kind of checked "*khes*" known as "*gabrún*" is made at Ludhiána. The native process of weaving is slow and the weavers are very poor. The Salvation Army is trying to introduce an improved hand loom. Fine "*lungís*" or turbans of cotton with silk borders are made at Ludhiána, Multán, Peshávar, and elsewhere. Effective cotton printing is carried on by very primitive methods at Kot Kamália and Lahore. Ludhiána and Lahore turn out cotton *darís* or rugs. Coarse woollen blankets or *loís* are woven at various places, and coloured felts or *namdas* are made at Ludhiána, Khusháb, and Peshávar. Excellent imitations of Persian carpets are woven at Amritsar, and the Srínagar carpets do credit to the Kashmírís' artistic

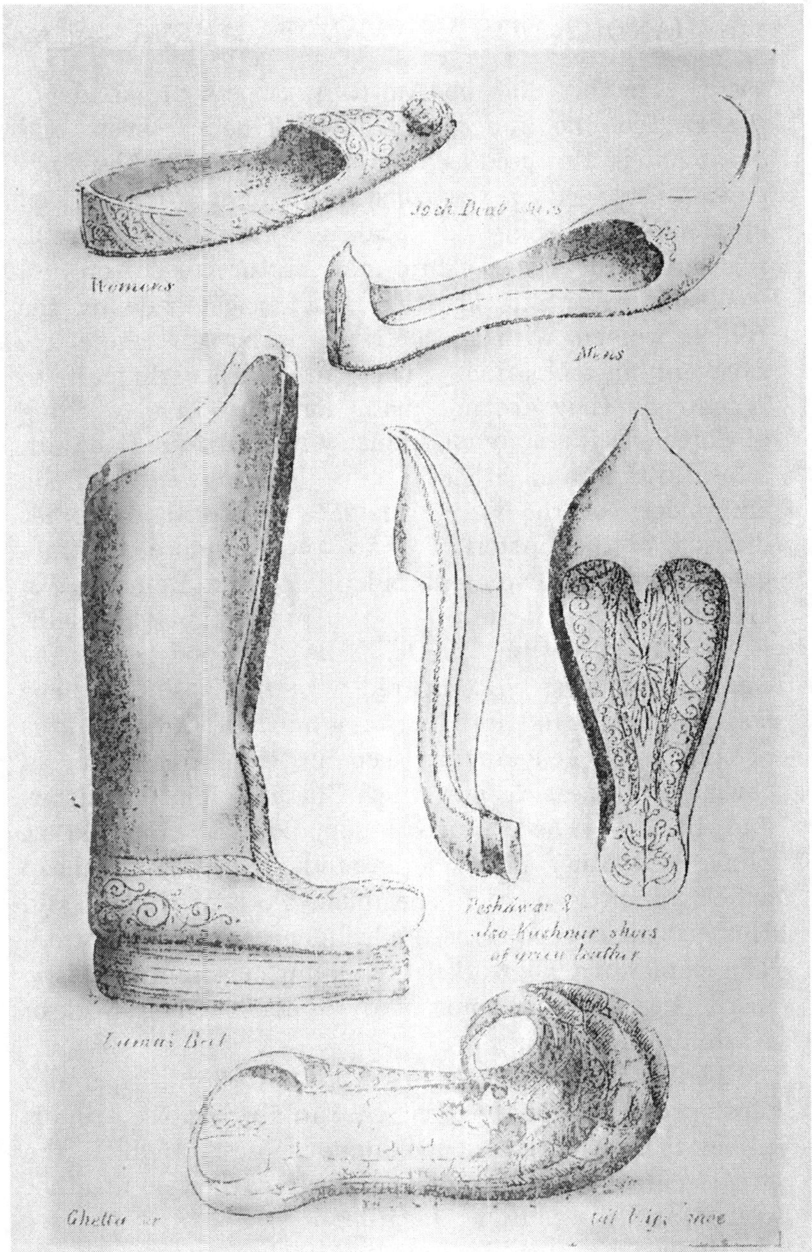


Fig. 53. Shoemaker's craft.

taste. The best of the Amritsar carpets are made of *pashm*, the fine underwool of the Tibetan sheep, and *pashmína* is also used as a material for *choghas* (dressing-gowns), etc. Coarse woollen cloth or *pattu* is woven in the Kángra hills for local use. At Multán useful rugs are made whose fabric is a mixture of cotton and wool. More artistic are the Biluch rugs made by the Biluch women with geometrical patterns. These are excellent in colouring. They are rather difficult to procure as they are not made for sale. The weaving of China silk is a common industry in Amritsar, Baháwalpur, Multán, and other places. The *phulkári* or silk embroidery of the village maidens of Hissár and other districts of the Eastern Panjáb, and the more elaborate gold and silver wire embroideries of the Delhi *bazárs*, are excellent. The most artistic product of the plains is the ivory carving of Delhi. As a wood-carver the Panjábí is not to be compared with the Kashmírí. His work is best fitted for doorways and the bow windows or *bokhárchas* commonly seen in the streets of old towns. The best carvers are at Bhera, Chiniot, Amritsar, and Batála. The European demand has produced at Simla and other places an abundant supply of cheap articles of little merit. The inlaid work of Chiniot and Hoshyárpur is good, as is the lacquer-work of Pákpattan. The papier maché work of Kashmír has much artistic merit (Fig. 55), and some of the repoussé silver work of Kashmír is excellent.

The craft of the *thathera* or brass worker is naturally most prominent in the Eastern Panjáb, because Hindus prefer brass vessels for cooking purposes. Delhi is the great centre, but the trade is actively carried on at other places, and especially at Jagádhrí.

Unglazed pottery is made practically in every village. The blue enamelled pottery of Multán and the glazed

Fig. 54. Carved windows.

Delhi china ware are effective. The manufacture of the latter is on a very petty scale.

**Factories.**—The factory industries of the Panjáb are still very small. In 1911 there were 268 factories employing 28,184 hands. The typical Panjáb factory is a little cotton ginning or pressing mill. The grinding of flour and husking of rice are sometimes part of the same

**Fig. 55. Papier maché work of Kashmír.**

business. The number of these mills rose in the 20 years ending 1911 from 12 to 202, and there are complaints that there are now too many factories. Cotton-spinning has not been very successful and the number of mills in 1911, eight, was the same as in 1903–4. The weaving is almost entirely confined to yarn of low counts. Part is used by the hand-loom weavers and part is exported to the United Provinces. Good woollen fabrics are turned out at a factory at Dháriwál in the Gurdáspur district. There were in 1911 fifteen flour mills, ten ironworks, three breweries, and one distillery.

**Joint-Stock Companies.**—The Panjáb has not reached the stage where the joint-stock business successfully takes the place of the family banking or factory business.

Fig. 56. The Potter.

*(From a picture book said to have been prepared for Mahárája Dalip Singh.)*

In 1911 there were 194 joint-stock companies. But many of these were provident societies, the working of which has been attended with such abuses that a special act has been passed for their control. A number of banks and insurance companies have also sprung up of late years. Of some of these the paid up capital is absurdly small, and the recent collapse of the largest and of two smaller native banks has drawn attention to the extremely risky nature of the business done. Of course European and Hindu family banking businesses of the old type stand on quite a different footing. Some of the cotton and other mills are joint-stock concerns.

# CHAPTER XVI

## EXPORTS AND IMPORTS

**Trade.**—In 1911–12 the exports from the Panjáb, excluding those by land to Central Asia, Ladákh, and Afghánistán, were valued at Rs. 27,63,21,000 (£18,421,000), of which 61 p.c. went to Karáchí and about 10 p.c. to Calcutta and Bombay. Of the total 27 p.c. consisted of wheat, nearly the whole of which was dispatched to Karáchí. All other grains and pulses were about equal in value to the wheat. "Gram and other pulses" (18 p.c. of total exports) was the chief item. Raw cotton accounts for 15, and oil-seeds for 10 p.c. The imports amounted in value to Rs. 30,01,28,000 (£20,008,000), little more than one-third being received from Karáchí. Cotton piece goods (Foreign 22, Indian 8½ p.c.) make up one-third of the total. The other important figures are sugar 12, and metals 11 p.c. The land trade with Afghánistán, Central Asia, and Ladákh is insignificant, but interesting as furnishing an example of modes of transport which have endured for many centuries, and of the pursuit of gain often under appalling physical difficulties.

# CHAPTER XVII

## HISTORY—PRE-MUHAMMADAN PERIOD, 500 B.C.–1000 A.D.

**In Hindu period relations of Panjáb were with western kingdoms.**—The large tract included in the British province of the Panjáb which lies between the Jamna and the Ghagar is, having regard to race, language, and past history, a part of Hindustán. Where "Panjáb" is used without qualification in this section the territories west of the Ghagar and south of Kashmír are intended. The true relations of the Panjáb and Kashmír during the Hindu period were, except for brief intervals, with Persia, Afghánistán, and Turkistán rather than with the great kingdoms founded in the valley of the Ganges and the Jamna.

**Normal division into petty kingdoms and tribal confederacies.**—The normal state of the Panjáb in early times was to be divided into a number of small kingdoms and tribal republics. Their names and the areas which they occupied varied from time to time. Names of kingdoms that have been rescued from oblivion are Gandhára, corresponding to Peshávar and the valley of the Kábul river, Urasa or Hazára, where the name is still preserved in the Orash plain, Táxila, which may have corresponded roughly to the present districts of Ráwalpindí and Attock with a small part of Hazára, Abhisara or the low hills of Jammu, Kashmír, and Trigartta, with its capital Jalandhara, which occupied most of the Jalandhar division north of the Sutlej and the states of Chamba, Suket, and Mandí. The historians of Alexander's campaigns introduce us also to the kingdoms of the elder Poros on both banks of the Jhelam, of the younger Poros east of the Chenáb, and of Sophytés (Saubhutí) in the neighbourhood of the Salt Range. We meet also with tribal confederacies, such as in Alexander's time those of the Kathaioi on the upper, and of the Malloi on the lower, Rávi.

**Invasion by Alexander, 327-325 B.C.**—The great Persian king, Darius, in 512 B.C. pushed out the boundary of his empire to the Indus, then running in a more easternly course than to-day[1]. The army with which Xerxes invaded Greece included a contingent of Indian bowmen[2]. When Alexander overthrew the Persian Empire and started on the conquest of India, the Indus was the boundary of the former. His remarkable campaign lasted from April, 327 B.C., when he led an army of 50,000 or 60,000 Europeans across the Hindu Kush into the Kábul valley, to October, 325, when he started from Sindh on his march to Persia through Makrán. Having cleared his left flank by a campaign in the hills of Buner and Swát, he crossed the Indus sixteen miles above Attock near Torbela. The King of Táxila, whose capital was near the Margalla pass on the north border of the present Ráwalpindí district, had prudently submitted as soon as the Macedonian army appeared in the Kábul valley. From the Indus Alexander marched to Táxila, and thence to the Jhelam (Hydaspes), forming a camp near the site now occupied by the town of that name in the country of Poros. The great army of the Indian king was drawn up to dispute the passage probably not very

[1] See Sykes' *History of Persia*, pp. 179–180; also Herodotos III. 94 and 98 and IV. 44.

[2] "The Indians clad with garments made of cotton had bows of cane and arrows of cane tipped with iron."—Herodotos VII. 65.

far from the eastern end of the present railway bridge. Favoured by night and a monsoon rain-storm—it was the month of July, 326 B.C.—Alexander succeeded in crossing some miles higher up into the Karrí plain under the low hills of Gujrát. Here, somewhere near the line now occupied by the upper Jhelam Canal, the Greek soldiers gave the first example of a feat often repeated since, the rout of a large and unwieldy Indian army by a small, but mobile and well-led, European force. Having defeated Poros, Alexander crossed the Chenáb (Akesines), stormed Sángala, a fort of the Kathaioi on the upper Rávi (Hydraotes) and advanced as far as the Biás (Hyphasis). But the weary soldiers insisted that this should be the bourn of their eastward march, and, after setting up twelve stone altars on the farther side, Alexander in September, 326 B.C., reluctantly turned back. Before he left the Panjáb he had hard fighting with the Malloi on the lower Rávi, and was nearly killed in the storm of one of their forts. Alexander intended that his conquests should be permanent, and made careful arrangements for their administration. But his death in June, 323 B.C., put an end to Greek rule in India. Chandra Gupta Maurya expelled the Macedonian garrisons, and some twenty years later Seleukos Nicator had to cede to him Afghánistán.

**Maurya Dominion and Empire of Aṣoka, 323-231 B.C.**— Chandra Gupta is the Sandrakottos, to whose capital at Pataliputra (Patna) Seleukos sent Megasthenes in 303 B.C. The Greek ambassador was a diligent and truthful observer, and his notes give a picture of a civilized and complex system of administration. If Chandra Gupta was the David, his grandson, Aṣoka, was the Solomon of the first Hindu Empire. His long reign, lasting from 273 to 231 B.C., was with one exception a period of profound peace deliberately maintained by an emperor who, after his conversion to the teaching of Gautama Buddha, thought war a sin. Aṣoka strove to lead his people into the right path by means of pithy abstracts of the moral law of his master graven on rocks and pillars. It is curious to remember that this missionary king was peacefully ruling a great empire in India during the twenty-four years of the struggle between Rome and Carthage, which we call the first Punic War. Of the four Viceroys who governed the outlying provinces of the empire one had his headquarters at Táxila. One of the rock edicts is at Mansehra in Hazára and another at Sháhbázgarhí in Pesháwar. From this time and for many centuries the dominant religion in the Panjáb was Buddhism, but the religion of the villages may then have been as remote from the State creed as it is to-day from orthodox Brahmanism.

**Graeco-Bactrian and Graeco-Parthian Rule.**—The Panjáb slipped from the feeble grasp of Aṣoka's successors, and for four centuries it looked not to the Ganges, but to the Kábul and the Oxus rivers.

Up to the middle of the first century of our era it was first under Graeco-Bactrian, and later under Graeco-Parthian, rule directly, or indirectly through local rulers with Greek names or Sáka Satraps. The Sákas, one of

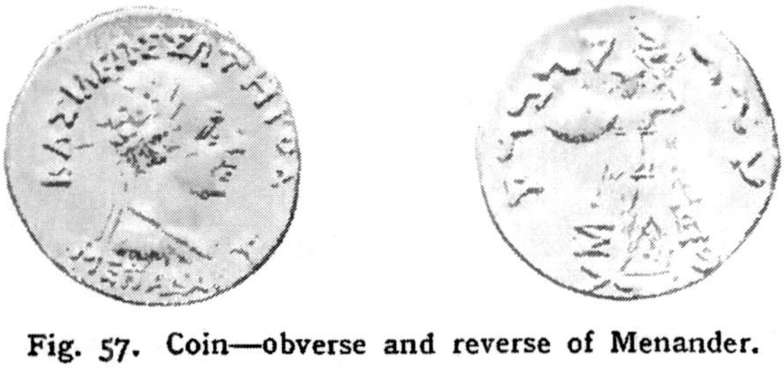

**Fig. 57. Coin—obverse and reverse of Menander.**

the central Asian shepherd hordes, were pushed out of their pastures on the upper Jaxartes by another horde.

the Yuechí. Shadowy Hellenist Princes have left us only their names on coins; one Menander, who ruled about 150 B.C., is an exception. He anticipated the feats of later rulers of Kábul by a temporary conquest of North-Western India, westwards to the Jamna and southwards to the sea.

**The Kushán Dynasty.**—The Yuechí in turn were driven southward to the Oxus and the Kábul valley and under the Kushán dynasty established their authority in the Panjáb about the middle of the first century. The most famous name is that of Kanishka, who wrested from China Kashgár, Yarkand, and Khotan, and assembled a notable council of sages of the law in Kashmír. His reign may be dated from 120 to 150 A.D. His capital was at Purushapura (Peshâwar), near which he built the famous relic tower of Buddha, 400 feet high. Beside the tower was a large monastery still renowned in the ninth and tenth centuries as a home of sacred learning. The rule of Kushán kings in the Panjáb lasted till the end of the first quarter of the third century. To their time belong the Buddhist sculptures found in the tracts near their Peshâwar capital (see also page 204).

**The Gupta Empire.**—Of the century preceding the establishment in 320 B.C. of the Gupta dynasty at Patna we know nothing. The Panjáb probably again fell under the sway of petty rájas and tribal confederacies, though the Kushán rule was maintained in Peshâwar till 465 A.D., when it was finally blotted out by the White Huns. These savage invaders soon after defeated Skanda Gupta, and from this blow the Gupta Empire never recovered. At the height of its power in 400 A.D. under Chandra Gupta II, known as Vikramaditya, who is probably the original of the Bikramajít of Indian legends, it may have reached as far west as the Chenáb.

**The White Huns or Ephthalites.**—In the beginning of

the sixth century the White Hun, Mahirakula, ruled the Panjáb from Sakala, the modern Siálkot. He was a worshipper of Şíva, and a deadly foe of the Buddhist cult, and has been described as a monster of cruelty.

The short-lived dominion of the White Huns was destroyed by the Turks and Persians about the year 565 A.D.

**Panjáb in seventh century A.D.**—From various sources, one of the most valuable being the Memoirs of the Chinese Buddhist pilgrim Hiuen Tsang, who travelled in India from 630 to 644 A.D., we know something of Northern India in the first half of the seventh century. Hiuen Tsang was at Kanauj as a guest of a powerful king named Harsha, whose first capital was at Thanesar, and who held a suzerainty over all the râjas from the Brahmaputra to the Biás. West of that river the king of Kashmír was also overlord of Táxila, Urasa, Parnotsa (Punch), Rájapurí (Rajaurí) and Sinhapura, which seems to have included the Salt Range. The Pesháwar valley was probably ruled by the Turkí Shahiya kings of Kábul. The rest of the Panjáb was divided between a kingdom called by Hiuen Tsang Tsekhia, whose capital was somewhere near Siálkot, and the important kingdom of Sindh, in which the Indus valley as far north as the Salt Range was included. Harsha died in 647 A.D. and his empire collapsed.

**Kashmír under Hindu Kings.**—For the next century China was at the height of its power. It established a suzerainty over Kashmír, Udyána (Swát), Yasín, and Chitrál. The first was at this period a powerful Hindu kingdom. Its annals, as recorded in Kalhana's Rájatarangini, bear henceforward a real relation to history. In 733 A.D. King Muktapida Lálitáditya received investiture from the Chinese Emperor. Seven years later he defeated the King of Kanauj on the Ganges. A ruler who carried his arms so far afield must have been very powerful in the Northern Panjáb. The remains of the wonderful Mártand temple, which he built in honour of the Sun God, are a standing memorial of his greatness. The history of Kashmír under its Hindu kings for the next 400 years is for the most part that of a wretched people ground down by cruel tyrants. A notable exception was

Fig. 58. Mártand Temple.

Avantidharman—855–883 A.D.—whose minister, Suyya, carried out very useful drainage and irrigation works.

**The Panjáb, 650-1000 A.D.**—We know little of Panjáb history in the 340 years which elapsed between the death of Harsha and the beginning of the Indian raids of the Sultáns of Ghazní in 986–7 A.D. The conquest of the kingdom of Sindh by the Arab general, Muhammad Kásim, occurred some centuries earlier, in 712 A.D. Multán, the city of the Sun-worshippers, was occupied, and part at least of the Indus valley submitted to the youthful conqueror. He and his successors in Sindh were tolerant rulers. No attempt was made to occupy the Central Panjáb, and when the Turkish Sultán, Sabaktagin, made his first raid into India in 986–7 A.D., his opponent was a powerful rája named Jaipál, who ruled over a wide territory extending from the Hakra to the frontier hills on the north-west. His capital was at Bhatinda. Just about the time when the rulers of Ghazní were laying the train which ended at Delhi and made it the seat of a great Muhammadan Empire, that town was being founded in 993–4 A.D. by the Tunwar Rájputs, who then held sway in that neighbourhood.

# CHAPTER XVIII

## HISTORY (*continued*). THE MUHAMMADAN PERIOD, 1000–1764 A.D.

**The Ghaznevide Raids.**—In the tenth century the Turks were the janissaries of the Abbaside Caliphs of Baghdád, and ambitious soldiers of that race began to carve out kingdoms. One Alptagin set up for himself at Ghazní, and was succeeded in 976 A.D. by his slave Sabaktagin, who began the long series of Indian raids which stained with blood the annals of the next half-century. His son, Mahmúd of Ghazní, a ruthless zealot and robber abroad, a patron of learning and literature at home, added the Panjáb to his dominions. In the first 26 years of the eleventh century he made seventeen marauding excursions into India. In the first his father's opponent, Jaipál, was beaten in a vain effort to save Pesháwar. Ten years later his successor, Anandpál, at the head of a great army, again met the Turks in the Khaibar. The valour of the Ghakkars had practically won the day, when Anandpál's elephant took fright, and this accident turned victory into rout. In one or other of the raids Multán and Lahore were occupied, and the temples of Kángra (Nagarkot) and Thanesar plundered. In 1018 the Turkish army marched as far east as Kanauj. The one permanent result of all these devastations was the occupation of the Panjáb. The Turks made Lahore the capital.

**Decline of Buddhism.**—The iconoclastic raids of Mahmúd probably gave the *coup de grâce* to Buddhism. Its golden age may be put at from 250 B.C. to 200 A.D. Brahmanism gradually emerged from retirement and reappeared at royal courts. It was quite ready to admit Buddha to its pantheon, and by so doing it sapped the doctrine he had taught. The Chinese pilgrim, Fahien, in the early part of the fifth century could still describe Buddhism in the Panjáb as "very flourishing," and he found numerous monasteries. The religion seems however to have largely degenerated into a childish veneration of relics.

**Conquest of Delhi.**—For a century and a quarter after the death of Mahmúd in 1030 A.D. his line maintained its sway over a much diminished empire. In 1155 the Afghán chief of Ghor, Alá ud dín, the "World-burner" (Jahán-soz), levelled Ghazní with the ground. For a little longer the Ghaznevide Turkish kings maintained themselves in Lahore. Between 1175 and 1186 Muhammad Ghorí, who had set up a new dynasty at Ghazní, conquered Multán, Pesháwar, Siálkot, and Lahore, and put an end to the line of Mahmúd. The occupation of Sirhind brought into the field Prithví Rája, the Chauhán Rájput king of Delhi. In 1191 he routed Muhammad Ghorí at Naráina near Karnál. But next year the Afghán came back with a huge host, and this time on the same battlefield fortune favoured him. Prithví Rája was taken and killed, and Muhammad's slave, Kutbuddín Aibak, whom he left to represent him in India, soon occupied Delhi. In 1203 Muhammad Ghorí had to flee for his life after a defeat near the Oxus. The Ghakkars seized the chance and occupied Lahore. But the old lion, though wounded, was still formidable. The Ghakkars were beaten, and, it is said, converted. A year or two later they murdered their conqueror in his tent near the Indus.

**Turkish and Afgháns Sultáns of Delhi.**—He had no son, and his strong viceroy, Kutbuddín Aibak, became in 1206 the first of the 33 Muhammadan kings, who in five successive dynasties ruled from Delhi a kingdom of varying dimensions, till the last of them fell at Pánipat in 1526, and Bábar, the first of the Moghals, became master of their red fort palace. The blood-stained annals of these 320 years can only be lightly touched on. Under vigorous rulers like the Turkí Slave kings, Altamsh (1210–1236) and Balban (1266–1287), a ferocious and masterful boor like Alá ud dín Khaljí (1296–1316), or a ferocious but able man of culture like Muhammad Tughlak (1325–1351), the local governors at Lahore and Multán were content to be servants. In the frequent intervals during which the royal authority was in the hands of sottish wastrels, the chance of independence was no doubt seized.

**Mongol Invasions.**—In 1221 the Mongol cloud rose on the north-west horizon. The cruelty of these camel-riding Tatars and the terror they inspired may perhaps be measured by the appalling picture given of their bestial appearance. In 1221, Chingiz Khán descended on the Indus at the heels of the King of Khwarizm (Khiva), and drove him into Sindh. Then there was a lull for twenty years, after which the Mongol war hordes ruined and ravaged the Panjáb for two generations. Two great Panjáb governors, Sher Khán under Balban and Tughlak under Alá ud dín Khaljí, maintained a gallant struggle against these savages. In 1297 and 1303 the Mongols came to the gates of Delhi, but the city did not fall, and soon after they ceased to harry Northern India. During these years the misery of the common people must often have been extreme. When foreign raids ceased for a time they were plundered by their own rulers. In the Panjáb the fate of the peasantry must have depended chiefly on the character of the governor for the time being, and of the local feudatories or *zamíndárs*, who were given the right to collect the State's share of the produce on condition of keeping up bodies of armed men for service when required.

**The Invasion of Timúr.**—The long reign of Muhammad Tughlak's successor, Firoz Sháh (1351–1388), son of a Hindu Rájput princess of Dipálpur, brought relief to all classes. Besides adopting a moderate fiscal policy, he founded towns like Hissár and Fatehábád, dug canals from the Jamna and the Sutlej, and carried out many other useful works. On his death the realm fell into confusion. In 1398–99 another appalling calamity fell upon it in the invasion of Timúrlang (Tamerlane), Khán of Samarkand. He entered India at the head of 90,000 horsemen, and marched by Multán, Dipálpur, Sirsa, Kaithal, and Pánipat to Delhi. What lust of blood was to the Mongols, religious hatred was to Timúr and his Turks. Ten thousand Hindus were put to the sword at Bhatner and 100,000 prisoners were massacred before the victory at Delhi. For the three days' sack of the royal city Timúr was not personally responsible. Sated with the blood of lakhs of infidels sent "to the fires of Hell" he marched back through Kángra and Jammu to the Indus. Six years later the House of Tughlak received a deadly wound when the Wazír, Ikbál Khan, fell in battle with Khizr Khán, the governor of Multán.

**The later Dynasties.**—The Saiyyids, who were in power from 1414 to 1451, only ruled a small territory round Delhi. The local governors and the Hindu chiefs made themselves independent. Sikandar Lodí (1488–1518) reduced them to some form of submission, but his successor, Ibrahím, drove them into opposition by pushing authority further than his power justified. An Afghán noble, Daulat Khán, rebelled in the Panjáb. There is always an ear at Kábul listening to the first sounds of discord and weakness between Pesháwar and Delhi. Bábar, a descendant of Timúr, ruled a little kingdom there. In 1519 he advanced as far as Bhera. Five years later his troops burned the Lahore *bazár*, and sacked Dipálpur. The next winter saw Bábar back again, and this time Delhi was his goal. On the 21st of April, 1526, a great battle at Pánipat again decided the fate of India, and Bábar entered Delhi in triumph.

**Akbar and** his successors.—He soon bequeathed his Indian kingdom to his son Humáyun, who lost it, but recovered it shortly before his death by defeating Sikandar Sur at Sirhind. In 1556 Akbar succeeded at the age of 13, and in the same year Bahram Khán won for his master a great battle at Pánipat and seated the Moghals firmly on the throne. For the next century and a half, till their power declined after the death of Aurangzeb in 1707, Kábul and Delhi were under one rule, and the Panjáb was held in a strong grasp. When it was disturbed the cause was rebellions of undutiful sons of the reigning Emperor, struggles between rival heirs on the Emperor's death, or attempts to check the growing power of the Sikh Gurus. The empire was divided into *súbahs*, and the area described in this book embraced *súbahs* Lahore and Multán, and parts of *súbahs* Delhi and Kábul. Kashmír and the trans-Indus tract were included in the last.

**The Sultáns of Kashmír.**—The Hindu rule in Kashmír had broken down by the middle of the twelfth century. A long line of Musalmán Sultáns followed. Two notable names emerge in the end of the fourteenth and the first half of the fifteenth century, Sikandar, the "Idol-breaker," who destroyed most of the Hindu temples and converted his people to Islám, and his wise and tolerant successor, Zain-ul-âbidín. Akbar conquered Kashmír in 1587.

**Moghal Royal Progresses to Kashmír.**—His successors often moved from Delhi by Lahore, Bhimbar, and the Pír

Panjál route to the Happy Valley in order to escape the summer heats. Bernier has given us a graphic account of Aurangzeb's move to the hills in 1665. On that occasion his total following was estimated to amount to 300,000 or 400,000 persons, and the journey from Delhi to Lahore occupied two months. The burden royal progresses on this scale must have imposed on the country is inconceivable. Jahángír died in his beloved Kashmír. He planted the road from Delhi to Lahore with trees, set up as milestones the *kos minárs*, some of which are still standing, and built fine *sarais* at various places.

**Prosperity of Lahore under Akbar, Jahángír, and Sháhjahán.**—The reigns of Akbar and of his son and grandson were the heyday of Lahore. It was the half-way house between Delhi and Kashmír, and between Agra and Kábul. The Moghal Court was often there. Akbar made the city his headquarters from 1584 to 1598. Jahángír was buried and Sháhjahán was born at Lahore. The mausoleum of the former is at Sháhdara, a mile or two from the city. Sháhjahán made the Shálimár garden, and Ali Mardán Khán's Canal, the predecessor of our own Upper Bárí Doáb Canal, was partly designed to water it. Lahore retained its importance under Aurangzeb, till he became enmeshed in the endless Deccan wars, and his successor, Bahádur Shah, died there in 1712.

**Bába Nának, the first Guru.**—According to Sikh legend Bábar in one of his invasions had among his prisoners their first Guru, Bába Nának, and tried to make him a Musalmán. Nának was born in 1469 at Talwandí, now known as Nankána Sáhib, 30 miles to the south-west of Lahore, and died twelve years after Bábar's victory at Pánipat. He journeyed all over India, and, if legend speaks true, even visited Mecca. His propaganda was a peaceful one. A man of the people himself, he had a

Fig. 59. Bába Nának and the Musician Mardána.

message to deliver to a peasantry naturally impatient of the shackles of orthodox Hinduism. Sikhism is the most important of all the later dissents from Brahmanism, which represent revolts against idolatry, priestly domination, and the bondage of caste and ritual. These things Nának unhesitatingly condemned, and in the opening lines of his Japjí, the morning service which every true Sikh must know by heart, he asserted in sublime language the unity of God.

**The Gurus between Nának and Govind.**—The first three successors of Nának led the quiet lives of great eastern saints. They managed to keep on good terms with the Emperor and generally also with his local representatives. The fifth Guru, Arjan (1581–1606), began the welding of the Sikhs into a body fit to play a part in secular politics. He compiled their sacred book, known as the *Granth Sáhib*, and made Amritsar the permanent centre of their faith. The tenets of these early Gurus chimed in with the liberal sentiments of Akbar, and he treated them kindly. Arjan was accused of helping Khusru, Jahángír's rebellious son, and is alleged to have died after suffering cruel tortures.

Hitherto there had been little ill-will between monotheistic Sikhs and Muhammadans. Henceforth there was ever-increasing enmity. The peasant converts to the new creed had many scores against Turk officials to pay off, while the new leader Hargovind (1606–1645), had the motive of revenge. He was a Guru of a new type, a lover of horses and hawks, and a man of war. He kept up a bodyguard, and, when danger threatened, armed followers flocked to his standard. The easy-going Jahángír (1605–1627) on the whole treated him well. Sháhjahán (1627–1659) was more strict or less prudent, and during his reign there were several collisions between the imperial troops and the Guru's followers. Hargovind

Fig. 60. Guru Govind Singh.

was succeeded by his grandson, Har Rai (1645–1661). The new Guru was a man of peace. Har Rai died in 1661, having nominated his younger son, Harkrishn, a child of six, as his successor. His brother, Rám Rai, disputed his claim, but Aurangzeb confirmed Harkrishn's appointment. He died of small pox in 1664 and was succeeded by his uncle, Teg Bahádur (1664–1675), whose chief titles to fame are his execution in 1675, his prophecy of the coming of the English, and the fact that he was the father of the great tenth Guru, Govind. It is said that when in prison at Delhi he gazed southwards one day in the direction of the Emperor's *zanána*. Charged with this impropriety, he replied: "I was looking in the direction of the Europeans, who are coming to tear down thy *pardas* and destroy thine empire."

**Guru Govind Singh.**—When Govind (1675–1708) succeeded his father, Aurangzeb had already started on the course of persecution which fatally weakened the pillars of Turkish rule. Govind grew up with a rooted hatred of the Turks, and a determination to weld his followers into a league of fighting men or *Khálsa* (Ar. *khális* = pure), admission into which was by the *pahul*, a form of military baptism. Sikhs were henceforth to be *Singhs* (lions). They were forbidden to smoke, and enjoined to wear the five k's, *kes, kangha, kripan, kachh,* and *kara* (uncut hair, comb, sword, short drawers, and steel bracelet). He established himself at Anandpur beyond the Hoshyárpur Siwáliks. Much of his life was spent in struggles with his neighbours, the Rájput Hill Rájas, backed from time to time by detachments of imperial troops from Sirhind. In 1705 two of his sons were killed fighting and two young grandsons were executed at Sirhind. He himself took refuge to the south of the Sutlej, but finally decided to obey a summons from Aurangzeb, and was on the way to the Deccan when the old Emperor died. The Guru took up his residence on the banks of the Godávarí, and died there in 1708.

**Bánda.**—Before his death he had converted the Hindu ascetic Bánda, and sent him forth on a mission of revenge. Bánda defeated and slew the governor of Sirhind, Wazír Khán, and sacked the town. Doubtless he dreamed of making himself Guru. But he was really little more than a condottiere, and his orthodoxy was suspect. He was defeated and captured in 1715 at Gurdáspur. Many of his followers were executed and he himself was tortured to death at Delhi, where the members of an English mission saw a ghastly procession of Sikh prisoners with 2000 heads carried on poles. The blow was severe, and for a generation little was heard of the Sikhs.

**Invasions of Nádir Sháh and Ahmad Sháh.**—The central power was weak, and a new era of invasions from the west began. Nádir Sháh, the Turkman shepherd, who had made himself master of Persia, advanced through the Panjáb. Zakaria Khán, the governor of Lahore, submitted and the town was saved from sack. A victory at Karnál left the road to Delhi open, and in March, 1738, the Persians occupied the capital. A shot fired at Nádir Sháh in the Chándní Chauk led to the nine hours' massacre, when the Daríba ran with blood, and 100,000 citizens are said to have perished. The Persians retired laden with booty, including the peacock throne and the Kohinur diamond. The Sikhs harassed detachments of the army on its homeward march. Nádir Sháh was murdered nine years later, and his power passed to the Afghán leader, the Durání Ahmad Sháh.

Between 1748 and 1767 this remarkable man, who could conquer but could not keep, invaded India eight times. Lahore was occupied in 1748, but at Sirhind the skill of Mír Mannu, called Muín ul Mulk, gave the advantage to the Moghals. Ahmad Sháh retreated, and

Muín ul Mulk was rewarded with the governorship of the Panjáb. He was soon forced to cede to the Afghán the revenue of four districts. His failure to fulfil his compact led to a third invasion in 1752, and Muín ul Mulk, after a gallant defence of Lahore, had to submit. In 1755–56 Ahmad Sháh plundered Delhi and then retired, leaving his son, Timúr, to represent him at Lahore. Meanwhile the Sikhs had been gathering strength. Then, as now, they formed only a fraction of the population. But they were united by a strong hatred of Muhammadan rule, and in the disorganized state of the country even the loose organization described below made them formidable. Owing to the weakness of the government the Panjáb became dotted over with forts, built by local chiefs, who undoubtedly lived largely by plunder. The spiritual organization under a Guru being gone, there gradually grew up a political and military organization into twelve *misls*, in which "a number of chiefs agreed, after a somewhat democratic and equal fashion, to fight under the general orders of some powerful leader" against the hated Muhammadans. The *misls* often fought with one another for a change. In the third quarter of the eighteenth century *Sardár* Jassa Singh of Kapúrthala, head of the Ahluwália *misl*, was the leading man among the Sikhs. Timúr having defiled the tank at Amritsar, Jassa Singh avenged the insult by occupying Lahore in 1756, and the Afghán prince withdrew across the Indus. Adína Beg, the governor of the Jalandhar Doáb, called in the Mahrattas, who drove the Sikhs out in 1758. Ahmad Sháh's fifth invasion in 1761 was rendered memorable by his great victory over the Mahratta confederacy at Pánipat. When he returned to Kábul, the Sikhs besieged his governor, Zín Khán, in Sirhind. Next year Ahmad Sháh returned, and repaid their audacity by a crushing defeat near Barnála.

They soon rallied, and, in 1763, under Jassa Singh Ahluwália and Rája Ala Singh of Patiála razed Sirhind to the ground. After the sack the Sikh horsemen rode over the plains between Sirhind and Karnál, each man claiming for his own any village into which in passing he had thrown some portion of his garments. This was the origin of the numerous petty chiefships and confederacies of horsemen, which, along with the Phulkian States, the British Government took under its protection in 1808. In 1764 the chiefs of the Bhangí *misl* occupied Lahore.

## CHAPTER XIX

### HISTORY (*continued*). THE SIKH PERIOD, 1764–1849 A.D.

**Rise of Ranjít Singh.**—The Bhangís held Lahore with brief intervals for 25 years. In 1799, Ranjít Singh, basing his claim on a grant from Sháh Zamán, the grandson of Ahmad Sháh, drove them out, and inaugurated the remarkable career which ended with his death in 1839. When he took Lahore the future Maháràja was only nineteen years of age. He was the head of the Sukarchakia *misl*, which had its headquarters at Gujránwála. Mean in appearance, his face marked and one eye closed by the ravages of smallpox, he was the one man of genius the Jat tribe has produced. A splendid horseman, a bold leader, a cool thinker untroubled with scruples, an unerring judge of character, he was bound to rise in such times. He set himself to put down every Sikh rival and to profit by the waning of the Duràní power to make himself master of their possessions in the Panjáb. Pluck, patience, and guile broke down all opposition among the Mánjha Sikhs. The Sikh chiefs to the south of the Sutlej were only saved from the same fate by throwing themselves in 1808 on the protection of the English, who six years earlier had occupied Delhi, and by taking under their protection the blind old Emperor, Sháh Álam, had virtually proclaimed themselves the paramount power in India. For 44 years he had been only a piece in the game played by Mahrattas,

Rohillas, and the English in alliance with the Nawáb Wazír of Oudh.

**British supremacy established in India.**—In the first years of the nineteenth century the Marquess of Wellesley had made up his mind that the time was ripe to grasp supreme power in India. The motive was largely self-

**Fig. 61. Mahárája Ranjít Singh.**

*(From a picture book said to have been prepared for Mahárája Dalip Singh.)*

preservation. India was included in Napoleon's vast plans for the overthrow of England, and Sindhia, with his army trained in European methods of warfare by French officers, seemed a likely confederate. Colonel Arthur Wellesley's hard-won battle at Assaye in September, 1803, and Lord Lake's victories on the Hindan and at Laswárí in the same year, decided the fate of India. Delhi was occupied, and Daulat Rao Sindhia ceded to the company territory reaching from Fázilka on the Sutlej to Delhi on the Jamna, and extending along that river northwards to Karnál and southwards to Mewát. Fázilka and a large part of Hissár then formed a wild desert tract called Bhattiána, over which no effective control was exercised till 1818. In 1832 "the Delhi territory" became part of the North-West Provinces, from which it was transferred to the Panjáb after the Mutiny.

**Relations of Ranjít Singh with English.**—In December, 1808, Ranjít Singh was warned that by the issue of the war with Sindhia the Cis-Sutlej chiefs had come under British protection. The Mahárája was within an ace of declaring war, or let the world think so, but his statesmanlike instincts got the better of mortified ambition, and in April, 1809, he signed a treaty pledging himself to make no conquests south and east of the Sutlej. The compact so reluctantly made was faithfully observed. In 1815, as the result of war with the Gurkhas, the Rájput hill states lying to the south of the Sutlej came under British protection.

**Extension of Sikh Kingdom in Panjáb.**—As early as 1806, when he reduced Jhang, Ranjít Singh began his encroachments on the possessions of the Duránís in the Panjáb. Next year, and again in 1810 and 1816, Multán was attacked, but the strong fort was not taken till 1818, when the old Nawáb, Muzaffar Khán, and five of his sons, fell fighting at the gate. Kashmír was first attacked in 1811 and finally annexed in 1819. Called in by the great Katoch Rája of Kángra, Sansár Chand, in 1809, to help him against the Gurkhas, Ranjít Singh duped both parties, and became master of the famous fort. Many years later he annexed the whole of the Kángra hill states. By 1820 the Mahárája was supreme from the

Sutlej to the Indus, though his hold on Hazára was weak. Peshávar became tributary in 1823, but it was kept in subjection with much difficulty. Across the Indus the position of the Sikhs was always precarious, and revenue was only paid when an armed force could be sent to collect it. As late as 1837 the great Sikh leader, Harí Singh Nalwa, fell fighting with the Afgháns at Jamrúd. The Barakzai, Dost Muhammad, had been the ruler of Kábul since 1826. In 1838, when the English launched their ill-starred expedition to restore Sháh Shuja to his throne, Ranjít Singh did not refuse his help in the passage through the Panjáb. But he was worn out by toils and excesses, and next year the weary lion of the Panjáb died. He had known how to use men. He employed Jat blades and Brahman and Muhammadan brains. Khatrís put both at his service. The best of his local governors was Diwán Sáwan Mal, who ruled the South-West Panjáb with much profit to himself and to the people. After 1820 the three Jammu brothers, Rájas Dhián Singh, Suchet Singh, and Guláb Singh, had great power.

**Successors of Ranjít Singh.**—From 1839 till 1846 an orgy of bloodshed and intrigue went on in Lahore. Kharak Singh, the Maháraja's son, died in 1840, and on the same day occurred the death of his son Nao Nihál Singh, compassed probably by the Jammu Rájas. Sher Singh, and then the child, Dalíp Singh, succeeded. In September, 1843, Maháraja Sher Singh, his son Partáb Singh, and Rája Dhián Singh were shot by Ajít Singh and Lehna Singh of the great Sindhanwália house. The death of Dhián Singh was avenged by his son, Híra Singh, who proclaimed Dalíp Singh as Maháraja and made himself chief minister. When he in turn was killed Rání Jindan, the mother of Dalíp Singh, her brother Jowáhir Singh, and her favourite, Lál Singh, took the reins.

Fig. 62. Mahárája Kharak Singh.

Fig. 63. Nao Nihál Singh.

Fig. 64. Mahárája Sher Singh.

(*From a picture book said to have been prepared for Mahárája Dalip Singh.*)

**The First Sikh War and its results.**—In 1845 these intriguers, fearing the *Khálsa* army which they could not control, yielded to its cry to be led across the Sutlej in the hope that its strength would be broken in its conflict with the Company's forces. The valour displayed by the Sikh soldiery on the fields of Mudkí, Ferozesháh (Pherushahr), and Sobráon was rendered useless by the treachery of its rulers, and Lahore was occupied in February, 1846. By the treaty signed on 9th March, 1846, the Mahárája ceded the territories in the plains between the Sutlej and Biás, and in the hills between the Biás and the Indus. Kashmír and Hazára were made over by the Company to Rája Guláb Singh for a payment of 75 lakhs, but next year he induced the Lahore Darbár to take over Hazára and give him Jammu in exchange. After Rája Lál Singh had been banished for instigating Shekḥ Imám ud din to resist the occupation of Kashmír by Guláb Singh, an agreement was executed, in December, 1846, between the Government and the chief Sikh *Sardárs* by which a Council of Regency was appointed to be controlled by a British Resident at Lahore. The office was given to Henry Lawrence.

**The Second Sikh War.**—These arrangements were destined to be short-lived. Diwán Sáwan Mal's son, Mulráj, mismanaged Multán and was ordered to resign. In April, 1848, two English officers sent to instal his Sikh successor were murdered. Herbert Edwardes, with the help of Muhammadan tribesmen and Baháwalpur troops, shut up Mulráj in Multán, but the fort was too strong for the first British regular force, which arrived in August, and it did not fall till January, 1849. During that winter a formidable Sikh revolt against English domination broke out. Its leader was *Sardár* Chatar Singh, Governor of Hazára. The troops sent by the *Darbár* to Multán under Chatar Singh's son, Sher Singh, marched northwards in September to join their co-religionists.

On the 13th of January, 1849, Lord Gough fought a very hardly contested battle at Chilianwála. If this was but a doubtful victory, that won six weeks later at Gujrát was decisive. On 12th March, 1849, the soldiers

Fig. 65. Zamzama Gun[1].

of the *Khálsa* in proud dejection laid down their weapons at the feet of the victor, and dispersed to their homes.

**Annexation.**—The cause they represented was in no sense a national one. The Sikhs were a small minority of the population, the bulk of the people being Muhammadans, to whom the English came as deliverers. On the 30th of March, 1849, the proclamation annexing the Panjáb was read at Lahore.

[1] This gun, known to the readers of *Kim*, stands on the Lahore Mall. Whoever possesses it is supposed to be ruler of the Panjáb.

# CHAPTER XX

## HISTORY (*continued*). THE BRITISH PERIOD, 1849–1913

**Administrative Arrangements in Panjáb.**—Lord Dalhousie put the government of the province under a Board of Administration consisting of the two Lawrences, Henry and John, and Charles Mansel. The Board was abolished in 1853 and its powers vested in a Chief Commissioner. A Revenue or Financial Commissioner and a Judicial Commissioner were his principal subordinates. John Lawrence, the first and only Chief Commissioner of the Panjáb, became its first Lieutenant-Governor on the 1st of January, 1859. The raising of the Panjáb to the full rank of an Indian province was the fitting reward of the great part which its people and its officers, with their cool-headed and determined chief, had played in the suppression of the Mutiny. The overthrow of the *Khálsa* left the contending parties with the respect which strong men feel for each other; the services of the Sikhs in 1857 healed their wounded pride and removed all soreness.

**Administration, 1849–1859.**—When John Lawrence laid down his office in the end of February, 1859, ten years of work by himself and the able officers drafted by Lord Dalhousie into the new province had established order on a solid foundation. A strong administration suited to a manly and headstrong people had been organised. In the greater part of the province rights in land had been determined and recorded. The principle of a moderate assessment of the land revenue had been laid down and partially carried out in practice. The policy of canal and railway development, which was to

Fig. 66. Sir John Lawrence.

have so great a future in the Panjáb, had been definitely started. The province had been divided into nine divisions containing 33 districts. The Divisional Commissioners were superintendents of revenue and police with power to try the gravest criminal offences and to hear appeals in civil cases. The Deputy Commissioner of districts had large civil, criminal, and fiscal powers. A simple criminal and civil code was enforced. The peace of the frontier was secured by a chain of fortified

**Fig. 67. John Nicolson's Monument at Delhi.**

outposts watching the outlets from the hills, behind which were the cantonments at the headquarters of the districts linked together by a military road. The posts and the cantonments except Pesháwar were garrisoned by the Frontier Force, a splendid body of troops consisting ultimately of seven infantry and five cavalry regiments, with some mule batteries. This force was till 1885 subject to the orders of the Lieutenant Governor. It never wanted work, for before the Mutiny troops had to be employed seventeen times against the independent tribesmen. East of the Indus order was secured by the disarmament of the people, the maintenance, in addition to civil police, of a strong body of military police, and the construction of good roads. Just before Lawrence left the construction of the Amritsar-Multán railway was begun, and a few weeks after his departure the Upper Bárí Doáb Canal was opened.

Fig. 68. Sir Robert Montgomery.

**Administration, 1859–1870.**—The next eleven years occupied by the administrations of Sir Robert Montgomery and Sir Donald Macleod were a quiet time in which results already achieved were consolidated. The Penal Code was extended to the Panjáb in 1862, and a Chief Court with a modest establishment of two judges in 1865 took the place of the Judicial Commissioner. In the same year a Settlement Commissioner was appointed to help the Financial Commissioner in the control of land revenue settlements. Two severe famines marked the beginning and the close of this period. Omitting the usual little frontier excitements, it is necessary to mention the troublesome Ambela campaign in 1863 in the country north of Pesháwar, which had for its object the breaking up of the power of a nest of Hindustání fanatics, and the Black Mountain expedition, in 1868, on the Hazára border, in which no fewer than 15,000 men were employed. Sir Henry Durand, who succeeded Sir Donald Macleod, after seven months of office lost his life by an accident in the beginning of 1871.

**Administration, 1871–1882.**—The next eleven years divided between the administrations of Sir Henry Davies (1871–1877) and Sir Robert Egerton (1877–1882) produced more striking events. In 1872 a small body of fanatics belonging to a Sikh sect known as Kúkas or Shouters marched from the Ludhiána district and attacked the headquarters of the little Muhammadan State of Malerkotla. They were repulsed and 68 men surrendered to the Patiála authorities. The Deputy Commissioner of Ludhiána blew 49 of them from the guns, and the rest were executed after summary trial by the Commissioner. Such strong measures were not approved by the Government, but it must be remembered that these madmen had killed ten and wounded seventeen men, and that their lives were justly forfeit. On the 1st of January,

1877, Queen Victoria's assumption of the title of Empress of India (*Kaisar-i-Hind*) was announced at a great *Darbár* at Delhi. In 1877 Kashmír, hitherto controlled by the Lieutenant-Governor, was put directly under the Government of India. The same year and the next the province was tried by famine, and in 1878–80 it was the base from

Fig. 69. Panjáb Camels—Lahore.

which our armies marched on Kábul and Kandahár, while its resources in camels were strained to supply transport. Apart from this its interest in the war was very great because it is the chief recruiting ground of the Indian army and its chiefs sent contingents to help their suzerain. The first stage of the war was closed by the treaty of Gandamak in May, 1879, by which Yakúb

Khán surrendered any rights he possessed over the Khaibar and the Kurram as far as Shutargardan.

**Administration, 1882–1892.**—During the Lieutenant-Governorships of Sir Charles Aitchison (1882–1887) and Sir James Lyall (1887–1892) there was little trouble on

Fig. 70. Sir Charles Aitchison.

the western frontier. In 1891 the need had arisen of making our power felt up to the Pamírs. The setting up of a British agency at Gilgit was opposed in 1891 by the fighting men of Hunza and Nagar. Colonel Durand advanced rapidly with a small force and when a determined assault reduced the strong fort of Nilt, trouble was at an end once and for all. Within the Panjáb the period was one of quiet development. The Sirhind Canal was opened in 1882, and the weir at Khánkí for the supply of the Lower Chenáb Canal was finished in 1892. New railways were constructed. Lord Ripon's policy of Local Self-government found a strong supporter in Sir Charles Aitchison, and Acts were passed dealing with the constitution and powers of municipal committees and district boards. In 1884 and 1885 a large measure of reorganization was carried out. A separate staff of divisional, district, and subordinate civil judges was appointed. The divisional judges were also sessions judges. The ten commissioners were reduced to six, and five of them were relieved of all criminal work by the sessions judges. The Deputy Commissioner henceforth was a Revenue Collector and District Magistrate with large powers in criminal cases. The revenue administration was at the same time being improved by the reforms embodied in the Panjáb Land Revenue and Tenancy Acts passed at the beginning of Sir James Lyall's administration.

**Administration, 1892–1902.**—The next two administrations, those of Sir Dennis Fitzpatrick (1892–97) and Sir Mackworth Young (1897–1902) were crowded with important events. Throughout the period the colonization of the vast area of waste commanded by the Lower Chenáb Canal was carried out, and the Lower Jhelam Canal was formally opened six months before Sir Mackworth Young left. The province suffered from famine in 1896–97 and again in 1899–1900. In October, 1897, a worse enemy appeared in the shape of plague, but its ravages were not very formidable till the end of the period. The Panjáb was given a small nominated Legislative Council in 1897, which speedily proved itself a valuable instrument for dealing with much-needed provincial legislation. But the most important Panjáb Act of the period, XIII of 1900, dealing with Land Alienation was passed by the Viceroy's Legislative Council. In 1901 a Political Agent was appointed as the intermediary between the Panjáb Government and the Phulkian States. On the frontier the conclusion of the Durand Agreement in 1893 might well have raised hopes of quiet times. But the reality was otherwise. The establishment of a British officer at Wána to exercise control over Southern Wazíristán in 1894 was forcibly resisted by the Mahsúd Wazírs, and an expedition had to be sent into their country. The Mehtar or Chief of Chitrál, who was in receipt of a subsidy from the British Government, died in 1892. A period of great confusion followed fomented by the ambitions of Umra Khán of Jandol. Finally we recognised as Mehtar the eldest son, who had come uppermost in the struggle, and sent an English officer as British Agent to Chitrál. Umra Khán got our protégé murdered, and besieged the Agent in the Chitrál fort. He withdrew however on the approach of a small force from Gilgit. Shuja-ul-Mulk was recognised as Mehtar. This little trouble occurred in 1895. Two years later a storm-cloud suddenly burst over the frontier, such as we had never before experienced. It spread rapidly from the Tochí to Swát, tribe after tribe rising and attacking our posts. It is impossible to tell here the story of the military measures taken against the different offending tribes. The most important was the campaign in Tirah against the Orakzais and Afrídís, in which 30,000 men were engaged for six months. In 1900 attacks on the peace of the border by the Mahsúd Wazírs had to be punished by a blockade, and in the cold weather of 1901–2 small columns harried the hill country to enforce their submission. By this time the connection of the Panjáb Government with frontier affairs, which had gradually come to involve responsibility with little real power, had ceased. On the 25th of October, 1901, the North-West Frontier Province was constituted and Colonel (afterwards Sir Harold) Deane became its first Chief Commissioner, an office which he held till 1908, when he was succeeded by Major (now Sir George) Roos Keppel.

**Administration, 1902–1913.**—The last eleven years have embraced the Lieutenant Governorship of Sir Charles Rivaz (1902–1907), the too brief administration of Sir Denzil Ibbetson (1907–1908), and that of Sir Louis Dane (1908–1913). Throughout the period plague has been a disturbing factor, preventing entirely the growth of population which the rapid development of the agricultural resources of the province would otherwise have secured. It was among the causes stimulating the unrest which came to a head in 1907. A terrible earthquake occurred in 1905. Its centre was in Kángra, where 20,000 persons perished under the ruins of their houses. The colonization of the Crown waste on the Lower Jhelam Canal was nearly finished during Sir Charles Rivaz's administration. Before he left the Triple Canal Project, now approaching completion, had been undertaken. Other measures of importance to the rural population were the passing of the Co-operative Credit Societies' Act in 1903, and the organization in 1905 of a provincial Agricultural Department. The seditious movement which troubled Bengal had its echo in some parts of the Panjáb in the end of 1906 and the spring of 1907. A bill dealing with the rights and obligations of the Crown tenants in the new Canal Colonies was at the time before the Local Legislature. Excitement fomented from outside spread among the prosperous colonists on the Lower Chenáb Canal. There was a disturbance in Lahore in connection with the trial of a newspaper editor, the ringleaders being students. When Sir Denzil Ibbetson took the reins into his strong hands in March, 1907, the position was somewhat critical. The disturbance at Lahore was followed by a riot at Rávalpindí. The two leading agitators were deported, a measure which was amply justified by their reckless

**Fig. 71. Sir Denzil Ibbetson.**

actions and which had an immediate effect. Lord Minto decided to withhold his assent from the Colony Bill, and it has recently been replaced by a measure which has met with general acceptance. When Sir Denzil Ibbetson took office he was already suffering from a mortal disease. In the following January he gave up the unequal struggle, and shortly afterwards died. Sir Louis Dane became Lieutenant Governor in May, 1908. A striking feature of his administration was the growth of co-operative credit societies or village banks. At the Coronation *Darbár* on 12th December, 1911, the King-Emperor announced the transfer of the capital of India to Delhi. As a necessary consequence the city and its suburbs were severed from the province, with which they had been connected for 55 years. In 1913 Sir Louis Dane was succeeded by Sir Michael O'Dwyer.

Fig. 72. Sir Michael O'Dwyer.

# CHAPTER XXI

## ARCHAEOLOGY AND COINS

**Hindu and Buddhist Remains.**—The scholar who ended his study of Indian history with the close of the first millennium of the Christian era would expect to find a fruitful field for the study of ancient monuments of the Hindu faith in the plains of the Panjáb. He would look for a great temple of the Sun God at Multán, and at places like Lahore and Kángra, Thanesar and Pihowa, for shrines rich with graven work outside and with treasures of gold and precious stones within. But he would look in vain. The Muhammadan invaders of the five centuries which elapsed between Mahmúd of Ghazní and the Moghal Bábar were above all things idol-breakers, and their path was marked by the destruction and spoliation of temples. Even those invaders who remained as conquerors deemed it a pious work to build their mosques with the stones of ruined fanes. The transformation, as in the case of the great Kuwwat ul Islám mosque beside the Kutb Minár, did not always involve the complete obliteration of idolatrous emblems. Kángra was not too remote to be reached by invading armies, and the visitor to Nurpur on the road from Pathánkot to Dharmsála can realize how magnificent some of the old Hindu buildings were, and how utterly they were destroyed. The smaller buildings to be found in the remoter parts of the hills escaped, and there are characteristic groups of stone temples at Chamba and still older shrines dating from the eighth century at Barmaur and Chitrádí in the same state. The ruins of the great temple of the Sun, built by Lálitáditya in the same period, at Mártand[1] near Islámábád in the Kashmír State are very striking. The smaller, but far better preserved, temple at Payer is probably of much later date. Round the pool of

**Fig. 73. Group of Chamba Temples.**

Katás, one of Ṣiva's eyes, a great place of Hindu pilgrimage in the Salt Range, there is little or nothing of antiquarian value, but there are interesting remains at Malot in the same neighbourhood. It is possible that when the mounds that mark the sites of ancient villages come to be excavated valuable relics of the Hindu period will be brought to light. The forces of nature or the violence of man have wiped out all traces of the numerous Buddhist monasteries

[1] See page 166.

which the Chinese pilgrims found in the Panjáb. Inscriptions of Aşoka graven on rocks survive at Sháhbázgarhí and Mansehra in the North-West Frontier Province. Two pillars with inscriptions of the Missionary Emperor stand at Delhi. They were brought from Topra near the Jamna in Ambála and from Meerut by Firoz Sháh. The traveller by train from Jhelam to Ráwalpindí can

Fig. 74. Payer Temple.

see to the west of the line at Mankiála a great *stúpa* raised to celebrate the self-sacrifice of the Bodhisattva who gave his life to feed a starving tigress. There is a ruined *stúpa* at Suí Vihár in the Baháwalpur State. The Chinese pilgrims described the largest of Indian *stúpas* built by Kanishka near Pesháwar to enshrine precious relics of Gautama Buddha and a great monastery beside it. Recent excavations have proved the truth of the conjecture that the two mounds at Sháhjí kí dherí covered the remains of these buildings, and the six-sided

Fig. 75. Reliquary.

crystal reliquary containing three small fragments of bone has after long centuries been disinterred and is now in the great pagoda at Rangoon. In the Lahore museum there is a rich collection of the sculptures recovered from the Peshäwar Valley, the ancient Gandhára. They exhibit strong traces of Greek influence. The best age of Gandhára sculpture was probably over before the reign of Kanishka. The site of the famous town of Táxila is now a protected area, and excavation there may yield a rich reward.

**Fig. 76. Colonnade in Kuwwat ul Islám Mosque.**

**Muhammadan Architecture.**—The Muhammadan architecture of North-Western India may be divided into three periods:

| | | | |
|---|---|---|---|
| (*a*) | The Pathán | .. | 1191–1320 |
| (*b*) | The Tughlak | .. | 1320–1556 |
| (*c*) | The Moghal | .. | 1556–1753 |

In the Pathán period the royal builders drew their inspiration from Ghazní, but their work was also much affected by Hindu influences for two reasons. They used the materials of Hindu temples in constructing their mosques and they employed masons imbued with the traditions of Hindu art. The best specimens of this period are to be found in the group of buildings in Old

Fig. 77. Kutb Minár.

Delhi or *Kila' Rai Pithora,* close to Mahraulí and eleven miles to the south of the present city. These buildings are the magnificent *Kuwwat ul Islám* (Might of Islám) Mosque (1191–1225), with its splendid tower, the *Kutb Minár* (1200–1220), from which the *mu'azzin* called the faithful to prayer, the tomb of the Emperor Altamsh (1238), and the great gateway built in 1310 by Alá ud dín Khaljí. In the second period, named after the house that occupied the imperial throne when it began, all traces of Hindu influence have vanished, and the buildings display the austere and massive grandeur suited to the faith of the desert prophet unalloyed by foreign elements. This style in its beginning is best seen in the cyclopean

**Fig. 78 Tomb of Emperor Tughlak Sháh.**

ruins of Tughlakábád and the tomb of the Emperor Tughlak Sháh, and in some mosques in and near Delhi. Its latest phase is represented by Sher Sháh's mosque in the Old Fort or *Purána Kila'*. To some the simple grandeur of this style will appeal more strongly than the splendid, but at times almost effeminate, beauty of the third period. Noted examples of Moghal architecture in the Panjáb are to be found in Sháhjahán's red fort

Fig. 79. Jama Masjid, Delhi.

Fig. 80. Tomb of Emperor Humáyun.

palace and *Jama' Masjid* at New Delhi or Sháhjahánábád, Humáyun's tomb on the road from Delhi to Mahraulí, the fort palace, the Bádsháhí and Wazír Khán's mosques, at Lahore, and Jahángír's mausoleum at Sháhdara. A very late building in this style is the tomb of Nawáb Safdar Jang (1753) near Delhi. A further account of some of the most famous Muhammadan buildings will be

**Fig. 81. Bádsháhí Mosque, Lahore.**

found in the paragraphs devoted to the chief cities of the province. The architecture of the British period scarcely deserves notice.

**Coins.**—Among the most interesting of the archaeological remains are the coins which are found in great abundance on the frontier and all over the Panjáb. These take us back through the centuries to times before the invasion of India by Alexander, and for the obscure period intervening between the Greek occupation of the Frontier and the Muhammadan conquest, they are our main source of history. The most ancient of the Indian monetary issues are the so-called punch-marked coins, some of which were undoubtedly in existence before the Greek invasion. Alexander himself left no permanent traces of his progress through the Panjáb and Sindh, but about the year 200 B.C., Greeks from Bactria, an outlying province of the Seleukidan Empire, once more appeared on the Indian Frontier, which they effectively occupied for more than a century. They struck the well-known Graeco-Bactrian coins; the most famous of the Indo-Greek princes were Apollodotos and Menander. Towards the close of this dynasty, parts of Sindh and Afghánistán were conquered by Sáka Scythians from Central Asia. They struck what are termed the Indo-Scythian and Indo-Parthian coins bearing names in legible Greek legends—Manes, Azes, Azilises, Gondophares, Abdagases. Both Greeks and Sákas were overthrown by the Kusháns. The extensive gold and copper Kushán currency, with inscriptions in the Greek script, contains the names of Kadphises, Kanishka, Huvishka, and others. In addition to the coins of these foreign dynasties, there are the purely Indian currencies, e.g. the coins of Táxila, and those bearing the names of such tribes as the Odumbaras, Kunindas, and Yaudheyas. The White Huns overthrew the Kushán Empire in the fifth century. After their own fall in the sixth century, there are more and more debased types of coinage such as the ubiquitous *Gadhiya paisa*, a degraded Sassanian type. In the ninth century we again meet with coins bearing distinct names, the "bull and horseman" currency of the Hindu kings of Kábul. We have now reached the beginning of the Muhammadan rule in India. Muhammad

Fig. 82. Coins.

1. Silver punch-marked coin. 2. Drachma of Sophytes (Panjáb Satrap about time of Alexander). 3. Hemidrachma of Azes. 4. Copper coin of Táxila. 5. Silver Kuninda coin. 6. Stater of Wema Kadphises. 7. Stater of Kanishka. 8. Later Kushán stater. 9. White Hun silver piece. 10. Gadhiya *paisa*. 11. Silver coin of Spalapati Deva, Hindu King of Kábul.

bin Sám was the founder of the first Pathán dynasty of Delhi, and was succeeded by a long line of Sultáns. The Pathán and Moghal coins bear Arabic and Persian legends. There were mints at Lahore, Multán, Háfizábád, Kalanaur, Deraját, Pesháwar, Srínagar and Jammu. An issue of coins peculiar to the Panjáb is that of the Sikhs. Their coin legends, partly Persian, partly Panjábí, are written in the Persian and Gurmúkhí scripts. Amongst Sikh mints were Amritsar, Lahore, Multán, Dera, Anandgarh, Jhang, and Kashmír.

# CHAPTER XXII

## ADMINISTRATION—GENERAL

**Panjáb Districts.**—The administrative unit in the Panjáb is the district in charge of a Deputy Commissioner. The districts are divided into *tahsíls*, each on the average containing four, and are grouped together in divisions managed by Commissioners. There are 28 districts and five divisions. An ordinary Panjáb district has an area of 2000 to 3000 square miles and contains from 1000 to 2000 village estates. Devon, the third in size of the English counties, is about equal to an average Panjáb district.

**Branches of Administration.**—The provincial governments of India are organized in three branches, Executive, Judicial, and Revenue, and a number of special departments, such as Forests and Irrigation. Under "Judicial" there are two subdivisions, civil and criminal. The tendency at first is for powers in all three branches to be concentrated in the hands of single individuals, development tends to specialization, but it is a matter of controversy how far the separation of executive and magisterial functions can be carried without jeopardy to the common weal.

**The Lieutenant Governor.**—At the head of the whole administration is the Lieutenant Governor, who holds office for five years. He has a strong Secretariat to help in the dispatch of business. The experiment of governing the Panjáb by a Board was speedily given up, and for sixty years it has enjoyed the advantage of one man government, the Lieutenant Governor controlling all subordinate authorities and being himself only controlled by the Governor General in Council. The independence of the Courts in the exercise of judicial functions is of course safeguarded.

**Official hierarchy.**—The following is a list of the official hierarchy in the different branches of the administration:

*A.* Lieutenant Governor.
*B.* Five Judges of Chief Court (*j*).
*C.* Two Financial Commissioners (*r*).
*D.* Five Commissioners, (*e*) and (*r*).
*E.* Sixteen Divisional and Sessions Judges (*j*).
*F.* Deputy Commissioners, (*e*), (*r*) and (*crim*).
*G.* District Judges (*civ*).
*H.* Subordinate Judges (*civ*).
*J.* Assistant and Extra Assistant Commissioners, (*e*), (*j*) and (*r*).
*K.* *Tahsíldárs* (*e*), (*r*) and (*crim*).
*L.* *Munsifs* (*civ*).
*M.* *Náib-Tahsíldárs*, (*e*) (*r*) and (*j*).

The letters in brackets indicate the classes of functions which the official concerned usually exercises. Translated into a diagram we have the following:

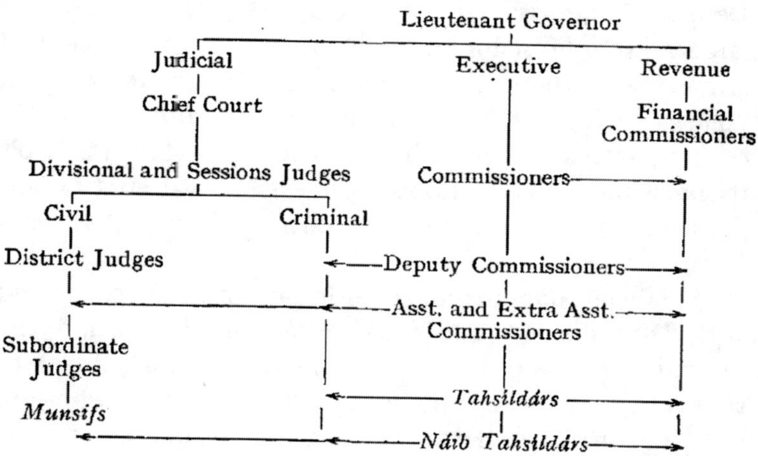

**Tahsíldárs and Assistant and Extra Assistant Commissioners.** Thus the chain of executive authority runs down to the *tahsíldár's* assistant or *náib* through the Commissioner and the Deputy Commissioner, the *tahsíldár* being directly responsible to the latter. The Assistant and Extra Assistant Commissioners are the Deputy Commissioner's Assistants at headquarters, and as such are invested with powers in all branches. The *tahsíldár*, a very important functionary, is in charge of a *tahsíl*. He is linked on to the village estates by a double chain, one official consisting of the *kanungos* and the *patwáris* or village accountants whom they supervise, the other non-official consisting of the village headmen and the *zaildárs*, each of whom is the intermediary between the revenue and police staffs and the villages.

**Subdivisional Officers.**—In some heavy districts one or more *tahsíls* are formed into a subdivision and put in charge of a resident Assistant or Extra Assistant Commissioner, exercising such independent authority as the Deputy Commissioner thinks fit to entrust to him.

**The Deputy Commissioner and his Assistants.**—As the officer responsible for the maintenance of order the Deputy Commissioner is District Magistrate and has large powers both for the prevention and punishment of crime. The District Superintendent is his Assistant in police matters. The Civil Surgeon is also under his control, and he has an Indian District Inspector of Schools to assist him in educational business. The Deputy Commissioner is subject to the control of the Divisional Commissioner.

**Financial Commissioners.**—In all matters connected with land, excise, and income tax administration the Commissioner and Deputy Commissioner are subject to the control of the Financial Commissioners, who are also the final appellate authority in revenue cases. As chief district revenue officer the Deputy Commissioner's proper title is "Collector," a term which indicates his responsibility for the realization of all Government revenues. In districts which are canal irrigated the amount is in some cases very large.

**Settlement Officers, etc.**—With the periodical revisions of the land revenue assessment the Deputy Commissioner has no direct concern. That very responsible duty is done by a special staff of Settlement Officers, selected chiefly from among the Assistant Commissioners and working under the Commissioners and Financial Commissioners. The Director of Land Records, the Registrar of Co-operative Credit Societies, and in some branches of his work the Director of Agriculture and Industries, are controlled by the Financial Commissioners.

**The Chief Court.**—It must be admitted that Panjábís are very litigious and that in some tracts they are extremely vindictive and reckless of human life. The volume of litigation is swollen by the fact that the country is one of small-holders subject as regards inheritance and other matters to an uncodified customary law, which may vary from tribe to tribe and tract to tract. A suit is to the Panjábí a rubber, the last game of which he will play in Lahore, if the law permits. It is not therefore extraordinary that the Chief Court constituted in 1865 with two judges has now five, and that even this number has in the past proved insufficient. In the same way the cadre of divisional and sessions judges had in 1909 to be raised from 12 to 16.

**Administration of N. W. F. Province.**—In the N. W. F. Province no Commissioner is interposed between the district officers and the Chief Commissioner, under whom the Revenue Commissioner and the Judicial Commissioner occupy pretty much the position of the Financial Commissioners and the Chief Court in the Panjáb.

**Departments.**—The principal departments are the Railway, Post Office, Telegraphs, and Accounts, under the Government of India, and Irrigation, Roads and Buildings, Forests, Police, Medical, and Education, under the Lieutenant Governor. In matters affecting the rural population, as a great part of the business of the Forest Department must do, the Conservator of Forests is subject to the control of the Financial Commissioners, whose relations with the Irrigation Department are also very intimate.

**Legislative Council.**—From 1897 to 1909 the Panjáb had a local Legislative Council of nine nominated members, which passed a number of useful Acts. Under 9 Edward VII, cap. 4, an enlarged council with increased powers has been constituted. It consists of 24 members of whom eight are elected, one by the University, one by the Chamber of Commerce, three by groups of Municipal and cantonment committees, and three by groups of district boards. The other sixteen members are nominated by the Lieutenant Governor, and at least six of them must be persons not in Government service. The right of interpellation has been given, and also some share in shaping the financial arrangements embodied in the annual budget.

# CHAPTER XXIII

## ADMINISTRATION—LOCAL

**Municipalities.**—It is matter for reflection that, while the effect of British administration has been to weaken self-government in villages, half a century of effort has failed to make it a living thing in towns and districts. The machinery exists, but outside a few towns the result is poor. The attempt was made on too large a scale, municipal institutions being bestowed on places which were no more than villages with a *bazár*. This has been partially corrected of late years. A new official entity, the "notified area," has been invented to suit the requirements of such places. While there were in 1904 139 municipalities and 48 notified areas, in 1911–12 the figures were 107 and 104 respectively. Even in the latter year 32 of the municipalities had incomes not exceeding £1000 (Rs. 15,000). The total income of the 104 towns was Rs. 71,41,000 (£476,000), of which Rs. 44,90,000 (£300,000) were derived from taxation. Nearly 90 p.c. of the taxation was drawn from octroi, a hardy plant which has survived much economic criticism. The expenditure was Rs. 69,09,000 (£461,000), of which Rs. 40,32,000 (£269,000) fall under the head of "Public Health and Convenience." The incidence of taxation was Rs. 2·6 or a little over three shillings a head.

**District Boards.**—The district boards can at present in practice only be treated as consultative bodies, and well handled can in that capacity play a useful rôle. Their income is mainly derived from the local rate, a surcharge of one-twelfth on the land revenue. In 1911–12 the income was Rs. 53,74,000 (£358,000) and the expenditure Rs. 54,44,500 (£363,000). The local rate contributed 51 p.c. and contributions from Government 23 p.c. of the former figure. Public works took up 41 and Education about 20 p.c. of the expenditure.

**Elections.**—Some of the seats in most of the municipalities and boards are filled by election when any one can be induced to vote. Public spirit is lacking and, as a rule, except when party or sectarian spirit is rampant, the franchise is regarded with indifference.

# CHAPTER XXIV

## REVENUE AND EXPENDITURE

**Financial Relations with Government of India.**—Local governments exercise their financial powers in strict subordination to the Government of India, which alone can borrow, and which requires the submission for its sanction of the annual provincial budgets. To ensure a reasonable amount of decentralization the Supreme Government has made financial contracts with the provinces under which they receive definite shares of the receipts, and are responsible for definite shares of the expenditure, under particular heads. The existing contract dates only from 1911–12 (see Table V).

**Income and Expenditure.**—Excluding income from railways, post offices, telegraphs, salt, and sales of excise opium, which are wholly imperial, the revenue of the Panjáb in 1911–12 was £5,057,000 (Rs. 758,56,000), of which the provincial share was £2,662,200 (Rs. 399,33,000), to which have to be added £251,800 (Rs. 37,77,000) on account of assignments made by the Government of India to the province. This brought up the total to £2,914,000 (Rs. 437,10,000). The expenditure was £2,691,933 (Rs. 403,79,000). This does not include £983,000 spent from loan funds on irrigation works, chiefly the great Triple Project. The large expenditure on railways is imperial. Of the gross income more than three-fourths is derived from the land (Land Revenue, 46 p.c., Irrigation, chiefly canal water rates, 29 p.c., and

Forests, $1\frac{3}{4}$ p.c.). The balance consists of Excise $8\frac{1}{2}$ p.c., Stamps, 7 p.c., Income Tax over 2 p.c., and other heads $5\frac{3}{4}$ p.c.

**Land Revenue.**—Certain items are included under the Land Revenue head which are no part of the assessment of the land. The real land revenue of the Panjáb is about £2,000,000 and falls roughly at the rate of eighteen pence per cultivated acre (Table II). It is not a land tax, but an extremely moderate quit rent. In India the ruler has always taken a share of the produce of the land from the persons in whom he recognised a permanent right to occupy it or arrange for its tillage. The title of the Rája to his share and the right of the occupier to hold the land he tilled and pass it on to his children both formed part of the customary law of the country. Under Indian rule the Rája's share was often collected in kind, and the proportion of the crop taken left the tiller of the soil little or nothing beyond what was needed for the bare support of himself and his family. What the British Government did was to commute the share in kind into a cash demand and gradually to limit its amount to a reasonable figure. The need of moderation was not learned without painful experience, but the Panjáb was fortunate in this that, except as regards the Delhi territory, the lesson had been learned and a reasonable system evolved in the United Provinces before the officers it sent to the Panjáb began the regular assessments of the districts of the new province. A land revenue settlement is usually made for a term of 20 or 30 years. Since 1860 the limit of the government demand has been fixed at one-half of the rental, but this figure is very rarely approached in practice. Between a quarter and a third would be nearer the mark. A large part of the land is tilled by the owners, and the rent of the whole has to be calculated from the data for the part, often not more than a third or two-fifths of the whole, cultivated by tenants at will. The calculation is complicated by the fact that kind rents consisting of a share of the crop are in most places commoner than cash rents and are increasing in favour. The determination of the cash value of the rent where the crop is shared is a very difficult task. There is a large margin for error, but there can be no doubt that the net result has almost always been undervaluation. It is probable that the share of the produce of the fields which the land revenue absorbs rarely exceeds one-seventh and is more often one-tenth or less. A clear proof of the general moderation of Panjáb assessments is furnished by the fact that in the three years ending 1910–11 the recorded prices in sales amounted to more than Rs. 125 per rupee of land revenue of the land sold, which may be taken as implying a belief on the part of purchasers that the landlord's rent is not double, but five or six times the land revenue assessment, for a man would hardly pay Rs. 125 unless he expected to get at least six or seven rupees annual profit.

**Fluctuating Assessments.**—The old native plan of taking a share of the crop, though it offered great opportunity for dishonesty on both sides, had at least the merit of roughly adjusting the demand to the character of the seasons. It was slowly realized that there were parts of the province where the harvests were so precarious that even a very moderate fixed cash assessment was unsuitable. Various systems of fluctuating cash assessment have therefore been introduced, and one-fourth of the total demand is now of this character, the proportion having been greatly increased by the adoption of the fluctuating principle in the new canal colonies.

**Suspensions and Remissions.**—Where fixity is retained the strain in bad seasons is lessened by a free use of suspensions, and, if the amounts of which the collection has been deferred accumulate owing to a succession of bad seasons, resort is had to remission.

**Irrigation Income and Expenditure.**—In a normal year in the Panjáb over one-fourth of the total crops is matured by the help of Government Canals, and this proportion will soon be largely increased. In 1911–12 the income from canals amounted to £1,474,000, and the working expenses to £984,000, leaving a surplus of £490,000. Nearly the whole of the income is derived from water rates, which represent the price paid by the cultivator for irrigation provided by State expenditure. The rates vary for different crops and on different canals. The average incidence may be roughly put at Rs. 4 or a little over five shillings per acre. In calculating the profit on canals allowance is made for land revenue dependent on irrigation, amounting to nearly £400,000.

Fig. 83. Skeleton District Map of Panjáb.

# CHAPTER XXV

## PANJÁB DISTRICTS AND DELHI

**Districts and Divisions.**—The Panjáb now consists of 28 districts grouped in five divisions. In descriptions of districts and states boundaries, railways, and roads, which appear on the face of the inset maps, are omitted. Details regarding cultivation and crops will be found in Tables II, III and IV, and information as to places of note in Chapter xxx. The revenue figures of Panjáb districts in this chapter relate to the year 1911–12.

**Delhi Enclave.**—On the transfer of the capital of India to Delhi part of the area of the old district of that name comprising 337 estates was removed from the jurisdiction of the Panjáb Government and brought under the immediate authority of the Government of India (Act No. XIII of 1912). The remainder of the district was divided between Rohtak and Gurgáon, and the headquarters of the Delhi division were transferred to Ambála.

The area of the new province is only 528 square miles, and the population including that of the City is estimated at 396,997. The cultivated area is 340 square miles, more than half of which is cultivated by the owners themselves. The principal agricultural tribe is the Hindu Játs, who are hard-working and thrifty peasant farmers. The land revenue is Rs. 4,00,203 (£26,680). The above figures only relate to the part of the enclave formerly included in the Panjáb[1]. The head of the administration has the title of Chief Commissioner.

[1] Some estates lying to the east of the Jamna and belonging to the United Provinces have recently been added to the enclave.

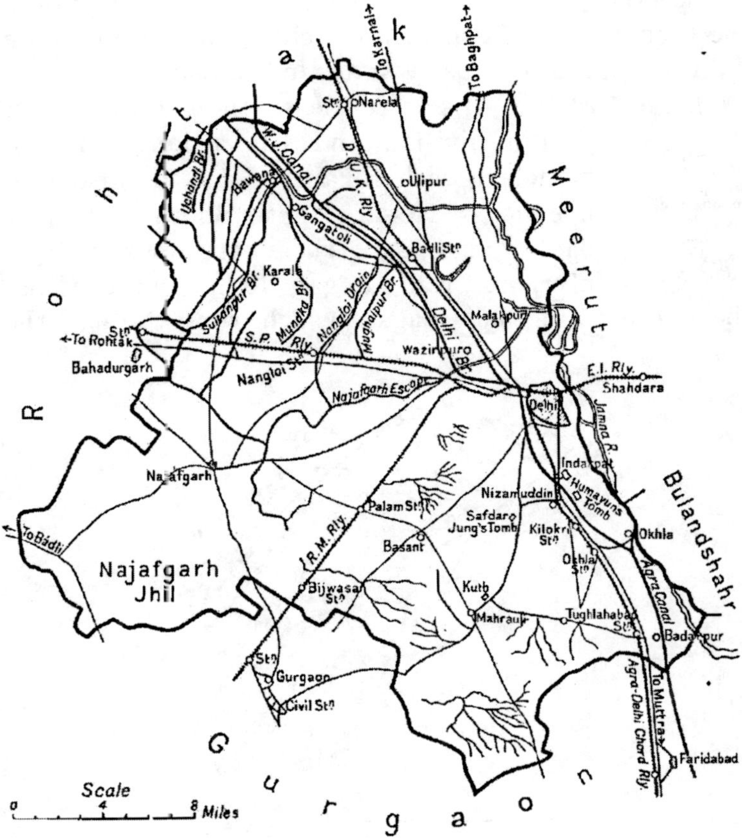


Fig. 84. Delhi Enclave.

Area, 14,832 sq. m. Cultd area, 10,650 sq. m. Pop. 3,704,608; 68 p. c. H.[1] Land Rev. Rs. 66,99,136 = £446,609.

**The Ambála division** includes four of the five districts of the South-Eastern Plains, the submontane district of Ambála, and the hill district of Simla. It is with the exception of Lahore the smallest division, but it ranks first in cultivated area and third in population. It

[1] H. = Hindu, M. = Muhammadan, S. = Sikh.

is twice the size of Wales and has twice its population. The Commissioner is in political charge of the hill state of Sirmúr and of five petty states in the plains.

Area, 5213 sq. m.
Cultd area, 4201 sq. m.
Pop. 804,809; 67 p. c. H.
Land Rev. Rs. 9,76,749 = £67,117.

**Hissár District.**—Hissár is the south-western district of the division and has a long common boundary with Bikaner. It is divided into five *tahsíls*, Hissár, Hánsi, Bhiwání, Fatehábád, and Sirsa. There are four natural divisions, Nálí, Bágar, Rohí, and Hariána. The overflow of the Ghagar, which runs through the

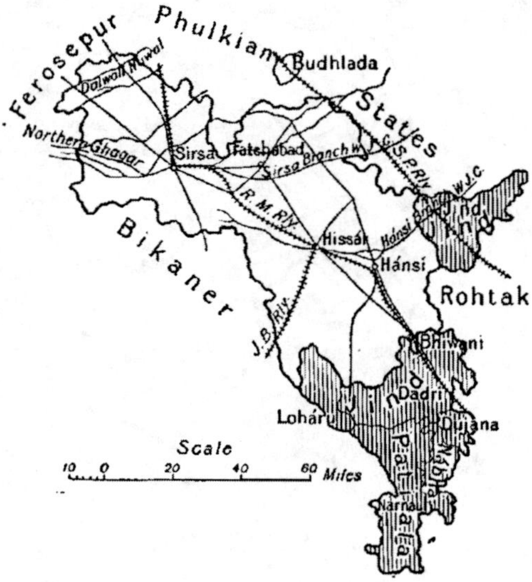


Fig. 85. Hissár with portions of Phulkian States etc.

north of the district has transformed the lands on either bank into hard intractable clay, which yields nothing to the husbandman without copious floods. This is the Nálí. The Bágar is a region of rolling sand stretching along the Bikaner border from Sirsa to Bhiwání. In Sirsa to the east of the Bágar is a plain of very light reddish loam known as the Rohí, partly watered by the Sirhind Canal. South of the Ghagar the loam in the east of the district is firmer, and well adapted to irrigation, which much of it obtains from branches of the Western Jamna Canal. This tract is known as Hariána, and has given its name to a famous breed of cattle. The Government cattle farm at Hissár covers an area of 65 square miles. North of the Fatehábád *tahsíl* and surrounded by villages belonging to the Phulkian States is an island of British territory called Budhláda. It belongs to the Jangal Dés, and has the characteristic drought-resisting sandy loam and sand of that tract. Much of Budhláda is watered by the Sirhind Canal. Of the total area of the district only about 9 p.c. is irrigated. The water level is so far from the surface that well irrigation is usually impossible, and the source of irrigation is canals.

Hissár suffered severely from the disorders which followed on the collapse of the Moghal Empire and its ruin was consummated by the terrible famine of 1783. The starving people died or fled and for years the country lay desolate. It passed into the hands of the British 20 years later, but for another 20 years our hold on this outlying territory was loose and ineffective. In 1857 the troops at Hánsi, Hissár, and Sirsa rose and killed all the Europeans who fell into their hands. The Muhammadan tribes followed their example, and for a time British authority ceased to exist. The district was part of the Delhi territory transferred to the Panjáb in 1858.

The rainfall is scanty, averaging 15 inches, and extremely capricious. No other district suffers so much from famine as Hissár. The crops are extraordinarily insecure, with a large surplus in a good season and practically nothing when the rains fail badly. They consist mainly of the cheap pulses and millets. With such fluctuating harvests it is impossible to collect the revenues with any regularity, and large sums have to be suspended in bad seasons.

Such industries as exist are mostly in Hánsi and Bhiwání, where there are mills for ginning and pressing cotton. Cotton cloths tastefully embroidered with silk, known as *phulkáris*, are a well-known local product.

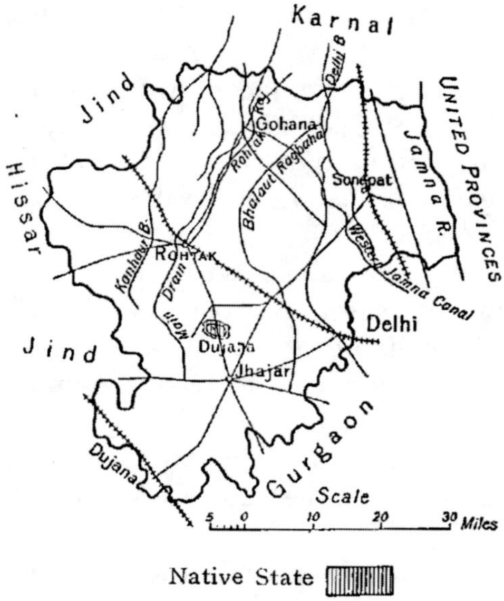


Fig. 86.

**Area, 2248 sq. m.**
**Cultd area, 1815 sq. m.**
**Pop. 714,834.**
**Land Rev. Rs. 16,66,364 = £111,091.**

**Rohtak** became a British possession in 1803, but it was not till after the Mutiny that it was brought wholly under direct British administration. The old district consisted of the three *tahsíls* of Rohtak, Gohána, and Jhajar, but on the breaking up of the Delhi district the Sonepat *tahsíl* was added.

Rohtak is practically a purely agricultural tract with

large villages, but no towns of any importance. By far the most important agricultural tribe is the Hindu Játs. They are strong-bodied sturdy farmers, who keep fine oxen and splendid buffaloes, and live in large and well organized village communities. 37 p.c. of the cultivation is protected by canal and well irrigation, the former being by far the more important. The district consists mainly of a plain of good loam soil. There have been great canal extensions in this plain, which under irrigation is very fertile, yielding excellent wheat, cotton, and cane. There is a rich belt of well irrigation in the Jamna valley, and in the south of the district there are parts where wells can be profitably worked. Belts of uneven sandy land are found especially in the west and south. The dry cultivation is most precarious, for the rainfall is extremely variable. In the old district it averages 20 inches. But averages in a tract like Rohtak mean very little. The chief crops are the two millets and gram.

Area, 2264 sq. m. Cultd area, 1701 sq. m. Pop. 729,167. Land Rev. Rs. 15,98,333 =£106,556.

**Gurgáon** contains six *tahsíls*, Rewárí, Gurgáon, Nuh, Firozpur, Palwal, and Ballabgarh. The southern part of the district projects into Rájputána, and in its physical and racial characteristics really belongs to that region.

Rewárí is the only town of any importance. It has a large trade with Rájputána. Apart from this the interests of the district are agricultural. In Gurgáon the Jamna valley is for the most part narrow and very poor. The plain above it in the Palwal *tahsíl* has a fertile loam soil and is irrigated by the Agra Canal. The Hindu Játs of this part of the district are good cultivators. The rest of Gurgáon consists mostly of sand and sandy loam and low bare hills. In Rewárí the skill and industry of the Hindu Ahírs have produced wonderful results considering that many of the wells are salt and much of the land very sandy. The lazy and thriftless Meos of the southern part of the district are a great contrast to the Ahírs. They are Muhammadans.

About a quarter of the area is protected by irrigation from wells, the Agra Canal, and embankments or "*bands*," which catch and hold up the hill drainages. Owing to the depth and saltness of many of the wells the cultivation dependent on them is far from secure, and the "*band*" irrigation is most precarious. The large dry area is subject to extensive and complete crop failures. The average rainfall over a series of years is 24 inches, but its

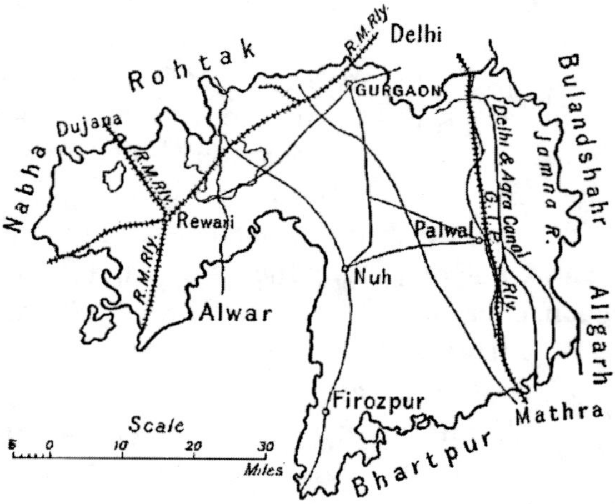


Fig. 87.

irregularities from year to year are extreme. The district is a poor one, and for its resources bears the heaviest assessment in the Panjáb. It requires the most careful revenue management. There are brine wells at Sultánpur, but the demand for the salt extracted is now very small.

**Karnál** is midway in size between Rohtak and Hissár. One-third of the cultivation is now protected by irrigation, two-fifths of the irrigation being from wells and three-fifths from the Western Jamna Canal. There are four *tahsíls*,

Area, 3153 sq. m.
Cultd area, 1744 sq. m.
Pop. 799,787; 70 p.c. H.
Land Rev. Rs. 12,92,620 = £86,175.

Thanesar, Karnál, Kaithal, and Pánipat. The peasantry consists mostly of hardworking Hindu Játs, but there are also many Hindu and Muhammadan Rájput villages. The chief towns are Pánipat, Karnál, and Kaithal.

The district falls broadly into two divisions, the boundary between them being the southern limit of the floods of the Sarustí in years of heavy rainfall. The marked features of the northern division is the effect which

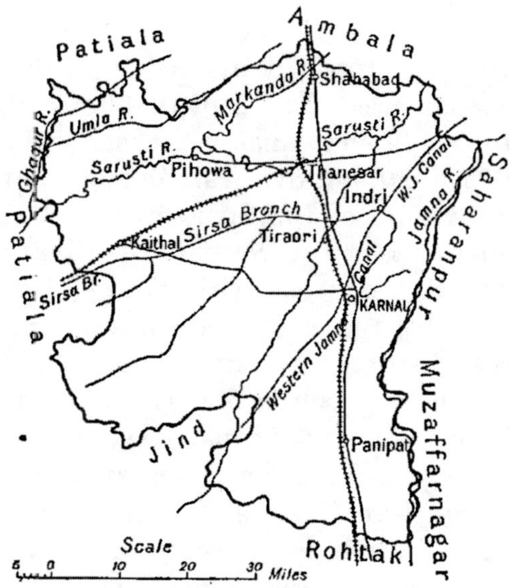


Fig. 88.

the floods of torrents of intermittent flow, the Sarustí, Márkanda, Umla, and Ghagar have on agriculture. Some tracts are included like the Andarwár and the outlying villages of the Powádh[1] in Kaithal which are fortunately unaffected by inundation, and have good well irrigation. The country between the Umla and Márkanda in Thanesar gets rich silt deposits and is generally fertile. The Kaithal Nailí is the tract affected by the overflow of the

[1] Not shown in map.

Sarustí, Umla, and Ghagar. It is a wretched fever-stricken region where a short lived race of weakly people reap precarious harvests. The southern division is on the whole a much better country. It includes the whole of Karnál and Pánipat, the south of Kaithal, and a small tract in the extreme east of the Thanesar *tahsíl*. North of Karnál the Jamna valley or Khádir is unhealthy and has in many parts a poor soil. South of Karnál it is much better in every respect. Above the Khádir is the Bángar, a plain of good loam. North of Karnál its cultivation is protected by wells and the people are in fair circumstances. South of that town it is watered by the Western Jamna Canal. Another slight rise brings one to the Nardak of the Karnál and Kaithal *tahsíls*. Till the excavation of the Sirsa branch of the Western Jamna Canal and of the Nardak Distributary much of the Nardak was covered with *dhák* jangal, and the cultivation was of the most precarious nature, for in this part of the district the rainfall is both scanty and capricious, and well cultivation is only possible in the north. The introduction of canal irrigation has effected an enormous change. Wheat and gram are the great crops.

Historically Karnál is one of the most interesting districts. The Nardak is the scene of the great struggle celebrated in the Mahábhárata. The district contains the holy city of Thanesar, once the capital of a great Hindu kingdom. It has found climate a more potent instrument of ruin than the sword of Mahmúd of Ghazní, who sacked it in 1014. It still on the occasion of Eclipse fairs attracts enormous crowds of pilgrims. Pihowa is another very sacred place. Naráina, a few miles to the north-west of Karnál, was the scene of two famous fights[1], and three times, in 1526, 1556, and 1761, the fate of India was decided at Pánipat.

[1] See page 169.

Area, 1851 sq. m. Cultd area, 1174 sq. m. Pop. 689,970. Land Rev. Rs. 11,47,688 = £76,513.

**Ambála** is a submontane district of very irregular shape. It includes two small hill tracts, Morní and Kasaulí. There is little irrigation, for in most parts the rainfall is ample. Wheat is the chief crop. The population has been declining in the past 20 years.

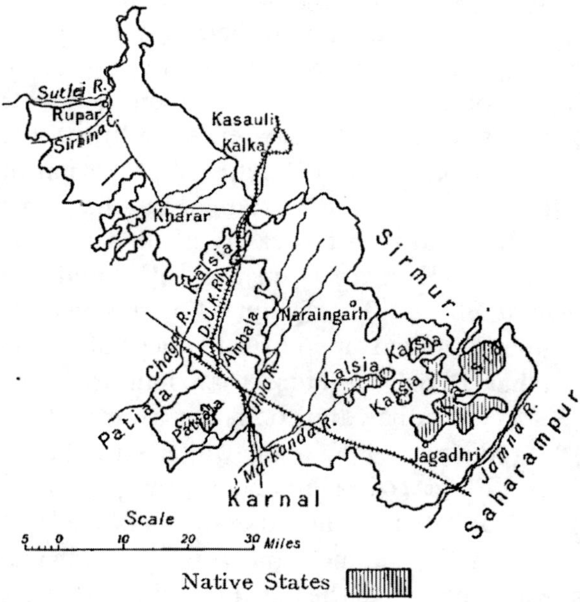


Fig. 89.

The only town of importance is Ambála. Jagádhrí is a busy little place now connected through private enterprise by a light railway with the N. W. Railway. The district consists of two parts almost severed from one another physically and wholly different as regards people, language, and agricultural prosperity. The Rúpar subdivision in the north-west beyond the Ghagar has a fertile soil, and, except in the Nálí, as the tract flooded by the Ghagar is called, a vigorous Ját peasantry, whose native tongue is Panjábí. The three south-eastern *tahsíls*,

Ambála, Naráingarh, and Jagádhrí, are weaker in every respect. The loam is often quite good, but interspersed with it are tracts of stubborn clay largely put under precarious rice crops. The Játs are not nearly so good as those of Rúpar, and Rájputs, who are mostly Musulmáns, own a large number of estates.

Area, 101 sq. m. Cultd area, 15 sq. m. Pop. in Feb. 1911, 39,320. Land Rev. Rs. 17,484 = £1166.

**Simla** consists of three little tracts in the hills known as Bharaulí, Kotkhai, and Kotgarh, and of patches of territory forming the cantonments of Dagshai, Subáthu, Solon, and Jutogh, the site of the Lawrence Military School at Sanáwar, and the great hill station of Simla. Bharaulí lies south-west of Simla in the direction of Kasaulí. Kotkhai is in the valley of the Girí, a tributary of the Jamna. Kotgarh is on the Sutlej and borders on the Bashahr State. The Deputy Commissioner of Simla is also Superintendent or Political Officer of 28 hill states.

Area, 19,934 sq. m. Cultd area, 7762 sq. m. Pop. 3,967,724. Land Rev. Rs. 61,64,172 = £410,945.

**Jalandhar Division.**—More than half the area of the Jalandhar division is contributed by the huge district of Kángra, which stretches from the Plains to the lofty snowy ranges on the borders of Tibet. The other districts are Hoshyárpur in the submontane zone, Jalandhar and Ludhiána, which belong to the Central Plains, and Ferozepore, which is part of the South-Eastern Panjáb. Sikhs are more numerous than in any other division, but are outnumbered by both Hindus and Muhammadans. The Commissioner has political charge of the hill states of Mandí and Suket and of Kapúrthala in the Plains.

Area, 9878 sq. m. Cultd area, 918 sq. m. Pop. 770,386; 94 p.c. H. Land Rev. Rs. 9,26,661 = £61,777.

**Kángra** is the largest district in the Panjáb. It includes three tracts of very different character:

(*a*) Spití and Lahul, area exceeding 4400 square miles, forming part of Tibet;

(*b*) Kulu and Saráj;

(*c*) Kángra proper, area 2939 square miles.

Fig. 90.

Lahul, Spití, Kulu, and Saráj form a subdivision in charge of an Assistant Commissioner. The people of Kángra are Hindus. Islám never penetrated into these hills as a religion, though the Rájput Rájas of Kángra became loyal subjects of the Moghal Emperors. In its last days Ranjít Singh called in as an ally against the Gurkhas remained as a hated ruler. The country was ceded to the British Government in 1846. The Rájas were chagrined that we did not restore to them their royal authority, but only awarded them the status of *jagírdárs*. An outbreak, which was easily suppressed, occurred in 1848. Since then Kángra has enjoyed 65 years of peace. A Gurkha regiment is stationed at the district headquarters at Dharmsála. The cultivation ranges from the rich maize and rice fields of Kulu and Kángra to the poor buckwheat and *kulath* on mountain slopes. Rice is irrigated by means of *kuhls*, ingeniously constructed channels to lead the water of the torrents on to the fields.

**Spití and Lahul.**—Spití, or rather Pití, is a country of great rugged mountains, whose bare red and yellow rocks rise into crests of everlasting snow showing clear under a cloudless blue sky. There is no rain, but in winter the snowfall is heavy. The highest of the mountains exceeds 23,000 feet. Pití is drained by the river of the same name, which after passing through Bashahr falls into the Sutlej at an elevation of 11,000 feet. Of the few villages several stand at a height of from 13,000 to 14,000 feet. The route to Pití from Kulu passes over the Hamtu Pass (14,200 feet) and the great Shigrí glacier. The people are Buddhists. They are governed by their hereditary ruler or Nono assisted by five elders, the Assistant Commissioner exercising a general supervision. Indian laws do not apply to the sparse population of this remote canton, which has a special regulation of its own. Lahul lies to the west of Pití, from which it is separated by a lofty range. It is entered from Kulu by the Rotang Pass (13,000 feet) and the road from it to Ladákh passes over the Baralácha (16,350 feet). The whole country is under snow from December to April, but there is very little rain. The two streams, the Chandra and Bhága, which unite to form the Chenáb, flow through Lahul and the few villages are situated at a height of 10,000 feet in their elevated valleys. The people are Buddhists. In summer the population is increased by "Gaddí" shepherds from Kángra, who drive lean flocks in the beginning of June over the Rotang and take them back from the

Alpine pastures in the middle of September fat and well liking.

**Kulu and Saráj.**—The Kulu Valley, set in a mountain frame and with the Biás, here a highland stream, running through the heart of it, is one of the fairest parts of the Panjáb Himálaya. Manálí, at the top of the Valley on the road to the Rotang, is a very beautiful spot. Kulu

Fig. 91. Biás at Manálí.

is connected with Kángra through Mandí by the Babbu and Dulchí passes. The latter is generally open the whole year round. The headquarters are at Sultánpur, but the Assistant Commissioner lives at Nagar. In Kulu the cultivation is often valuable and the people are well off. The climate is good and excellent apples and pears are grown by European settlers. Inner and outer Saráj are connected by the Jalaori Pass on the watershed of the Sutlej and Biás. Saráj is a much rougher and poorer country than Kulu. There are good *deodár* forests in the Kulu subdivision. In 1911 the population of Kulu, Saráj, Lahul, and Pití, numbered 124,803. The Kulu people are a simple folk in whose primitive religion local godlings of brass each with his little strip of territory take the place of the Brahmanic gods. It is a quaint sight to see their ministers carrying them on litters to the fair at Sultánpur, where they all pay their respects to a little

Fig. 92. Religious Fair in Kulu.

silver god known as Raghunáthjí, who is in a way their suzerain.

**Kángra proper** is bounded on the north by the lofty wall of the Dhaula Dhár and separated from Kulu by the mountains of Bara Bangáhal. It consists of the five *tahsíls* of Kángra, Palampur, Nurpur, Dera, and Hamírpur. The first two occupy the rich and beautiful Kángra Valley. They are separated from the other three *tahsíls* by a medley of low hills with a general trend from

Fig. 93. Kulu Women.

N.W. to S.E. They are drained by the Biás, and are much more broken and poorer than the Kángra Valley. The tea industry, once important, is now dead so far as carried on by English planters. The low hills have extensive *chír* pine forests. They have to be managed mainly in the interests of the local population, and are so burdened with rights that conservation is a very difficult problem. In 1911 the population of the five *tahsíls* amounted to 645,583. The most important tribes

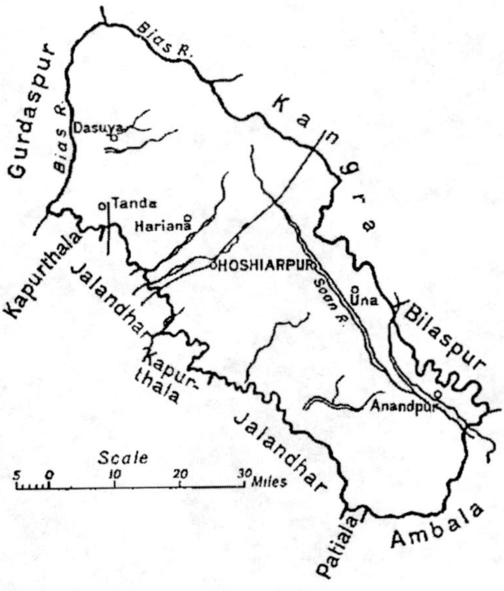


Fig. 94.

are Brahmans, Rájputs, and hardworking Gírths. The hill Brahman is usually a farmer pure and simple.

Area, 2247 sq. m. Cultd area, 1128 sq. m. Pop. 918,569; 54 p.c. H. Land Rev. Rs. 14,22,527 = £94,835.

**Hoshyárpur** became a British possession in 1846 after the first Sikh War. It is a typically submontane district. A line of low bare hills known as the Solasinghí Range divides it from Kángra. Further west the Katár dhár, a part of the Siwáliks, runs through the heart of the district. Between these two ranges lies the fertile Jaswan Dun corresponding to the Una *tahsíl*. The other three *tahsíls*, Garhshankar, Hoshyárpur, and Dasúya, are to the west of the Katár dhár. Una is drained by the Soan, a tributary of the Sutlej. The western *tahsíls* have a light loam soil of great fertility, except where it has been overlaid by sand from the numerous *chos* or torrents which issue from the Siwáliks. The denudation of that range was allowed to go on for an inordinate time with disastrous results to the plains below. At last the Panjáb Land Preservation (*Chos*) Act II of 1890 gave the Government power to deal with the evil, but it will take many years to remedy the mischief wrought by past inaction. The rainfall averages about 32 inches and the crops are secure. The population has fallen off by 93,000 in 20 years, a striking instance of the ravages of plague. The chief tribes are Játs, Rájputs, and Gújars.

Area, 1431 sq. m.
Cultd area, 1069 sq. m.
Pop. 801,920; 45 p.c. M. 33 p.c. H. 22 p.c. S.
Land Rev. Rs. 14,77,661 = £98,511.

**Jalandhar District.**—Modern though the town of Jalandhar looks it was the capital of a large Hindu kingdom, which included also Hoshyárpur, Mandí, Suket, and Chamba, and in the ninth century was a rival of Kashmír (page 160). The present district is with the exception of Simla the smallest, and for its size the richest, in the province. It contains four *tahsíls*, Nawashahr, Phillaur, Jalandhar, and Nakodar. About 45 p.c. of the cultivation is protected by 28,000 wells. Behind the long river frontage on the Sutlej is the Bet, divided by a high bank from the more fertile uplands. The soil of the latter is generally an excellent loam, but there is a good deal of sand in the west of the district. The rainfall averages about 26 inches and the climate is healthy. The well cultivation is the best in the Panjáb. Between 1901 and 1911 the population declined by 13 p.c.

Játs and Arains, both excellent cultivators, are the predominant tribes. British rule dates from 1846.

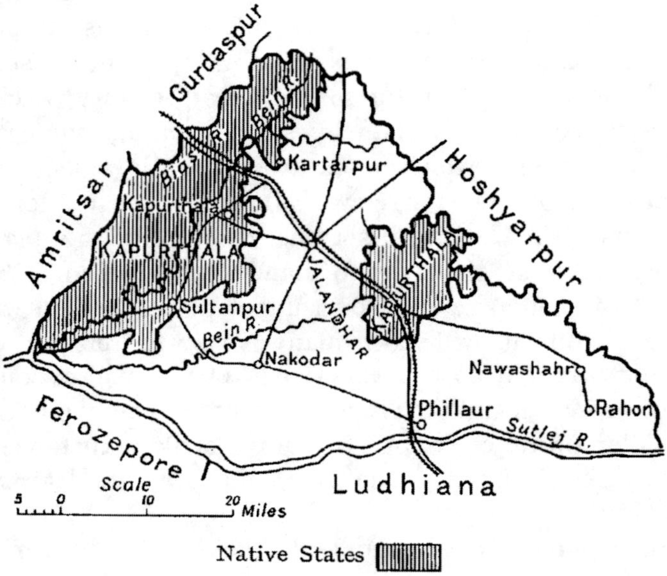


Fig. 95.

Ludhiána on the opposite bank of the Sutlej is also a very small district. It consists of a river Bet and Uplands with generally speaking a good loam soil. But there are very sandy outlying estates in the Jangal Des surrounded by Patiála and Jínd villages. There are three *tahsíls*, Samrála, Ludhiána, and Jagráon. Of the cultivated area 26 p.c. is irrigated, from wells (19) and from the Sirhind Canal (7). Wheat and gram are the principal crops. Between 1901 and 1911 the population fell from 673,097 to 517,192, the chief cause of decline being plague.

Area, 1452 sq. m.
Cultd area, 1143 sq. m.
Pop. 517,192; 40 p.c. S. 35 p.c. M. 25 p.c. H.
Land Rev. Rs. 11,57,399 = £77,160.

Sturdy hard-working Játs are the backbone of the peasantry. They furnish many recruits to the Army.

Ludhiána is a thriving town and an important station on the N.W. Railway. Our connection with Ludhiána began in 1809, and the district assumed practically its present shape in 1846 after the first Sikh War.

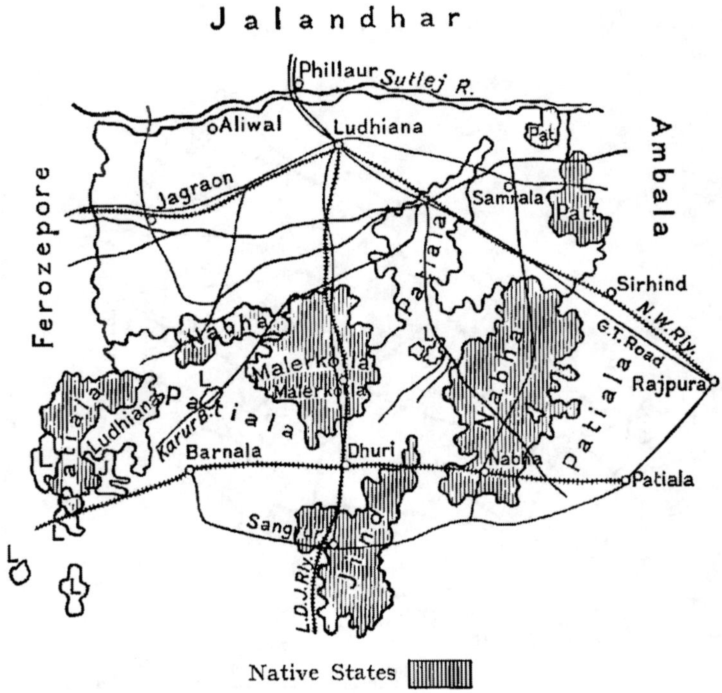


Fig. 96.

**Ferozepore** is a very large district. The Farídkot State nearly cuts it in two. The northern division includes the *tahsíls* of Ferozepore, Zíra, and Moga, the last with an outlying tract known as Mahráj, which forms an island surrounded by the territory of several native states. The southern division contains the *tahsíls* of Muktsar and Fázilka. Our connection with

Area, 4286 sq. m.
Cultd area, 3504 sq. m.
Pop. 959,657;
44 p.c. M.
29 p.c. H.
27 p.c. S.
Land Rev. Rs. 11,79,924 = £78,661.

Ferozepore began in 1809, and, when the widow of the last Sikh chief of Ferozepore died in 1835, we assumed direct responsibility for the administration of a considerable part of the district. Two of the great battles of the first Sikh War, Mudkí and Ferozesháh or more properly Pherushahr, were fought within its borders. Mamdot with

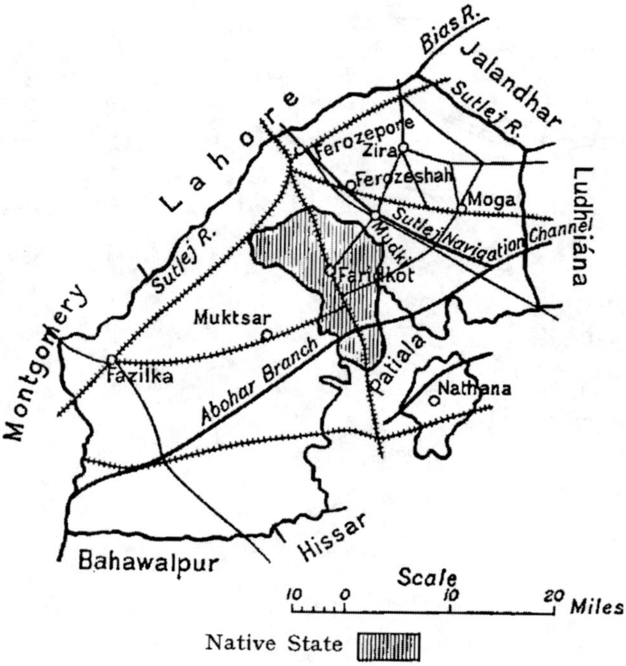


Fig. 97.

an area of about 400 square miles ceased to be independent in 1855, but the descendant of the last ruler still holds it in *jagír*. Fázilka was added in 1864 when the Sirsa district was broken up. Of the cultivated area 47½ p.c. is irrigated by the Sirhind Canal, the Grey Inundation Canals, and wells. For the most part the district is divided into three tracts, the riverain, Hithár or Bet, with a poor clay soil and a weak population, the Utár, representing river deposits of an older date when the Sutlej ran far west of its present bed, and the Rohí, an upland plain of good sandy loam, now largely irrigated by the Sirhind Canal. The Grey Canals furnish a far less satisfactory source of irrigation to villages in the Bet and Utár. In different parts of this huge district the rainfall varies from 10 to 22 inches. The chief crops are gram and wheat. The Játs are the chief tribe. In the Uplands they are a fine sturdy race, but unfortunately they are addicted to strong drink, and violent crime is rife. Ferozepore has a large cantonment and arsenal and a big trade in grain. It is an important railway junction.

Area, 12,387 sq. m. Cultd area, 7924 sq. m. Pop 4,656,629; 57 p.c. M. 24 „ H. 16 „ S. Land Rev. Rs. 70,53,856 =£470,257.

**Lahore Division.**—Lahore is the smallest division, but the first in population. Its political importance is great as the home of the Sikhs of the Mánjha, and because the capital of the province and the sacred city of the *Khálsa* are both within its limits. It contains the five districts of Gurdáspur, Siálkot, Gujránwála, Lahore, and Amritsar. The Commissioner is in political charge of the Chamba State.

Area, 1809 sq. m. Cultd area, 1281 sq. m. Pop. 836,771; 49 p.c. M. 34 „ H. 14½ „ S. Land Rev. Rs. 17,68,412 = £117,894.

**Gurdáspur** is a submontane district with a good rainfall and a large amount of irrigation. The crops are secure except in part of the Shakargarh *tahsíl.* 27 p.c. of the cultivated area is irrigated, 16 by wells and 11 by the Upper Bárí Doáb Canal. Irrigation is only allowed from the Canal for the Autumn harvest. The chief crop is wheat and the area under cane is unusually large. Of late years plague has been very fatal and the population fell from 940,334 in 1901 to 836,771 in 1911. Játs, Rájputs, Arains, Gújars, and Brahmans, are the chief agricultural tribes, the first being by far the most important element. There are four *tahsíls*, Batála, Gurdáspur, and Pathánkot in the Bárí Doáb, and Shakargarh to the west of the Rávi. Batála is one of the most fertile and prosperous tracts in the Panjáb and Gurdáspur is also thriving. Pathánkot is damp, fever stricken, and unprosperous. It lies mostly

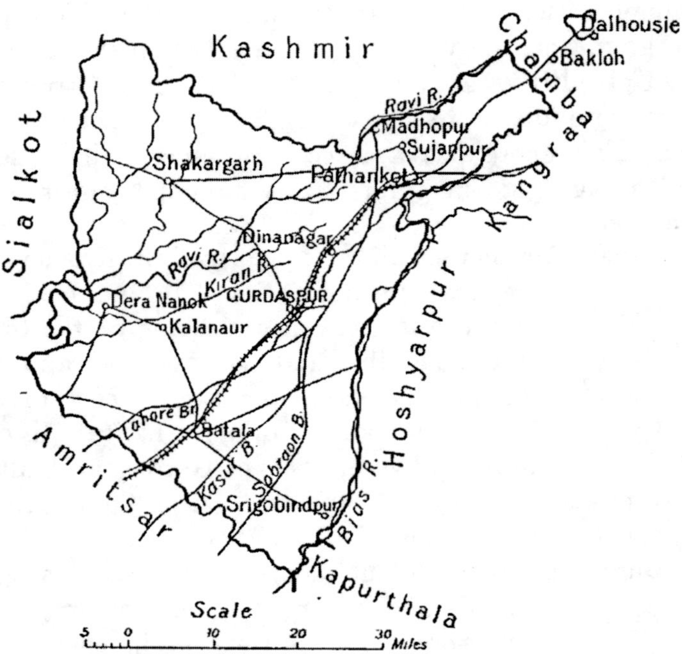


Fig. 98.

in the plains but contains a considerable area in the low hills and higher up two enclaves, Bakloh and Dalhousie, surrounded by Chamba villages. Shakargarh is much more healthy, and is better off than Pathánkot. There is good duck and snipe shooting to be got in some parts of the district, as the drainage from the hills collects in swamps and *jhíls*.

Area, 1991 sq. m.
Cultd area, 1427 sq. m.
Pop. 979,553; 62 p.c. M. 25 „ H. 8 „ S.
Land Rev. Rs. 14,79,390 = £98,626.

**Siálkot** is another secure and fully cultivated submontane district. It lies wholly in the Rechna Doáb and includes a small well-watered hilly tract, Bajwát, on the borders of Jammu. The Rávi divides Siálkot from Amritsar and the Chenáb separates it from Gujrát. The Degh and some smaller torrents run through the district. In the south there is much hard

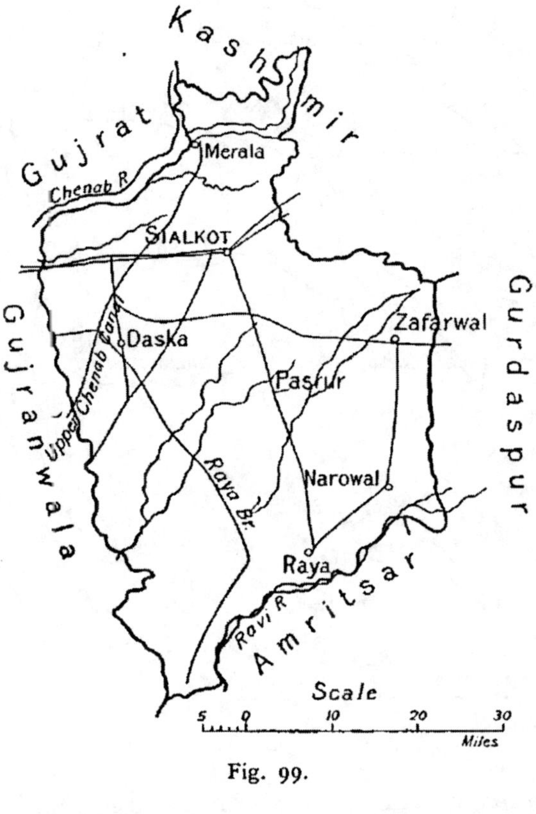


Fig. 99.

sour clay, part hitherto unculturable. But irrigation from the Upper Chenáb Canal will give a new value to it. There are five *tahsíls*, Zafarwál, Siálkot, Daska, Pasrúr, and Raya. The chief crop is wheat which is largely grown on the wells, numbering 22,000. The pressure of the population on the soil was considerable, but since 1891 the total has fallen from 1,119,847 to 979,553 as the result of plague and emigration to the new canal colonies.

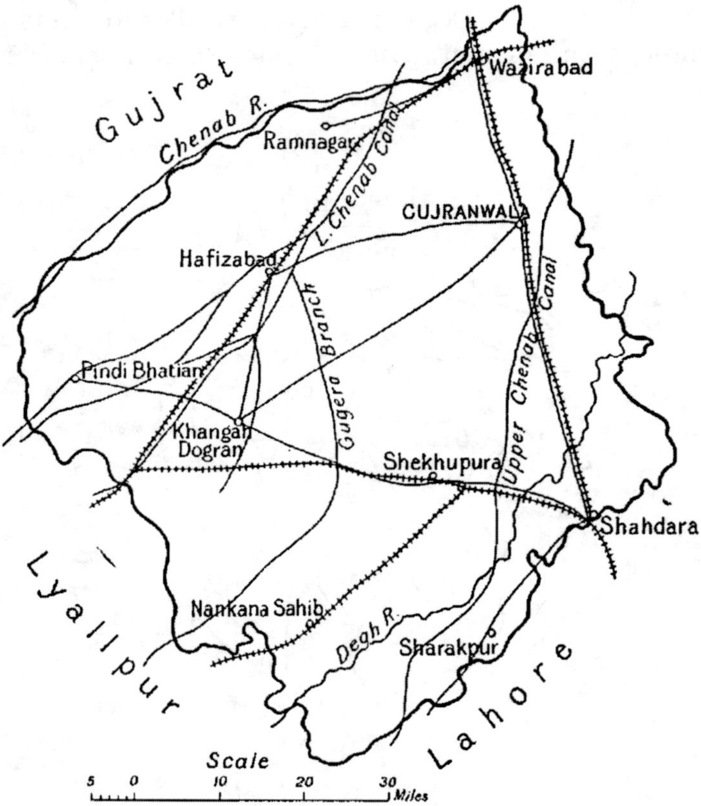


Fig. 100.

Christianity has obtained a considerable number of converts in Siálkot. The Játs form the backbone of the peasantry. Rájputs and Arains are also important tribes, but together they are not half as numerous as the Játs.

Area, 4802 sq. m.
Cultd area, 2166 sq. m.
Pop. 923,419.
Land Rev. Rs. 15,43,440 = £102,896.

**Gujránwála** is a very large district in the Rechna Doáb, with five *tahsíls*, Wazírábád, Gujránwála, Sharakpur, Háfizábád, and Khángáh Dográn. The rainfall varies from 20 inches on the Siálkot border to ten or eleven in the extreme south-west corner of the district. Gujránwála is naturally divided into three tracts: the Riverain of the Rávi and Chenáb, the Bángar or well tract, and the Bár once very partially cultivated, but now commanded by the Lower and Upper Chenáb Canals. Enormous development has taken place in the Háfizábád and Khángáh Dográn *tahsíls* in the 20 years since the Lower Chenáb Canal was opened. Of late years the rest of the district has suffered from plague and emigration, and has not prospered. But a great change will be effected by irrigation from the Upper Chenáb Canal, which is just beginning. In the east of the district much sour clay will become culturable land, and the Bár will be transformed as in the two *tahsíls* watered by the older canal. Of the cultivated area 73½ p.c. is irrigated, 36½ from wells and 37 from canals. The chief crops are wheat and gram. There is, as is usual in the Western Panjáb, a great preponderance of Spring crops. The Játs are far and away the strongest element in the population.

Area, 1601 sq. m.
Cultd area, 1184 sq. m.
Pop. 880,728; 46 p.c. M. 29 ,, S. 24 ,, H.
Land Rev. Rs. 12,70,799 = £84,720.

**Amritsar** is a small district lying in the Bárí Doáb between Gurdáspur and Lahore. 62 p.c. of the cultivated area is irrigated, half from 12,000 wells and half from the Upper Bárí Doáb Canal. Unfortunately much waterlogging exists, due to excessive use of canal water and defective drainage. Measures are now being taken to deal with this great evil, which has made the town of Amritsar and other parts of the district liable to serious outbreaks of fever. There are two small riverain tracts on the Biás and Rávi and a poor piece of country in Ajnála flooded by the Sakkí. The main part of the district is a monotonous plain of fertile loam. The two western *tahsíls*, Amritsar and Tarn Táran, are prosperous, Ajnála is depressed. The rainfall is moderate averaging 21 or 22 inches, and the large amount of irrigation makes the harvests secure. The chief crops are wheat and gram.

Fig. 101.

The Sikh Játs of the Mánjha to the south of the Grand Trunk Road form by far the most important element in the population. Between 1901 and 1911 there was a falling off from 1,023,828 to 880,728. Besides its religious importance the town of Amritsar is a great trade centre.

**Lahore** lies in the Bárí Doáb to the south-west of Amritsar. It is a much larger district, though, like Amritsar, it has only three *tahsíls*, Lahore, Kasúr, and Chúnian. 76 p.c. of the cultivated area is irrigated, 23 from wells and 53 from canals. There has been an enormous

Area, 2824 sq. m. Cultd area, 1866 sq. m. Pop. 1,036,158. Land Rev. Rs. 991,815 =£66,121.

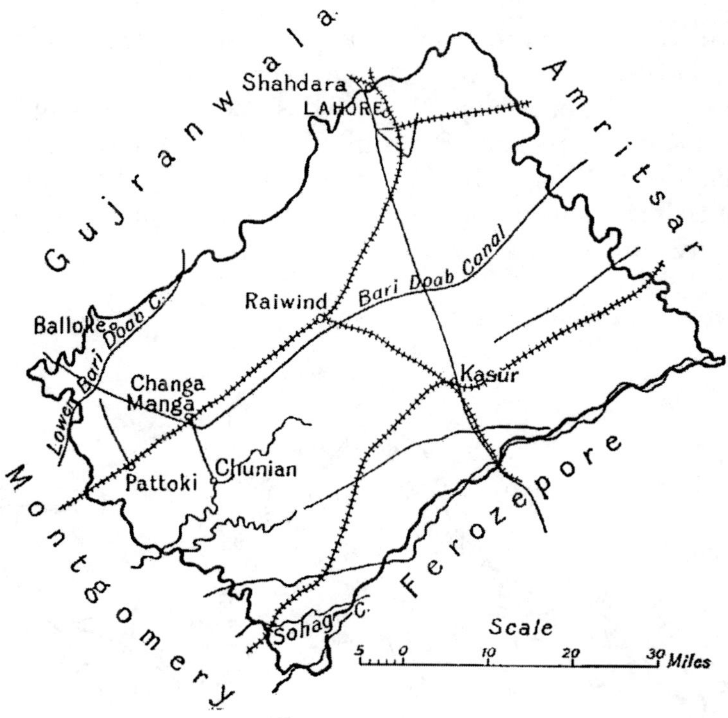


Fig. 102.

extension of irrigation from the Upper Bárí Doáb Canal in the past 30 years. Accordingly, though the rainfall is somewhat scanty, the crops are generally secure. The principal are wheat and gram. The district consists of the Riverain on the Biás and Rávi, the latter extending to both sides of the river, and the plain of the Mánjha, largely held by strong and energetic Sikh Játs. In the Rávi valley industrious Arains predominate. Railway communications are excellent. Trade activity is not confined to the city of Lahore. Kasúr, Chúnian, and Raiwind are important local centres.

Area, 21,361 sq. m. Cultd area, 8099 sq. m. Pop. 3,353,052; 87 p.c. M. Land Rev. Rs. 50,43,587 =£336,239.

The **Ráwalpindí Division** occupies the N.W. of the Panjáb. It is in area the second largest division, but in population the smallest. Five-sixths of the people profess the faith of Islám. It includes six districts, Gujrát, Jhelam, Ráwalpindí, Attock, Mianwálí, and Sháhpur. This is the division from which the Panjáb Musalmáns, who form so valuable an element in our army, are drawn.

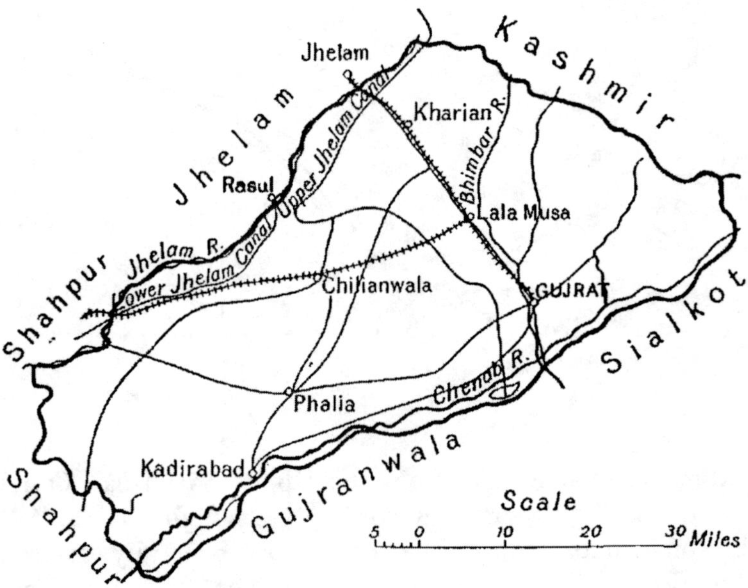


Fig. 103.

Gujrát lies in the Jech Doáb. The two northern *tahsíls*, Gujrát and Kharián, have many of the features of a submontane tract. In the former the Pabbí, a small range of low bare hills, runs parallel to the Jhelam, and the outliers of the Himálaya in Kashmír are not far from the northern border of the district. The uplands of these two *tahsíls* slope pretty rapidly from N.E. to S.W., and contain much light soil. They are traversed by sandy torrents, dry in winter, but sometimes very destructive in the rains. Phália on the other hand is a typical plain's *tahsíl*. It has on the Chenáb a wide riverain, which also separates the uplands of the Gujrát *tahsíl* from that river. The Jhelam valley is much narrower. Above the present Chenáb alluvial tract there is in Phália a well tract known as the Hithár whose soil consists of older river deposits, and at a higher level a Bár, which will now receive irrigation from the Upper Jhelam Canal and become a rich agricultural tract. 26 p.c. of the cultivated area is irrigated from wells. Játs and Gújars are the great agricultural tribes, the former predominating. The climate is mild and the rainfall sufficient. The chief crops are wheat and *bájra*.

Area, 2357 sq. m. Cultd area, 1369 sq. m. Pop. 784,011. Land Rev. Rs. 887,220 = £59,148.

The Jhelam district lies to the north of the river of the same name. The district is divided into three *tahsíls*, Jhelam, Chakwál, Pind Dádan Khán. The river frontage is long, extending for about 80 miles, and the river valley is about eight miles wide. The district contains part of the Salt Range, from the eastern end of which the Nílí and Tilla spurs strike northwards, enclosing very broken ravine country called the Khuddar. The Pabbí tract, embracing the Chakwál *tahsíl* and the north of the Jhelam *tahsíl*, is much less broken, though it too is scored by deep ravines and traversed by torrents, mostly flowing

Area, 2813 sq. m. Cultd area, 1162 sq. m. Pop. 511,575; 88 p.c. M. Land Rev. Rs. 752,758 = £50,183.

north-west into the Sohán river. Two large torrents, the Kahá and the Bunhár, drain into the Jhelam. There are some fertile valleys enclosed in the bare hills of the Salt Range. The average rainfall is about 20 inches and the climate is good. It is hot in summer, but the cold weather is long, and sometimes for short periods severe. There is little irrigation and the harvests are by no means secure. The chief crops are wheat and *bájra*. The country

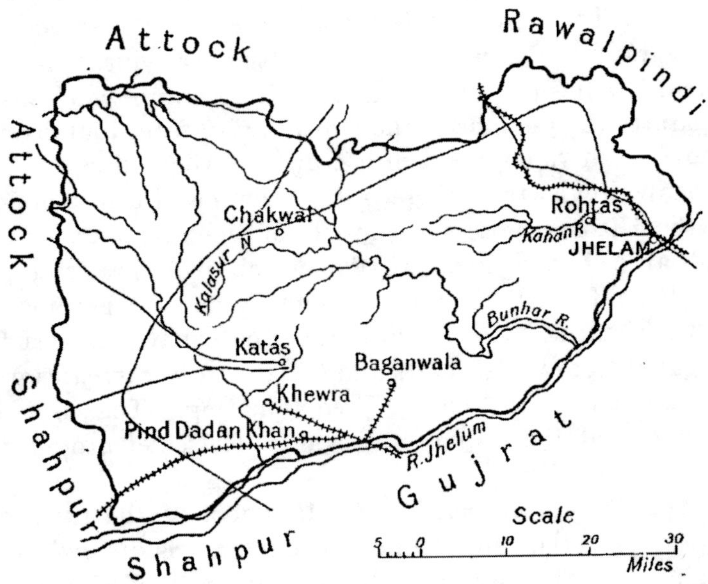


Fig. 104.

breeds fine horses, fine cattle, and fine men. Numerically Játs, Rájputs, and Awáns are the principal tribes, but the Janjuas and Gakkhars, though fewer in number, are an interesting element in the population, having great traditions behind them. Awáns, Janjuas, and Gakkhars supply valuable recruits to the army. Most of the villages are far from any railway.

**Ráwalpindí** is the smallest district in the division. Along the whole eastern border the Jhelam, which runs in a deep gorge, divides it from Kashmír. There are four *tahsíls*, Murree, Kahúta, Ráwalpindí, and Gújar Khán. The first is a small wedge of mountainous country between Kashmír and Hazára. The hills are

Area, 2010 sq. m.
Cultd area, 937 sq. m.
Pop. 547,827; 83 p.c. M.
Land Rev. Rs. 674,650 = £44,977.

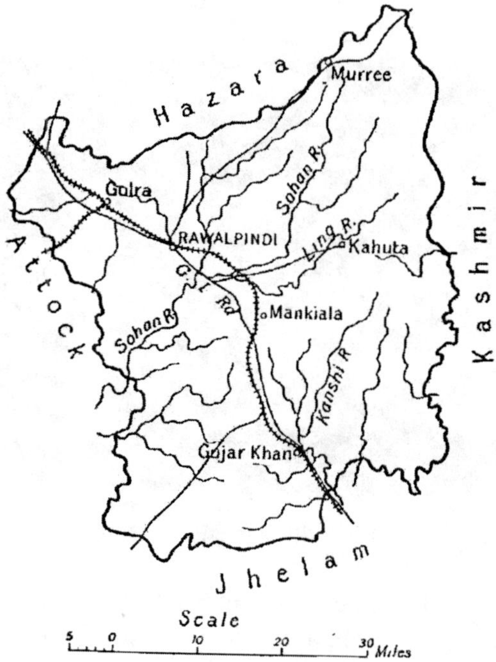


Fig. 105.

continued southwards at a lower level in the Kahúta *tahsíl* parallel with the Jhelam. The greater part of the district consists of a high plateau of good light loam, in parts much eaten into by ravines. Where, as often happens, it is not flat the fields have to be carefully banked up. The plateau is drained by the Sohán and the Kánshí. The latter starting in the south of Kahúta runs through the south-east of the Gújar Khán *tahsíl,* and for some miles forms the boundary of the Ráwalpindí and Jhelam districts. The district is very fully cultivated except in the hills. In the plains the rainfall is sufficient and the soil very cool and clean, except in the extreme west, where it is sometimes gritty, and, while requiring more, gets less, rain. The chief crops are wheat, the *Kharíf* pulses and *bájra.* The

Fig. 106. Shop in Murree Bazár.

climate is good. The cold weather is long, and, except in January and February, when the winds from the snows are very trying, it is pleasant. In the plains the chief tribes are Rájputs and Awáns. Gakkhars are of some importance in Kahúta. In the Murree the leading tribes are the Dhúnds and the Sattís, the latter a fine race, keen on military service.

**Ráwalpindí** is the largest cantonment in Northern India. From it the favourite hill station of Murree is easily reached, and soon after leaving Murree the traveller crosses the Jhelam by the Kohála bridge and enters the territory of the Mahárája of Kashmír.

Area, 4025 sq. m. Cultd area, 1678 sq. m. Pop. 519,273; 91 p.c. M. Land Rev. Rs. 672,851 =£44,857.

**Attock district.**—Though Attock is twice the size of Ráwalpindí it has a smaller population. Nature has decreed that it should be sparsely peopled. The district stretches from the Salt Range on the south to the Hazára border on the north. It contains itself the fine

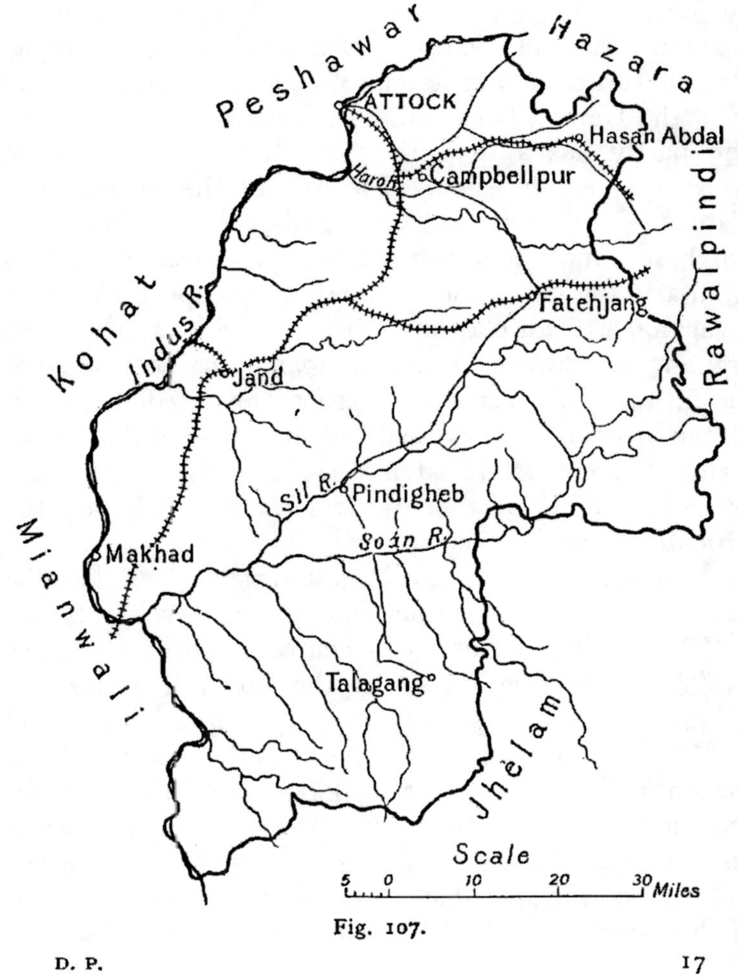


Fig. 107.

Kálachitta range in the north, the small and barren Khairí Múrat range in the centre, and a line of bare hills running parallel with the Indus in the west. That river forms the western boundary for 120 miles, dividing Attock from Pesháwar and Kohát. It receives in the Attock district two tributaries, the Haro and the Soán. There are four *tahsíls*, Attock, Fatehjang, Pindigheb, and Talagang. The northern *tahsíl* of Attock is most favoured by nature. It contains the Chach plain, part of which has a rich soil and valuable well irrigation, also on the Hazára border a small group of estates watered by cuts from the Haro. The south of the *tahsíl* is partly sandy and partly has a dry gritty or stony soil. Here the crops are very insecure. The rest of the district is a plateau. The northern part consists of the *tahsíls* of Fatehjang and Pindigheb drained by the Soán and its tributary the Sil. The southern is occupied by *tahsíl* Talagang, a rough plateau with deep ravines and torrents draining northwards into the Soán. In the valleys of the Sil and Soán some good crops are raised. The soil of the plateau is very shallow, and the rainfall being scanty the harvest is often dried up. The chief crops are wheat and *bájra*. Awáns form the bulk of the agricultural population.

**Mianwálí** is one of the largest districts, but has the smallest population of any except Simla. The Indus has a course of about 180 miles in Mianwálí. In the north it forms the boundary between the Mianwálí *tahsíl* and the small Isakhel *tahsíl* on the right bank. In the south it divides the huge Bhakkar *tahsíl*, which is bigger than an average district, from the Dera Ismail Khán district of the N.W.F. Province. It is joined from the west by the Kurram, which has a short course in the south of the Isakhel *tahsíl*. The Salt Range extends into the

**Area, 5395 sq. m. Cultd area, 1020 sq. m. Pop. 341,377; 88 p.c. M. Land Rev. Rs. 359,836 = £23,989.**

district, throwing off from its western extremity a spur which runs north to the Indus opposite Kálabágh. Four tracts may be distinguished, two large and two small. North and east of the Salt Range is the Khuddar or ravine country, a little bit of the Awánkárí or Awán's

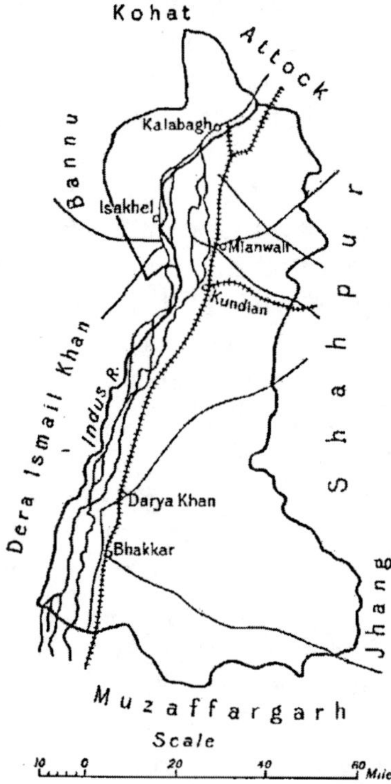


Fig. 108.

land, which occupies a large space in Attock. West of the Indus in the north the wild and desolate Bhangí Khel glen with its very scanty and scattered cultivation runs north to the Kohát Hills. The rest of the district consists of the wide and flat valley of the Indus and the Thal or Uplands. In the north the latter includes an area of strong thirsty loam, but south of the railway it is a huge expanse of sand rising frequently into hillocks and ridges with some fertile bottoms of better soil. Except in the north the Thal people used to make their living almost entirely as shepherds and camel owners. There were scattered little plots of better soil where wells were sunk, and the laborious and careful cultivation was and is Dutch in its neatness. Some millets were grown in the autumn and the sandhills yielded melons. The people have now learned that it is worth while to gamble with a spring crop of gram, and this has led to an enormous extension of the cultivated area. But even now in Mianwálí this is a comparatively small fraction of the total area. There is a small amount of irrigation from wells and in the neighbourhood of Isakhel from canal cuts from the Kurram. Owing to the extreme scantiness of the rainfall the riverain depends almost entirely on the Indus floods, to assist the spread of which a number of embankments are maintained. Everywhere in Mianwálí the areas both of crops sown and of crops that ripen fluctuate enormously, and much of the revenue has accordingly been put on a fluctuating basis. The chief crops are wheat, *bájra*, and gram. Jats[1] are in a great majority Cis-Indus, but Patháns are important in Isakhel.

Area, 4791 sq. m.
Cultd area, 1933 sq. m.
Pop. 648,989.
Land Rev. Rs. 16,96,272 = £113,085.

**Sháhpur** is also a very large district with the three *tahsíls* of Bhera, Sháhpur, and Sargodha in the Jech Doáb, and on the west of the Jhelam the huge Khusháb *tahsíl*, which in size exceeds the other three put together. The principal tribes are Jats Cis-Jhelam, Awáns in the Salt Range, and Jats and Tiwánas in Khusháb. The Tiwána Maliks have large estates on both sides of the river and much local influence. East of the Jhelam the colonization of the Bár after the opening of the Lower Jhelam Canal has led to a great increase of population

[1] This leading tribe in the Panjáb is known as Ját in the Hindi-speaking Eastern districts and as Jat elsewhere.

and a vast extension of the cultivated area, 71 p.c. of which is irrigated. The part of the district in the Jech Doáb consists of the river valleys of the Chenáb and Jhelam, the Utár, and the Bár. The Chenáb riverain is poor, the Jhelam very fertile with good well irrigation. In the north of the district the Utár, a tract of older alluvium, lies between the present valley of the

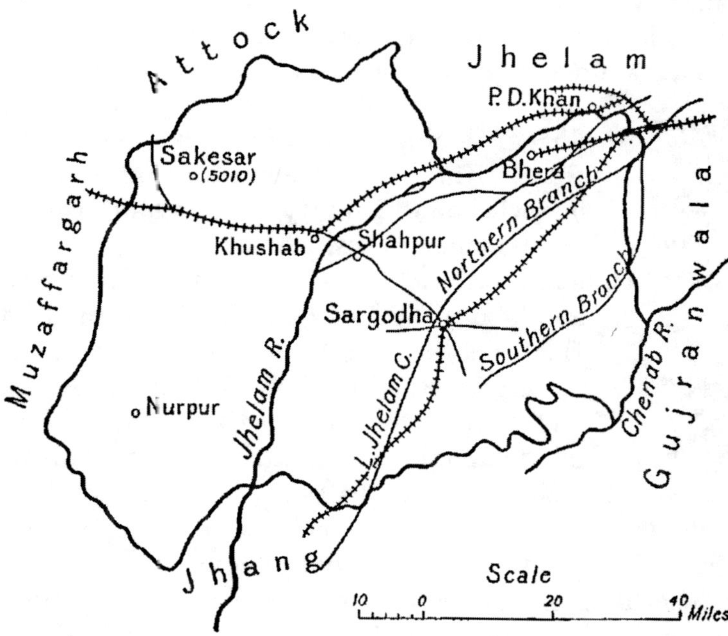


Fig. 109.

Jhelam and the Bár. It has hitherto been largely irrigated by public and private inundation canals, but this form of irrigation may be superseded by the excavation of a new distributary from the Lower Jhelam Canal. Till the opening of that canal the Bár was a vast grazing area with a little cultivation on scattered wells and in natural hollows. North of the Kirána Hill the soil is excellent and the country is now a sheet of cultivation. In the south of the Bár much of the land is too poor to be worth tillage. The Khusháb *tahsíl* consists of the Jhelam riverain, the Salt Range with some fertile valleys hidden amid barren hills, the Mohár below the hills with a thirsty soil dependent on extremely precarious torrent floods, and the Thal, similar to that described on page 260. The rainfall of the district is scanty averaging eleven or twelve inches. The chief crops are wheat, *bájra* and *jowár, charí* and cotton.

Area, 28,652 sq. m. Cultd area, 9160 sq. m. Pop. 3,772,728; 78 p.c. M. Land Rev. Rs. 81,48,103 = £542,872.

The **Multán division** consists of the six districts of the S.W. Panjáb, Montgomery, Lyallpur, Jhang, Multán, Muzaffargarh, and Dera Ghází Khán. Muhammadans are in an overwhelming majority. Wheat and cotton are the chief crops.

Area, 4649 sq. m. Cultd area, 1080 sq. m. Pop. 535,299; 75 p.c. M. Land Rev. Rs. 434,563 = £28,971.

The **Montgomery district** takes its name from Sir Robert Montgomery (page 192). It lies in the Bárí Doáb between the Sutlej and the Ráví. It consists of the two Ráví *tahsíls* of Gugera and Montgomery, and the two Sutlej *tahsíls* of Dipálpur and Pákpattan. The trans-Ráví area of the Montgomery district was transferred to Lyallpur in April, 1913. It is included in the figures for area and population given in the margin.

The backbone of the district is a high and dry tract known as the Ganjí or Bald Bár. The advent of the Lower Bárí Doáb Canal will entirely change the character of this desert. Its south-eastern boundary is a high bank marking the course of the old bed of the Biás. Below this is the wide Sutlej valley. The part beyond the influence of river floods depends largely on the Khánwáh and Sohág Pára inundation Canals. The Ráví valley to the north-west of the Bár is naturally fertile and has good well irrigation. But it has suffered much by the failure of the Ráví floods.

The peasantry belongs largely to various tribes described vaguely as Jats. The most important are Káthias,

Fig. 110.

Wattús, and Kharrals. The last gave trouble in 1857 and were severely punished. The Dipálpur Kambohs are much more hard-working than these semi-pastoral Jats. There is already a small canal colony on the Soháḡ Pára Canals and arrangements for the colonization of the Ganjí Bár are now in progress.

The **Lyallpur district** occupies most of the Sándal Bár, which a quarter of a century ago was a desert producing scrub jungle and, if rains were favourable, excellent grass. It was the home of a few nomad graziers. The area of the district, which was formed in 1904 and added to from time to time, has been taken out of the Crown Waste of the Jhang and Montgomery districts on its colonization after the opening of the Lower

Area, 3156 sq. m. Cultd area, 2224 sq. m. Pop. 857,711; 61 p.c. M. 18 „ H. 17 „ S. 4 „ Ch.[1] Land Rev. Rs. 37,55,139 = £237,009.

[1] Ch. = Christian.

Chenáb Canal. Some old villages near the present borders of these two districts have been included. The colonization of the Sándal Bár has been noticed on pages 139–140.

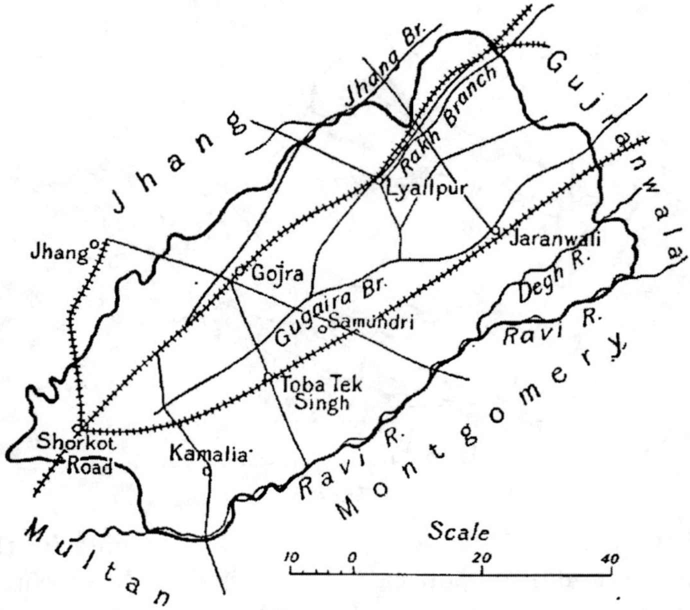


Fig. 111.

The figures for area and population given in the margin are for the district as it was before the addition of the trans-Rávi area of Montgomery.

Lyallpur is divided into the four *tahsils* of Lyallpur, Járanwala, Samundrí, and Toba Tek Singh. It consists almost entirely of a flat plain of fertile loam with fringes of poor land on the eastern, western, and southern edges. The cultivated area is practically all canal irrigated. The rainfall of 10 inches does not encourage dry cultivation. The chief crops are wheat, the oil seed called *toria*, cotton, and gram. The area of the first much exceeds that of the other three put together. There is an enormous export of wheat and oil seeds to Karáchí.

Jhang now consists of a wedge of country lying between Lyallpur on the east and Sháhpur, Mianwálí, and Muzaffargarh on the west. It contains the valleys of the Chenáb and Jhelam rivers, which unite to the south-west of the district headquarters and flow as a single stream to the southern boundary. The valley of the Jhelam

Area, 3363 sq. m. Cultd area, 1214 sq. m. Pop. 515,526; 82 p.c. M. Land Rev. Rs. 11,67,965 = £77,864.

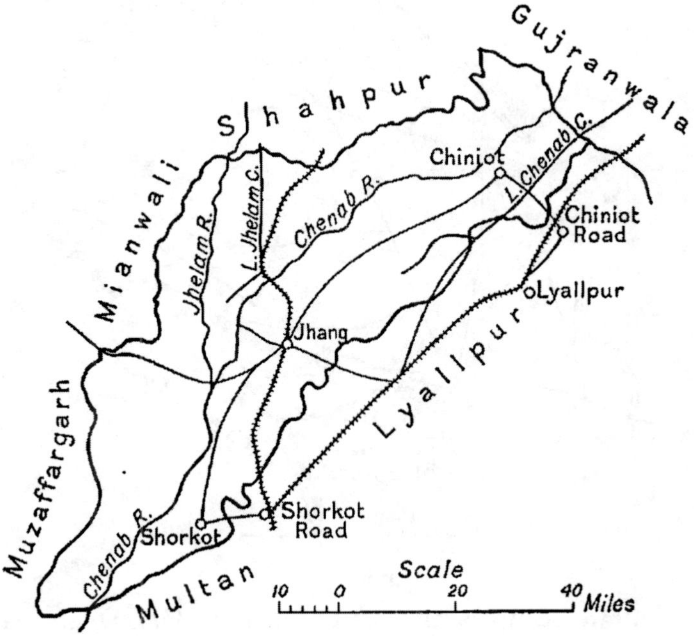


Fig. 112.

is pretty and fertile, that of the Chenáb exactly the reverse. In the west of the district part of the Thal is included in the boundary. The high land between the river valleys is much of it poor. Irrigation from the Lower Jhelam Canal is now available. There is a fringe of high land on the east of the Chenáb valley, partly commanded by the Lower Chenáb Canal. Jhang is divided into the three large *tahsíls* of Jhang, Chiniot, and Shorkot.

The rainfall is about ten inches and the summer long and very hot. The chief crops are wheat, *jowár*, and *charí*. The Siáls are few in number, but are the tribe that stands highest in rank as representing the former rulers.

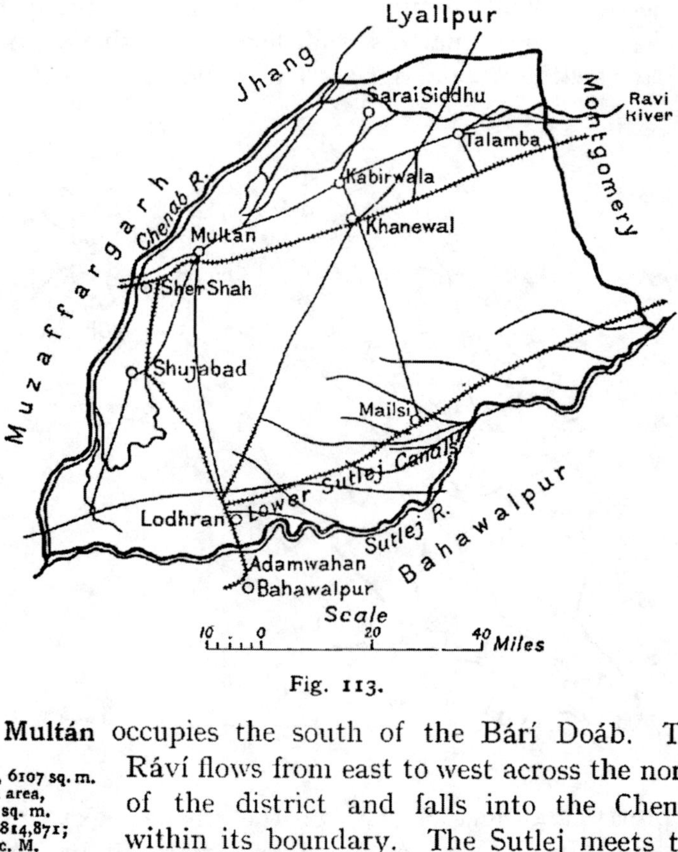


Fig. 113.

**Multán** occupies the south of the Bárí Doáb. The Ráví flows from east to west across the north of the district and falls into the Chenáb within its boundary. The Sutlej meets the combined stream of the Jhelam, Chenáb, and Ráví at the south-west corner of the district.

Area, 6107 sq. m. Cultd area, 1756 sq. m. Pop. 814,871; 82 p.c. M. Land Rev. Rs. 13,74,472 = £91,631.

A part of the Kabírwála *tahsíl* lies beyond the Ráví. The other four *tahsíls* are Multán, Shujábád, Lodhran, and Mailsí. In a very hot district with an average rainfall of six inches cultivation must depend on irrigation or river floods. The present sources of irrigation are inundation canals from the Chenáb and Sutlej supplemented by well irrigation, and the Sidhnai Canal from the Rávi. The district consists of the river valleys, older alluvial tracts slightly higher than these valleys, but which can be reached by inundation canals[1], and the high central Bár, which is a continuation of the Ganjí Bár in Montgomery. Part of this will be served by the new Lower Bárí Doáb Canal. The population consists mainly of miscellaneous tribes grouped together under the name of Jats, the ethnological significance of which in the Western Pánjab is very slight. They are Muhammadans. The district is well served by railways.

Area, 6052 sq. m. Cultd area, 1163 sq. m. Pop. 569,461; 87 p.c. M. Land Rev. Rs. 873,491 = £58,233.

**Muzaffargarh** is with the exception of Kángra the biggest Panjáb district. It forms a large triangle with its apex in the south at the junction of the Indus and Panjnad. On the west the Indus forms the boundary for 180 miles. On the east Muzaffargarh has a river boundary with Baháwalpur and Multán, but, where it marches with Jhang, is separated from it by the area which that district possesses in the Sind Ságar Doáb. There are four *tahsíls*, Leia, Sinánwan, Muzaffargarh, and Alipur, the first being equal in area to a moderately sized district. The greater part of Leia and Sinánwan is occupied by the Thal. The southern tongue of the Thal extends into the Muzaffargarh *tahsíl*. The rest of that district is a heavily inundated or irrigated tract, the part above flood level being easily reached by inundation canals. Dry cultivation is impossible with a yearly rainfall of about six inches. The chief crop is wheat. In the south of the district the people live in frail grass huts,

[1] There is a project for improving the water-supply of inundation canals in the west of the district by building a weir across the Chenáb below its junction with the Jhelam.

and when the floods are out transfer themselves and their scanty belongings to wooden platforms.

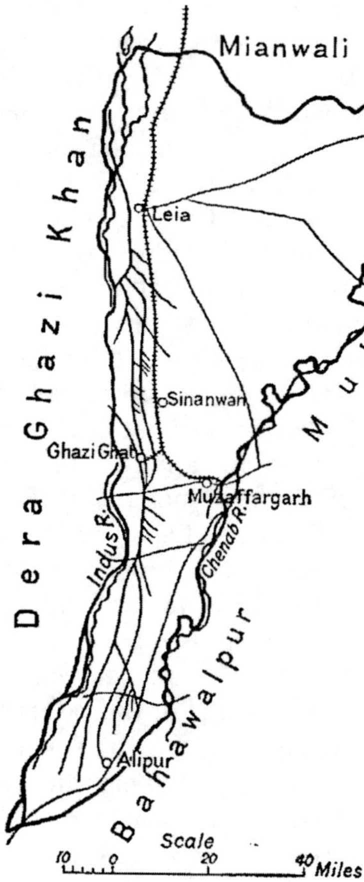


Fig. 114.

**Dera Ghází Khán district.**—When the N.W. Frontier Province was separated from the Panjáb, the older province retained all the trans-Indus country in which Biluches were the predominant tribe. The Panjáb therefore kept Dera Ghází Khán. It has a river frontage

Area, 5325 sq. m. Cultd area, 1723 sq. m. Pop. 499,860; 88 p.c. M. Land Rev. Rs. 542,473 = £36,165.

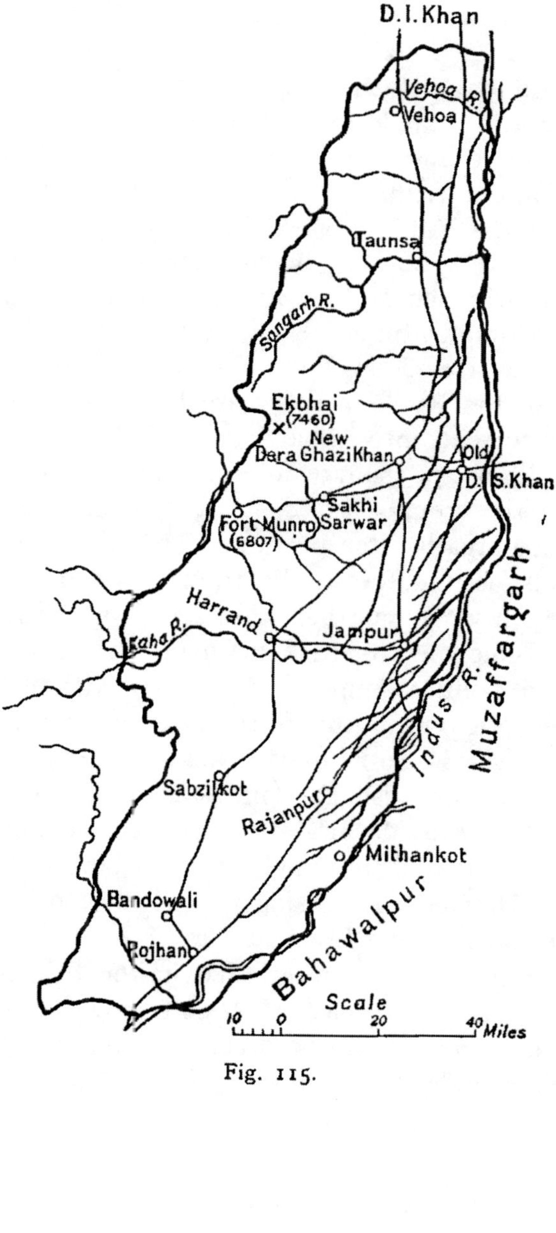
D.I. Khan
Vehoa R.
Vehoa
Taunsa
Sangarh R.
Ekbhai
(7460)
New
Dera Ghazi Khan
Old
D. G. Khan
Sakhi
Sarwar
Fort Munro
(6807)
Harrand
Kaha R.
Jampur
Indus R.
Muzaffargarh
Sabzilkot
Rajanpur
Mithankot
Bandowali
Rojhan
Bahawalpur
Scale
10
0
20
40 Miles

Fig. 115.

on the Indus about 230 miles in length and on the west is bounded by the Sulimán Range, part of which is included within the district. The Deputy Commissioner of Dera Ghází Khán and the Commissioner of Multán spend part of the hot weather at Fort Munro. The wide Indus valley is known as the Sindh. The tract between it and the Hills is the Pachádh. It is seamed by hill torrents, three of which, the Vehoa, the Sangarh, and the Kahá, have a thread of water even in the cold season. The heat in summer is extreme, and the *luh*, a moving current of hot air, claims its human victims from time to time. The cultivation in the Sindh depends on the river floods and inundation canals, helped by wells. In the Pachádh dams are built to divert the water of the torrents into embanked fields. The cultivated area is recorded as 1723 square miles, but this is enormously in excess of the cropped areas, for a very large part of the embanked area is often unsown. The encroachments of the Indus have enforced the transfer of the district headquarters from Dera Ghází Khán to a new town at Choratta. Biluches are the dominant tribe both in numbers and political importance. They with few exceptions belong to one or other of the eight organized clans or tumans, Kasránis, Sorí Lunds, Khosas, Laghárís, Tibbí Lunds, Gurchánís, Drishaks, and Mazárís. The most important clans are Mazárís, Laghárís, and Gurchánís. Care has been taken to uphold the authority of the chiefs. The Deputy Commissioner is political officer for such of the independent Biluch tribes across the administrative frontier as are not included in the Biluchistán Agency. Regular troops have all been removed from the district. The peace of the borderland is maintained by a tribal militia under the command of a British officer.

# CHAPTER XXVI

## THE PANJÁB NATIVE STATES

### 1. *The Phulkian States*

Area, 7599 sq. m.
Pop. 1,928,724.
Rev.
Rs. 118,00,000
=£786,666.

**Phulkian States.**—The three Phulkian States of Patiála, Jínd, and Nábha form a political agency under the Panjáb Government. They occupy, with Baháwalpur and Hissár, the bulk of that great wedge of light loam and sand which Rájputána, physically considered, pushes northwards almost to the Sutlej. In the Phulkian States this consists of two tracts, the Powádh and the Jangal Des. The former, which occupies the north and north-east of their territory, possesses a light fertile loam soil and a very moderate natural water level, so that well irrigation is easy. The Jangal Des is a great tract of sandy loam and sand in the south-west. Water lies too deep for the profitable working of wells, but the harvests are far less insecure than one would suppose looking to the scantiness of the rainfall. The soil is wonderfully cool and drought-resisting. The dry cultivation consists of millets in the Autumn, and of gram and mixed crops of wheat or barley and gram in the Spring, harvest. The three states have rather more than a one-third share in the Sirhind Canal, their shares *inter se* being Patiála 83·6, Nábha 8·8, and Jínd 7·6. Portions of the Powádh and Jangal Des are irrigated. In the case of the Powádh there has been in some places over irrigation

Fig. 116. Mahárája of Patiála.

considering how near the surface the water table is. The Nirwána *tahsil* in Patiála and the part of Jínd which lies between Karnál and Rohtak is a bit of the Bángar tract of the south-eastern Panjáb, with a strong loam soil and a naturally deep water level. The former receives irrigation from the Sirsa, and the latter from the Hánsi, branch of the Western Jamna Canal. The outlying tracts to the south of Rohtak and Gurgáon, acquired after the Mutiny, are part of the dry sandy Rájputána desert, in which the *Kharíf* is the chief harvest, and the millets and gram the principal crops. In addition Patiála has an area of 294 square miles of territory immediately below and in the Simla Hills. The territory of the Phulkian States is scattered and intermixed, and they have islands in British districts and *vice versa*, a natural result of their historic origin and development.

Phul was the sixth in descent from Baryám, a Sidhu Ját, to whom Bábar gave the *Chaudhráyat* of the wild territory to the south-west of Delhi, making him in effect a Lord of the Marches.

*Tree showing relationship of the three Houses.*

- Phul
  - Tiloka
    - Gurditta
      - Suratya
        - Raja Hamír Singh of Nábha
    - Sukhchen
      - Raja Gajpat Singh of Jínd
  - Ráma
    - Raja Ála Singh of Patiála

The century and more which elapsed between the grant and Phul's death in 1652 were filled with continual fighting with the Bhattís. Phul's second son Ráma obtained from the Governor of Sirhind the *Chaudhráyat* of the Jangal Des. When Ahmad Sháh defeated the Sikhs near Barnála in 1762, Ráma's son, Ála Singh, was one of his prisoners. He was a chief of such importance that his conqueror gave him the title of Rája and the right to coin money. But Ála Singh found it prudent to join next year in the capture of Sirhind. From the division of territory which followed the separate existence of the Phulkian States begins. The manner in which they came in 1809 under British protection has already been related. The Rája of Patiála was our ally in the Gurkha War in 1814, and received the Pinjaur *tahsíl*. The active loyalty displayed in 1857 was suitably rewarded by accessions of territory. The right of adoption was conferred, and special arrangements made to prevent lapse, if nevertheless the line in any state failed.

**Area, 5412 sq. m.**
**Cultd area, 4515 sq. m.**
**Pop. 1,407,659; 40 p.c. H. 38 ,, S. 22 ,, M.**
**Rev. Rs. 82,00,000 =£546,666.**

**Patiála** occupies five-sevenths of the Phulkian inheritance. The predominant agricultural tribe is the Játs, over three-fourths of whom are Sikhs. The cultivated area is four-fifths of the total area. Over one-fourth of the former is irrigated, 27 p.c. from wells, and the rest from the two canals. In an area extending with breaks from Simla to the Rájputána desert the variations of agriculture are of course extreme. The state is excellently served by railways.

**Nizámats.**—There are five *nizámats* or districts, Pinjaur, Amargarh, Karmgarh, Anáhadgarh, and Mohindargarh. Their united area is equivalent to that of two ordinary British districts. The Pinjaur *nizámat* with headquarters at Rájpura covers only 825 square miles. Of its four *tahsíls* Pinjaur contains the submontane and hill tract, part of the latter being quite close to Simla. The other three *tahsíls* Rájpura, Bannur, and Ghanaur are in the Powádh. The Amargarh *nizámat* with an area of 855 square miles comprises the three *tahsíls* of Fatehgarh, Sáhibgarh, and Amargarh. The first two are rich and fertile well tracts. Amargarh is in the Jangal Des to the south-west of Sáhibgarh. It receives irrigation from the Kotla branch of the Sirhind Canal. The Karmgarh *nizámat* with an area of 1835 square miles contains the four *tahsíls* of Patiála, Bhawánigarh, Sunám, and Nirwána. The headquarters are at Bhawánigarh. The first three are partly in the Powádh, and partly in the Jangal Des. Nirwána is in the Bángar. There is much irrigation from the Sirhind and Western Jamna Canals. The Anáhadgarh *nizámat* lies wholly in the Jangal Des. It has an area of 1836 square miles, and is divided into three *tahsíls*, Anáhadgarh, Bhikhi, and Govindgarh. The headquarters are at Barnála or Anáhadgarh. The Mohindarpur *nizámat* lies far away to the south on the borders of Jaipur and Alwar (see map on page 226). Its area is only 576 miles and it has two *tahsíls*, Mohindargarh or Kánaud and Narnaul. Kánaud is the headquarters.

The history down to 1763 has already been related. Rája Ála Singh died in 1765 and was succeeded by his grandson Amar Singh (1765–1781), who was occupied in continual warfare with his brother and his neighbours, as became a Sikh chieftain of those days. His son, Sáhib Singh (1781–1813), came under British protection in 1809. Karm Singh (1813–1845), his successor, was our ally in the Gurkha War. Mahárája Narindar Singh, K.C.S.I. (1845–1862), was a wise and brave man, who gave manful and most important help in 1857. His son, Mahárája Mohindar Singh (1862–1876), succeeded at the age of ten and died 14 years later. His eldest son, Mahárája Rajindar Singh (1876–1900), was only four when he succeeded and died at the age of 28. Another long minority, that of the present Mahárája Bhupindar Singh, only came to an end a few years ago. In the last fifty years Patiála has in consequence of three minorities been governed, and as a rule successfully governed, for long periods by Councils of Regency. The State in 1879 sent a contingent of 1100 men to the Afghán War. It maintains an Imperial Service Force consisting of two fine regiments of infantry and one of cavalry. Maháraja Rajindar Singh went with one of these regiments to the Tirah Expedition.

Area, 1259 sq. m.
Cultd area, 1172 sq. m.
Pop. 248,887; 78 p.c. H. and J.[1]
14 ,, M.
8 ,, S.
Rev. Rs. 19,00,000 =£126,666.

**Jínd.**—A third of the population of Jínd consists of Hindu and Sikh Játs. There are two *nizámats*, Sangrúr and Jínd, the latter divided into the *tahsíls* of Jínd and Dádrí (map on page 226). The Sangrúr villages are interspersed among those of the other Phulkian States, and form a part of the Jangal Des. Jínd is in the Bángar, and Dádrí, separated from Jínd by the Rohtak district, is partly in Hariána and partly in the sandy Rájputána desert. The rainfall varies from 17 inches at Sangrúr to ten inches at Dádrí. Sangrúr is irrigated by the Sirhind, and Jínd by the Western Jamna, Canal. Dádrí is a dry sandy tract, in which the Autumn millets are the chief crop. The revenue in 1911–12 was 19 *lákhs* (£126,700). For imperial service Jínd keeps up a fine battalion of infantry 600 strong. The real founder of the state was Gajpat Singh, who was a chief of great vigour. He conquered Jínd and in 1774 deprived his relative, the chief of Nábha, of Sangrúr. He died in 1789. His successor, Rája Bhág Singh, was a good ally of the British Government. He died after a long and successful career in 1819. His son, Fateh Singh, only survived him by three years. Sangat Singh succeeded to troublous times and died childless in 1834. His second cousin, Rája Sarúp Singh, was only allowed to inherit the territory acquired by Gajpat Singh, from whom he derived his claim. But the gallant and valuable services rendered by Rája Sarúp

[1] J.=Jain.

Singh in 1857 enabled him to enlarge his State by the grant of the Dádrí territory and of thirteen villages near Sangrúr. He died in 1864. His son Raghubír Singh (1864–1887) was a vigorous and successful ruler. He gave loyal help in the Kúka outbreak and in the Second Afghán War. His grandson, the present Mahárája Ranbir Singh, K.C.S.I., was only eight when he succeeded, and Jínd was managed by a Council of Regency for a number of years. Full powers were given to the chief in 1899.

Fig. 117. Mahárája of Jínd.

Area, 928 sq. m.
Cultd area, 806 sq. m.
Pop. 248,887; 51 p.c. H. and J. 31 „ S. 18 „ M.
Rev. Rs. 17,00,000 = £113,300.

**Nábha** consists of twelve patches of territory in the north scattered among the possessions of Patiála, Jínd, and Farídkot, and two other patches in the extreme south on the border of Gurgáon. The northern section of the state is divided into the eastern *nizámat* of Amloh in the Powádh and the western *nizámat* of Phul in the Jangal Des. Both now receive irrigation from the Sirhind Canal. The Báwal *nizámat* is part of the arid Rájputána desert. Játs, who are mostly Sikhs, constitute 30 p.c. of the population.

The State is well served by railways, Nábha itself being on the Rájpura-Bhatinda line. The Mahárája maintains a battalion of infantry for imperial service. Hamír Singh, one of the chiefs who joined in the capture of Sirhind, may be considered the first Rája. He died in 1783 and was succeeded by his young son, Jaswant Singh. When he grew to manhood Jaswant Singh proved a very capable chief and succeeded in aggrandising his State, which he ruled for 57 years. His son, Deoindar

Singh (1840-47), was deposed, as he was considered to have failed to support the British Government when the Khalsa army crossed the Sutlej in 1845. A fourth of the Nábha territory was confiscated. Bharpur Singh, who became chief in 1857, did excellent service at that critical time, and the Báwal *nizámat* was his reward. He was succeeded by his brother, Bhagwán Singh, in 1863. With Bhagwán Singh the line died out in 1871, but under the provisions of the *sanad* granted after the Mutiny a successor was selected from among the Badrúkhan chiefs in the person of the late Mahárája Sir Hira Singh. No choice could have been more happy. Hira Singh for 40 years ruled his State on old fashioned lines with much success. Those who had the privilege of his friendship will not soon forget the alert figure wasted latterly by disease, the gallant bearing, or the obstinate will of a Sikh chieftain of a type now departed. His son, Mahárája Ripudaman Singh, succeeded in 1911.

Fig. 118. Mahárája Sir Hira Singh.

## 2. *Other Sikh States*

Area, 630 sq. m. Cultd area, 424 sq. m. Pop. 268,163. Rev. Rs. 14,00,000 = £93,333, exclusive of Rs. 13,00,000 = £86,666 derived from the Oudh estates.

**Kapúrthala.**—The main part consists of a strip of territory mostly in the valley of the Biás, and interposed between that river and Jalandhar. This is divided into the four *tahsíls* of Bholath, Dhilwan, Kapúrthala, and Sultánpur. There is a small island of territory in Hoshyárpur, and a much larger one, the Phagwára *tahsíl*, projecting southwards from the border of that district into Jalandhar. Two-thirds of the area is cultivated and the proportion of high-class crops is large. The chief agricultural tribes are the Muhammadan Arains and the Játs, most of whom are Sikhs.

The real founder of the Kapúrthala house was Sardár Jassa Singh Ahluwália, who in 1763, when Sirhind fell, was the leading Sikh chief in the Panjáb. He captured Kapúrthala in 1771 and made it his headquarters, and died in 1783. A distant relative, Bágh Singh, succeeded. His successor, Fateh Singh, was a sworn brother of Ranjít Singh, with whom he exchanged turbans. But an alliance between the weak and the strong is not free from fears, and in 1826 Fateh Singh, who had large possessions south of the Sutlej, fled thither and asked the protection of the British Government. He returned however to Kapúrthala in 1827, and the Mahárája never pushed matters with Fateh Singh to extremities. The latter died in 1836. His successor, Nihál Singh, was a timid man, and his failure to support the British in 1845 led to the loss of his Cis-Sutlej estates. In 1849 he took the English side and was given the title of Rája. Randhír Singh succeeded in 1852. His conspicuous services in the Mutiny were rewarded with the grant of estates in Oudh. The present Mahárája, Sir Jagatjít Singh Bahádur, G.C.S.I., is a grandson of Randhír Singh. He was a young child when he succeeded in 1877. The State maintains a battalion of infantry for imperial service.

Fig. 119. Mahárája Sir Jagatjít Singh Bahádur, G.C.S.I.

**Farídkot** is a small wedge of territory which almost divid s the Ferozepore district in two. The population is composed of Sikhs 42½, Hindus and Jains 29, and Musalmans 28½ p.c. Sikh Jats are the strongest tribe. The country is flat. In the west it is very sandy, but in the east the soil is firmer and is irrigated in part by the Sirhind Canal. The Chief, like the Phulkians, is a Sidhu Barár Ját, and, though not a descendant of Phul, unites his line with the Phulkians further back. The present Rája, Brijindar Singh, is 17 years of age, and the State is managed by a Council of Regency.

Area, 642 sq. m.
Pop. 130,925.
Rev.
Rs. 11,50,000
= £76,666.

Fig. 120. Rája Brijindar Singh.

**Kalsia** consists of a number of patches of territory in Ambála and an enclave in Ferozepore known as Chirak. The founder of the State was one of the Játs from the Panjáb, who swept over Ambála after the capture of Sirhind in 1763, and carved out petty principalities, of which Kalsia is the only survivor (page 180). The capital is Chachraulí, eight or nine miles north-west of Jagádhrí. The present Chief, Sardár Ráví Sher Singh, is a minor.

Area, 168 sq. m.
Pop. 55,915.
Rev.
Rs. 221,000
= £14,733.

### 3. *The Muhammadan States*

**Baháwalpur** is by far the largest of the Panjáb States. But the greater part of it is at present desert, and the population, except in the river tract, is very sparse. Baháwalpur stretches from Ferozepore on the north to the Sindh border. It has a river frontage

Area,
15,917 sq. m.
Cultd area,
1853 sq. m.
Pop. 780,641;
84 p.c. M.
Rev.
Rs. 35,00,000
= £233,333.

exceeding 300 miles on the Sutlej, Panjnad, and Indus. The cultivated area in 1903–4 was 1451 square miles, and of this 83 p.c. was irrigated and 10 p.c. flooded. The rainfall is only five inches and the climate is very hot. South and east of the rivers is a tract of low land known as the "Sindh," which

Fig. 121. Nawáb Sadik Muhammad Khán.

widens out to the south. It is partly flooded and partly irrigated by inundation canals with the help of wells. Palm groves are a conspicuous feature in the Sindh. Behind it is a great stretch of strong loam or "*pat*," narrow in the south, but widening out in the north. It is bounded on the south-east by a wide depression known as the Hakra, probably at one time the bed of the Sutlej. At present little cultivation is possible in the *pat*, but there is some hope that a canal taking out on the right bank of the Sutlej in Ferozepore may bring the water of that river back to it. South of the Hakra is a huge tract of sand and sand dunes, known as the Rohí or Cholistán, which is part of the Rájputána desert. There are three *nizámats*, Minchinábád in the north, Baháwalpur in the middle, and Khánpur in the south. The capital, Baháwalpur, is close to the bridge at Adamwáhan by which the N.W. Railway crosses the Sutlej. The ruling family belongs to the Abbásí Dáudpotra clan, and came originally from Sindh. Sadik Muhammad Khán, who received the title of Nawáb from Nádir Sháh, when he invaded the Deraját in 1739, may be considered the real founder of the State. The Nawáb Muhummad Baháwal Khan III, threatened with invasion by Mahárája Ranjít Singh, made a treaty with the British Government in 1833. He was our faithful ally in the first Afghán War, and gave valuable help against Diwán Mulráj in 1848. The next three reigns extending from 1852 to 1866 were brief and troubled. Nawáb Sadik Muhummad Khán IV, who succeeded in 1866, was a young child, and for the next thirteen years the State was managed by Captain Minchin and Captain L. H. Grey as Superintendents. The young Nawáb was installed in 1879, and henceforth ruled with the help of a Council. In the Afghán War of 1879–1880 Baháwalpur did very useful service. The Nawáb died in 1899. A short minority followed during which Colonel L. H. Grey again became Superintendent. The young Nawáb, Muhammad Baháwal Khán V, had but a brief reign. He was succeeded by the present Chief, Nawáb Sadik Muhummad Khán V, a child of eight or nine years. The State is managed by a Council aided by the advice of the political Agent. From 1903 to 1913, the Agent for the Phulkian States was in charge, but a separate Agent has recently been appointed for Baháwalpur and Farídkot. An efficient camel corps is maintained for imperial service.

**Malerkotla** consists of a strip of territory to the south of the Ludhiána district. The capital is connected with Ludhiána by railway. The Nawáb keeps up a company of Sappers and Miners for imperial service. He is an Afghán, and his ancestor held a position of trust under the Moghal Empire, and became independent on its decline. The independence of his successor was menaced by Mahárája Ranjít Singh when Malerkotla came under British protection in 1809.

Area, 167 sq. m.
Pop. 71,144.
Rev.
Rs. 900,000
= £60,000.

**Pataudí, Dujána, and Loháru.**—The three little Muhammadan States of Lohárú, Dujána, and Pataudí are relics of the policy which in the opening years of the nineteenth century sought rigorously to limit our responsibilities to the west of the Jamna. Together they have an area of 275 square miles, a population of 59,987 persons, and a revenue of Rs. 269,500 (£18,000). The Chief of Lohárú, Nawáb Amír ud dín Ahmad Khán, K.C.I.E., is a man of distinction.

## 4. *Hindu Hill States*

**Mandí** is a tract of mountains and valleys drained by the Biás. With Suket, with which for many generations it formed one kingdom, it is a wedge thrust up from the Sutlej between Kángra and Kulu. Three-fifths of the area is made up of forests and grazing lands. The *deodár* and blue pine forests on the Kulu border are valuable. At Guma and Drang an impure salt, fit for cattle, is extracted from shallow cuttings. A considerable part of the revenue is derived from the price and duty. The

Area, 1200 sq. m.
Pop. 181,110.
Rev.
Rs. 500,000
= £33,333.

chiefs are Chandarbánsí Rájputs. The direct line came to an end in 1912 with the death of Bhawání Sen, but to prevent lapse the British Government has chosen as

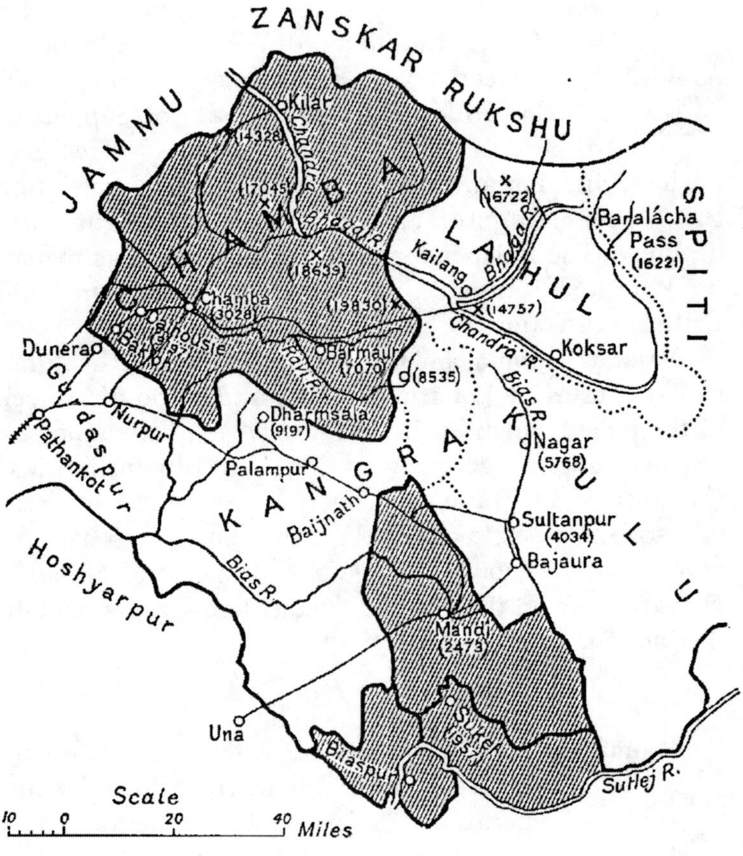


Native States

Fig. 122.

successor a distant relative, Jogindar Singh, who is still a child.

**Suket** lies between Mandí and the Sutlej. Its Rája, Ugar Sen, like his distant relative, the Rája of Mandí, came under British protection in 1846. His great-grandson, Rája Bhim Sen, is the present chief.

Area, 420 sq. m.
Pop. 54,928.
Rev.
Rs. 200,000
= £13,333.

**Sirmúr** (Náhan) lies to the north of the Ambála district, and occupies the greater part of the catchment area of the Girí, a tributary of the Jamna. It is for the most part a mountain tract, the Chor to the north of the Girí rising to a height of 11,982 feet. The capital, Náhan (3207 feet), near the southern border is in the Siwálik range. In the south-east of the State is the rich valley known as the Kiárda Dún, reclaimed and colonized by

Area, 1198 sq. m.
Pop. 138,520.
Rev.
Rs. 600,000
= £40,000.

Fig. 123. The late Rája Surindar Bikram Parkásh, K.C.S.I., of Sirmúr.

Rája Shamsher Parkásh. There are valuable *deodár* and *sál* forests. A good road connects Náhan with Barára on the N.W. Railway. In 1815 the British Government having driven out the Gurkhas put Fateh Parkásh on the throne of his ancestors. His troops fought on the English side in the first Sikh War. His successors, Rája Sir Shamsher Parkásh, G.C.S.I. (1856–98), and Rája Sir Surindar Bikram Parkásh, K.C.S.I. (1898–1911), managed their State with conspicuous success. The present Rája, Amar Parkásh, is 25 years of age. In the second Afghán War in 1880, Sirmúr sent a contingent to the frontier, and the Sappers and Miners, which it keeps up for imperial service, accompanied the Tirah Expedition of 1897.

Area, 3216 sq. m. Pop. 135,989. Rev. 4 *lákhs* = £26,700.

**Chamba** lies to the N. of Kángra from which it is divided by the Dhauladhár (map, p. 284). The southern and northern parts of the State are occupied respectively by the basins of the Rávi and the Chandrabhágá or Chenáb. Chamba is a region of lofty mountains with some fertile valleys in the south and west. Only about one-nineteenth of the area is cultivated. The snowy range of the Mid-Himálaya separates the Rávi valley from that of the Chandrabhágá, and the great Zánskár chain with its outliers occupies the territory beyond the Chenáb, where the rainfall is extremely small and Tibetan conditions prevail. The State contains fine forests and excellent sport is to be got in its mountains. There are five *wazárats* or districts, Brahmaur or Barmaur, Chamba, Bhattoyat, Chaura, and Pángí.

The authentic history of this Súrajbansí Rájput principality goes back to the seventh century. It came into the British sphere in 1846. During part of the reign of Rája Shám Singh (1873–1904), the present Rája, Sir Bhure Singh, K.C.S.I., C.I.E., administered the State as

Wazír, filling a difficult position with loyalty and honour. He is a Rájput gentleman of the best type. The Rája

Fig. 124. Rája Sir Bhure Singh, K.C.S.I., C.I.E.

owns the land of the State, but the people have a permanent tenant right in cultivated land.

**Simla Hill States.**—The Deputy Commissioner of Simla is political officer with the title of Superintendent of nineteen, or, including the tributaries of Bashahr, Keonthal, and Jubbal, of 28 states with a total area of 6355 square miles, a population of 410,453, and revenues amounting to a little over ten *lákhs* (£66,000). The States vary in size from the patch of four square miles ruled by the Thákur of Bija to the 3881 square miles included in Bashahr. Only four other States have areas exceeding 125 square miles, namely, Biláspur (448), Keonthal (359), Jubbal (320), and Hindúr or Nalagarh (256). Excluding feudatories the revenues vary from Rs. 900 (or a little over £1 a week) in Mangal to Rs. 190,000

(£12,666) in Bilâspur. The chiefs are all Rájputs, who came under our protection at the close of the Gurkha War.

The watershed of the Sutlej and Jamna runs through the tract. The range which forms the watershed of the Sutlej and the Jamna starts from the Shinka Pass on the south border of Bashahr and passes over Hattu and Simla. In Bashahr it divides the catchment areas of the Rupín and Pábar rivers, tributaries of the Tons and therefore of the Jamna, from those of the Báspa and the Noglí, which are affluents of the Sutlej. West of Bashahr the chief tributary of the Jamna is the Girí and of the Sutlej the Gámbhar, which rises near Kasaulí. In the east Bashahr has a large area north of the Sutlej drained by its tributary the Spití and smaller streams. In the centre the Sutlej is the northern boundary of the Simla Hill States. In the west Biláspur extends across that river. The east of Bashahr is entirely in the Sutlej basin.

Area, 448 sq. m.
Pop. 93,107.
Rev. Rs. 190,000 = £12,666.

**Biláspur.**—This is true also of Biláspur or Kahlúr (map, p. 284), which has territory on both banks of the river. The capital, Biláspur, is on the left bank only 1455 feet above sea level. The present Rája Bije Chand, C.S.I., succeeded in 1889.

Area, 3881 sq. m.
Pop. 93,203.
Rev. Rs. 95,000 = £6233.

**Bashahr.**—The chain which forms the watershed of the Sutlej and Jamna rises from about 12,000 feet at Hattu in the west to nearly 20,000 feet on the Tibet border. Two peaks in the chain exceed 20,000 feet. Further north Raldang to the east of Chíní is 21,250 feet high, and in the north-east on the Tibet border there are two giants about 1000 feet higher. Generally speaking the Sutlej runs in a deep gorge but at Chíní and Saráhan the valley widens out. The main valley of the Pábar is not so narrow as that of the Sutlej, while the side valleys descend in easy slopes to the river beds. The Báspa has a course of 35 miles. In the last ten miles it falls 2000 feet and is hemmed in by steep mountains. Above this gorge the Báspa valley is four or five miles wide and consists of a succession of plateaux rising one above the other from the river's banks. Bashahr is divided into

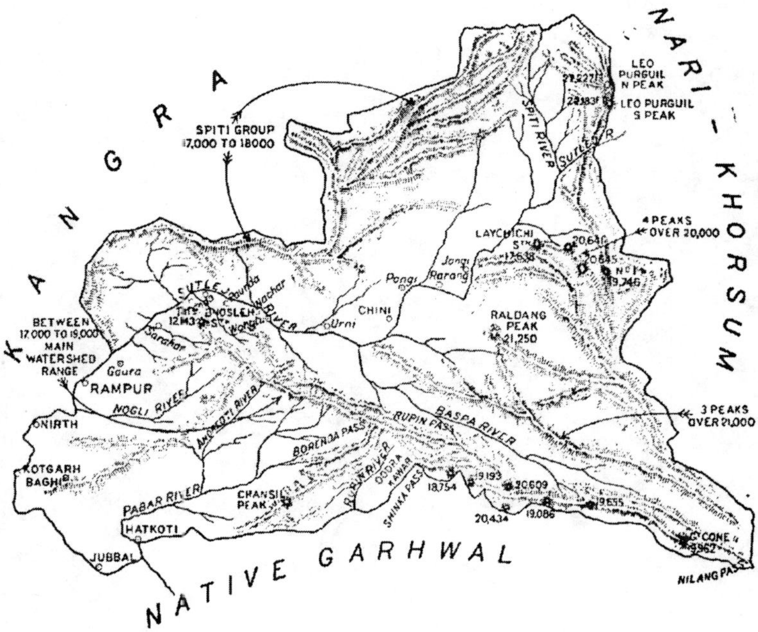


Fig. 125. Bashahr.

two parts, Bashahr proper and Kunáwar. The latter occupies the Sutlej valley in the north-east of the State. It covers an area of about 1730 square miles and is very sparsely peopled. In the north of Kunáwar the predominant racial type is Mongoloid and the religion is Buddhism. The capital of Bashahr, Rámpur, on the left bank of the Sutlej is at an elevation of 3300 feet. The Gurkhas never succeeded in conquering Kunáwar.

They occupied Bashahr, but in 1815 the British Government restored the authority of the Rája. The present chief, Shamsher Singh, is an old man, who succeeded as long ago as 1850. He is incapable of managing the State and an English officer is at present in charge.

# CHAPTER XXVII

## THE NORTH WEST FRONTIER PROVINCE

### 1. *Districts*

**The Province.**—The N. W. F. Province consists of five British districts, Dera Ismail Khán, Bannu, Kohát, Pesháwar, and Hazára with a total area of 13,193 square miles, of which rather less than one-third is cultivated. Of the cultivated area 70 p.c. depends solely on the rainfall. In addition the Chief Commissioner as Agent to the Governor General controls beyond the administrative boundary territory occupied by independent tribes, which covers approximately an area of 25,500 square miles. In 1911 the population of British districts was 2,196,933 and that of tribal territory is estimated to exceed 1,600,000. In the districts 93 persons in every hundred profess the creed of Islam and over 38 p.c. are Patháns.

Area, 3780 sq. m. Cultd area, 851 sq. m. Pop. 256,120. Land Rev. Rs. 306,240 = £20,416.

**Dera Ismail Khán** lies to the north of Dera Ghází Khán and is very similar to it in its physical features. It is divided into the three *tahsíls* of Tánk, Dera Ismail Khán, and Kuláchi. It has a long river frontage on the west, and is bounded on the east by the Sulimán Range. The Kachchhí of Dera Ismail Khán corresponds to the Sindh of Dera Ghází Khán, but is much narrower and is not served by inundation canals, except in the extreme north, where the Pahárpur

Fig. 126. Sir Harold Deane.

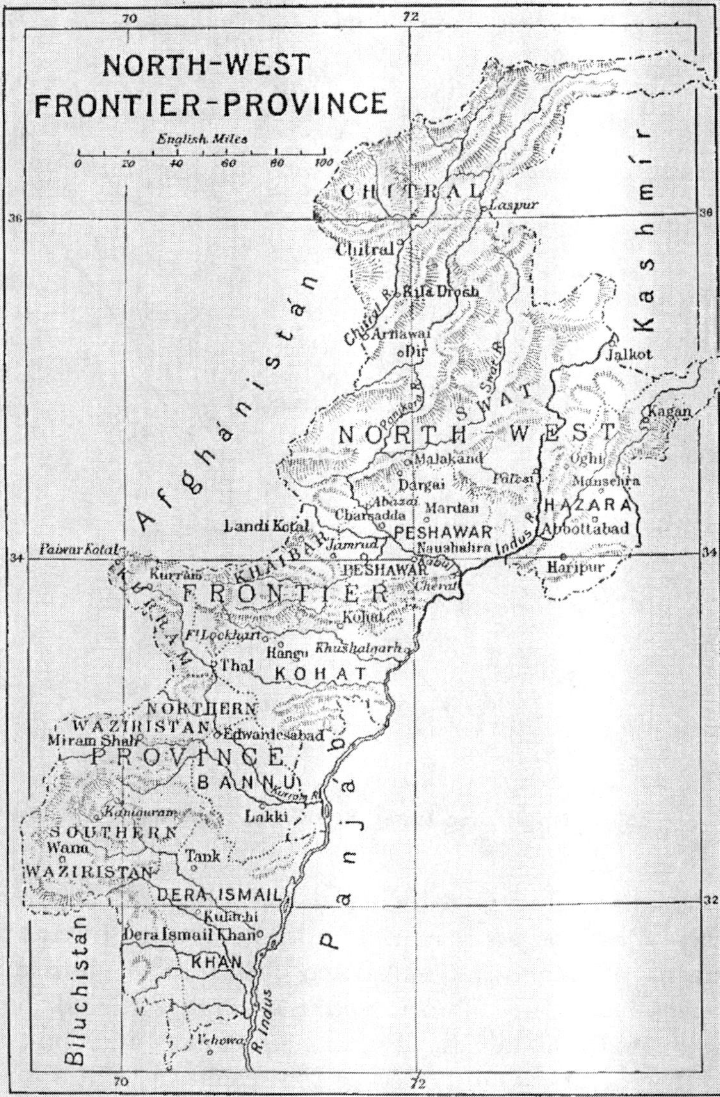
NORTH-WEST
FRONTIER-PROVINCE
English Miles
0 20 40 60 80 100
70
72
36
34
32
CHITRAL
Laspur
Chitral
Kila Drosh
Arnawai
Dir
Kashmír
Jalkot
Kagan
SWAT
NORTH-WEST
Malakand
Oghi
Mansehra
Dargai
Abazai
Mardan
HAZARA
Charsadda
PESHAWAR
Abbottabad
Landi Kotal
Jamrud
Naushahra
Indus R.
Paiwar Kotal
Kurram
KHAIBAR
PESHAWAR
Haripur
Cherat
FRONTIER
Kohat
Ft. Lockhart
Hangu
Khushalgarh
Thal
KOHAT
NORTHERN
WAZIRISTAN
Edwardesabad
Miram Shah
PROVINCE
BANNU
Kanigoram
Lakki
SOUTHERN
Wana
Tank
WAZIRISTAN
DERA ISMAIL
Kulachi
Dera Ismail Khan
KHAN
Panjáb
Afghánistán
Biluchistán
Vehowa
R. Indus

Fig. 127.

Canal has recently been dug. It depends on floods and wells. The Dáman or "Skirt" of the hills is like the

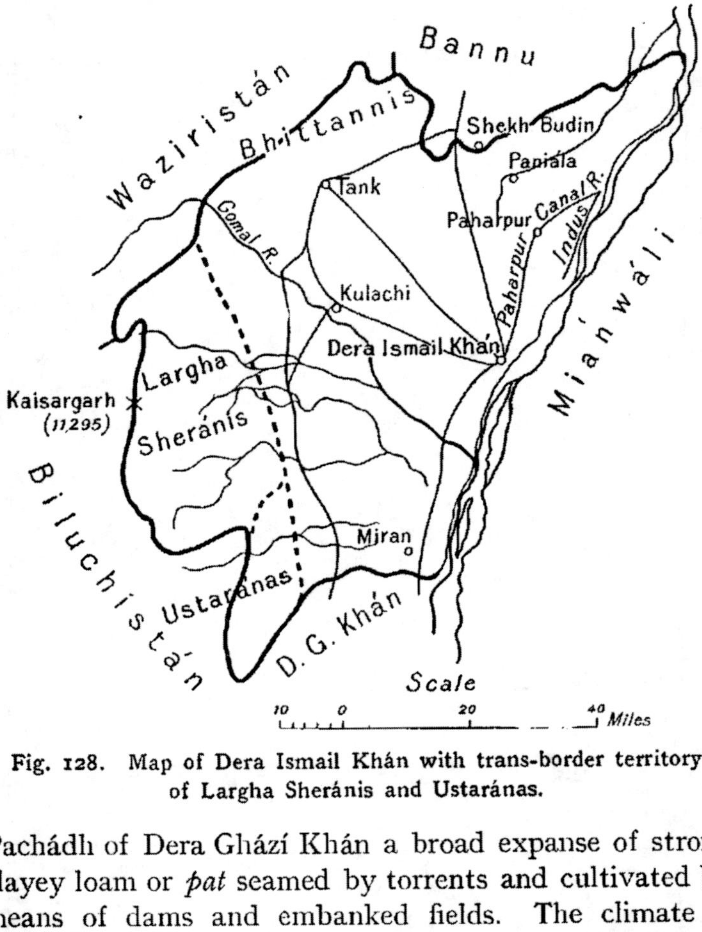


**Fig. 128. Map of Dera Ismail Khán with trans-border territory of Largha Sheránis and Ustaránas.**

Pachádh of Dera Ghází Khán a broad expanse of strong clayey loam or *pat* seamed by torrents and cultivated by means of dams and embanked fields. The climate is intensely hot in summer, and the average rainfall only amounts to ten inches. Between one-fourth and one-fifth of the area is cultivated. The Pachádh is a camel-breeding tract.

Patháns predominate in the Dáman and Jats in the Kachchhí. The Bhittannís in the north of the district are an interesting little tribe. The hill section lies outside our administrative border, but like the Lárgha Sheránís in the south are under the political control of the Deputy Commissioner. A good metalled road, on which there is a *tonga* service, runs northwards from Dera Ismail Khán to Bannu.

Area, 1641 sq. m.
Cultd area, 818 sq. m.
Pop. 250,086.
Land Rev. Rs. 304,004 = £20,267.

**Bannu.**—The small Bannu district occupies a basin surrounded by hills and drained by the Kurram and its affluent, the Tochí. It is cut off from the Indus by the Isakhel *tahsíl* of Mianwálí and by a horn of the Dera Ismail Khán district. Bannu is now connected with

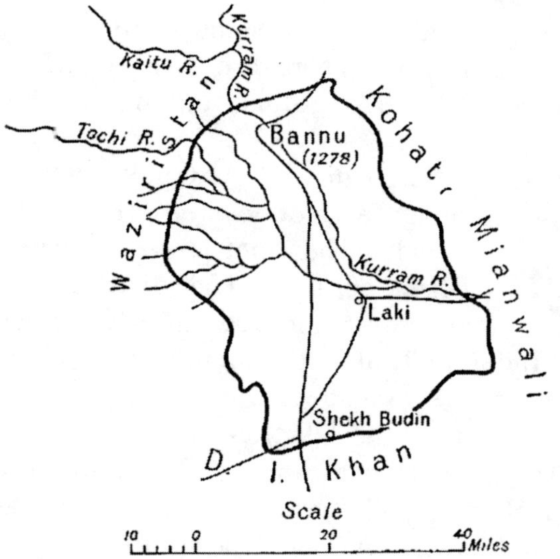


Fig. 129.

Kálabágh in Mianwálí by a narrow gauge railway. An extension of this line from Laki to Tánk in the Dera Ismail Khán district has been sanctioned. There are two *tahsíls*, Bannu and Marwat. The cultivated area is about one-half of the total area. About 30 p.c. of the cultivation is protected by irrigation from small canals taking out of the streams. Most of the irrigation is in the Bannu *tahsíl*. The greater part of Marwat is a dry sandy tract yielding in favourable seasons large crops of gram. But the harvests on unirrigated land are precarious, for the annual rainfall is only about 12 inches. The irrigated land in Bannu is heavily manured and is often double-cropped. Wheat accounts for nearly half of the whole crops of the district. The Marwats are a frank manly race of good physique. The Bannúchís are hard-working, but centuries of plodding toil on a wet soil has spoiled their bodily development, and had its share in imparting to their character qualities the reverse of admirable. The Deputy Commissioner has also political charge of some 17,884 tribesmen living across the border. There are good metalled roads to Dera Ismail Khán and Kohát, and also one on the Tochí route.

Area, 2973 sq. m.
Cultd area, 512 sq. m.
Pop. 222,690.
Land Rev. Rs. 275,462 = £18,364.

**Kohát** is a large district, but most of it is unfit for tillage and only one-sixth is actually cultivated. The chief crops are wheat, 44, and *bájra*, 26 p.c. The district stretches east and west for 100 miles from Khushálgarh on the Indus to Thal at the mouth of the Kurram valley. The two places are now connected by a railway which passes through the district headquarters at Kohát close to the northern border. There are three *tahsíls*, Kohát, Hangu, and Terí, the last a wild tract of bare hills and ravines occupying the south of the district and covering more than half its area. Two small streams, the Kohát Toi and the Terí Toi, drain into the Indus. The rainfall is fair, but very capricious. The cold weather lasts long and the chill winds that blow during part of it are very trying. The chief tribes are the Bangash Patháns of Hangu and the Khattak Patháns of Terí. The Khán of Terí is head of the Khattaks, a manly race which sends many soldiers to our army. He enjoys the revenue of the *tahsíl* subject to a quit rent of Rs. 20,000.

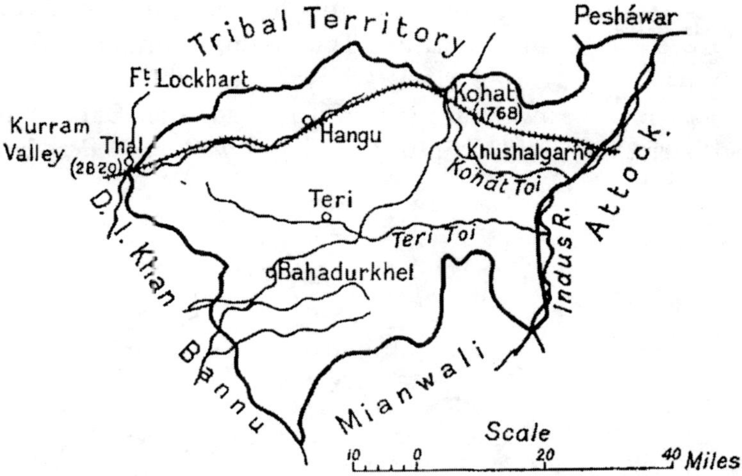


Fig. 130.

Hangu contains in Upper and Lower Miranzai the most fertile land in the district, but the culturable area of the *tahsíl* is small and only one-tenth of it is under the plough. Perennial streams run through the Miranzai valleys, and the neighbouring hills support large flocks of sheep and goats. Kohát contains a number of salt quarries, the most important being at Bahádur Khel near the Bannu border. The Thal subdivision consisting of the Hangu *tahsíl* is in charge of an Assistant Commissioner who manages our political relations with trans-frontier tribes living west of Fort Lockhart on the Samána Range. The Deputy Commissioner is in direct charge of the Pass Afrídís and the Jowákís and Orakzais in the neighbourhood of Kohát. He and his Assistant between them look after our relations with 144,000 trans-border Patháns. The Samána Rifles, one of the useful irregular corps which keep the peace of the Borderland, have their headquarters at Hangu.

Area, 2611 sq. m.
Cultd area, 1398 sq. m.
Pop. 865,009
Land Rev Rs. 11,37,504 = £75,834.

**Peshâwar** is a large basin encircled by hills. The gorge of the Indus separates it from Attock and Hazára. The basin is drained by the Kábul river, whose chief affluents in Peshâwar are the Swát and the Bára. The district is divided into the five *tahsíls* of Pesháwar,

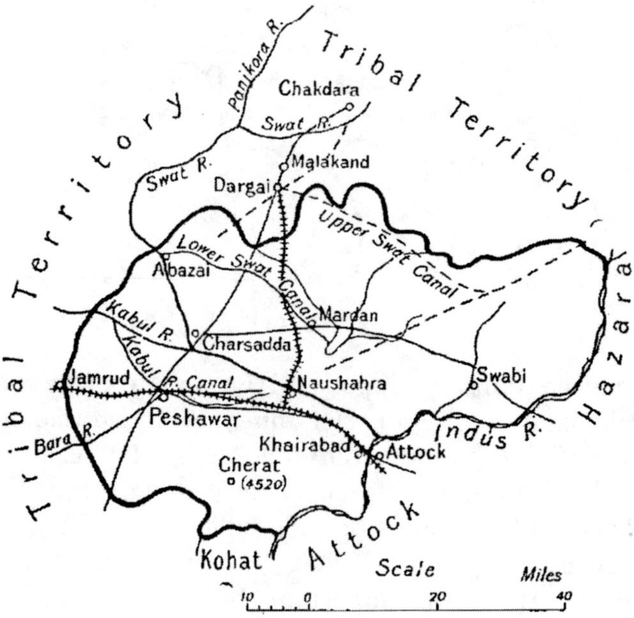


Fig. 131.

Charsadda, Naushahra, Mardán, and Swábí. The last two form the Mardán subdivision. Nearly 40 p.c. of the cultivation is protected by irrigation mainly from canals large and small. The most important are the Lower Swát, the Kábul River, and the Bára River, Canals. The irrigated area will soon be much increased by the opening of the Upper Swát Canal. The cold weather climate is on the whole pleasant, though too severe in December and January. The three months from August to October are a very unhealthy time. The soil except in the stony lands near the hills is a fertile loam. The cold weather rainfall is good, and the Spring harvest is by far the more important of the two. Wheat is the chief crop. Half of the people are Patháns, the rest are known generically as Hindkís. The principal Hindkí tribe is that of the Awáns. Besides managing his own people the Deputy Commissioner has to supervise our relations with 240,000 independent tribesmen across the border. The Assistant Commissioner at Mardán, where the Corps of Guides is stationed, is in charge of our dealings with the men of Buner and the Yúsafzai border. The N.W. Railway runs past the city of Pesháwar to Jamrúd, and there is a branch line from Naushahra to Dargai at the foot of the Malakand Pass.

**Area, 2858 sq. m. Cultd area, 673 sq. m. Pop. 603,028. Land Rev. Rs. 512,897 = £34,193.**

**Hazára** is a typical montane and submontane district with a copious rainfall and a good climate. It has every kind of cultivation from narrow terraced *kalsí* fields built laboriously up steep mountain slopes to very rich lands watered by canal cuts from the Dor or Haro. Hazára is divided into three *tahsíls*, Haripur, Abbottábád, and Mansehra. Between a fourth and a fifth of this area is culturable and cultivated. In this crowded district the words are synonymous. The above figure does not include the 204 square miles of Feudal Tanáwal. The rainfall is copious and the crops generally speaking secure. The principal are maize 42 and wheat 25 p.c. Hazára was part of the territory made over to Rája Guláb Singh in 1846, but he handed it back in exchange for some districts near Jammu. The maintenance of British authority in Hazára in face of great odds by the Deputy Commissioner, Captain James Abbott, during the Second Sikh War is a bright page in Panjáb history; honourable alike to himself and his faithful local

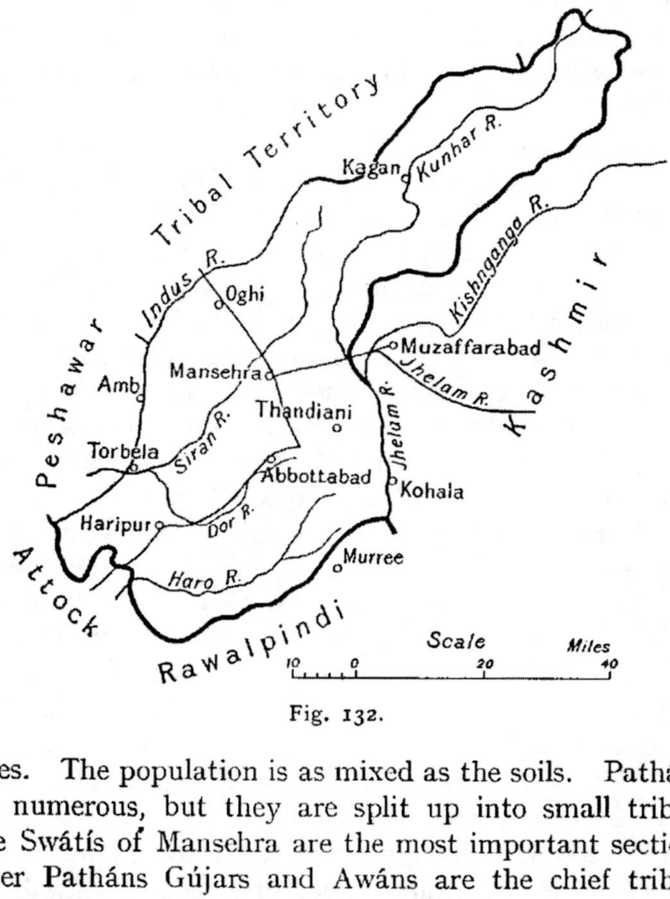


Fig. 132.

allies. The population is as mixed as the soils. Patháns are numerous, but they are split up into small tribes. The Swátís of Mansehra are the most important section. After Patháns Gújars and Awáns are the chief tribes. The Gakkhars, though few in number, hold much land and a dominant position in the Khánpur tract on the Ráwalpindí border. The Deputy Commissioner is also responsible for our relations with 98,000 trans-border tribesmen. The district is a wedge interposed between Kashmír on the east and Pesháwar and the tribal territory north of Pesháwar on the west. The Indus becomes the border about eight miles to the north of Amb, and the district consists mainly of the areas drained by its tributaries the Unhár, Siran, Dor, and Haro. On the eastern side the Jhelam is the boundary with Kashmír from Kohála to a point below Domel, where the Kunhár meets it. Thence the Kunhár is the boundary to near Garhí Habíbullah. To the south of Garhí the watershed of the Kunhár and Jhelam is close to these rivers and the country is very rough and poor. West of Garhí it is represented by the chain which separates the Kunhár and Siran Valleys and ends on the frontier at Musa ká Musalla (13,378 feet). This chain includes one peak over 17,000 feet, Málí ká Parvat, which is the highest in the district. The Kunhár rises at the top of the Kágan Glen, where it has a course of about 100 miles to Bálakot. Here the glen ends, for the fall between Bálakot and Garhí Habíbullah is comparatively small. There is a good mule road from Garhí Habíbullah to the Bábusar Pass at the top of the Kágan Glen, and beyond it to Chilás. There are rest-houses, some very small, at each stage from Bálakot to Chilás. The Kágan is a beautiful mountain glen. At places the narrow road looks sheer down on the river hundreds of feet below, rushing through a narrow gorge with the logs from the *deodár* forests tossing on the surface, and the sensation, it must be confessed, is not wholly pleasant. But again it passes close to some quiet pretty stretch of this same Kunhár. There are side glens, one of which opposite Naran contains the beautiful Safarmulk Lake. Near the top of the main glen the Lulusar Lake at a height of 11,167 feet and with an average depth of 150 feet is passed on the left. In the lower part of the glen much maize is grown. As one ascends almost the last crop to be seen is a coarse barley sown in June and reaped in August. Where the trees and the crops end the rich grass pastures begin. Kágan covers between one-third and one-fourth of the whole district. The Siran flows through the beautiful Bhogarmang Glen, at the foot of which it receives from the west the drainage of the Konsh Glen. Forcing its way through the rough Tanáwal hills, it leaves Feudal Tanáwal and Badhnak on its right, and finally after its junction with the Dor flows round the north of the Gandgarh Range and joins the Indus below Torbela. The bare Gandgarh Hills run south from Torbela parallel with the Indus. The Dor rises in the hills to the south of Abbottábád and drains the Haripur plain. A range of rough hills divides the Dor valley from that of the Haro, which again is separated from Ráwalpindí by the Khánpur Range. To the west of the Siran the Unhár flows through Agror and Feudal Tanáwal, and joins the Indus a little above Amb. Irrigation cuts are taken from all these streams, and the irrigated cultivation is often of a very high character. The best cultivation of the district is in the Haripur plain and the much smaller Orash and Pakhlí plains and in the Haro valley. There is much unirrigated cultivation in the first, and it is generally secure except in the dry tract in the south-west traversed by the new railway from Sarai Kála. The little Orash plain below Abbottábád is famous for its maize and the Pakhlí plain for its rice.

Feudal Tanáwal is a very rough hilly country between the Siran on the east and the Black Mountain and the river Indus on the west. It is the appanage of the Kháns of Amb and Phulra.

North of Feudal Tanáwal is Agror. In 1891 the rights of the last Khán were declared forfeit for abetment of raids by trans-bordermen.

There are fine forests in Hazára, but unfortunately the *deodár* is confined to the Kágan Glen and the Upper Siran. Nathiagalí, the summer headquarters of the Chief Commissioner, is in the Dungagalí Range. The

Serai Kála-Srínagar railway will run through Hazára. There is a good mule road from Murree to Abbottábád through the Galís.

## 2. *Tribal Territory*

Feudal Tanáwal mentioned above occupies the southern corner of the tract of independent tribal territory lying between the Hazára border and the Indus. North of Tanáwal on the left bank of the river a long narrow chain known as the Black Mountain rises in its highest

Fig. 133. Sir George Roos Keppel.

peaks to a height of nearly 10,000 feet. The western slopes are occupied by Hasanzais, Akazais, and Chagarzais, who are Patháns belonging to the great Yúsafzai clan, and these three sections also own lands on the right bank

Fig. 134.

of the Indus. They have been very troublesome neighbours to the British Government. The eastern slopes of the Black Mountain are occupied by Saiyyids and Swátís, and the latter also hold the glens lying further north, the chief of which is Allai.

The mountainous tract on the Pesháwar border lying to the west of Tanáwal and the territory of the Black Mountain tribes formed part of the ancient Udyána, and its archaeological remains are of much interest. It is drained by the Barandu, a tributary of the Indus. Its people are mainly Yúsafzai Patháns, the principal section being the Bunerwáls. These last bear a good character for honesty and courage, but are slaves to the teachings of their *mullas*. The Yúsafzais have been bad neighbours. The origin of the trouble is of old standing, dating back to the welcome given by the tribesmen in 1824 to a band of Hindústání fanatics, whose leader was Saiyyid Ahmad Sháh of Bareilly. Their headquarters, first at Sitána and afterwards at Malka, became Caves of Adullam for political refugees and escaped criminals, and their favourite pastime was the kidnapping of Hindu shopkeepers. In 1863 a strong punitive expedition under Sir Neville Chamberlain suffered heavy losses before it succeeded in occupying the Ambela Pass. The door being forced the Yúsafzais themselves destroyed Malka as a pledge of their submission. Our political relations with the Yúsafzais are managed by the Assistant Commissioner at Mardán.

The rest of the tribal territory between the Pesháwar district and the Hindu Kush is included in the Dir, Swát, and Chitrál political agency. It is a region of mountains and valleys drained by the Swát, Panjkora, and Chitrál or Yárkhun rivers, all three affluents of the Kábul river. Six tracts are included in the Agency.

(*a*) **Swát.**—A railway now runs from Naushahra in the Pesháwar district to Dargai, which lies at the foot of the Malakand, a little beyond our administrative boundary. An old Buddhist road crosses the pass and descends on the far side into Swát. We have a military post at Chakdarra on the Swát river, and a military road passing through Dir connects Chakdarra with Kila Drosh in Chitrál. Most of the Swátís, who are Yúsafzais of the Akozai section, occupy a rich valley above 70 miles in length watered by the Swát river above its junction with the Panjkora. Rice is extensively grown, and a malarious environment has affected the physique and the character of the people. The Swátí is priest-ridden and treacherous. Even his courage has been denied, probably unjustly. Swátí fanaticism has been a source of much trouble on the Pesháwar border. The last serious outbreak was in 1897, when a determined, but unsuccessful, attack was made on our posts at Chakdarra and the Malakand Pass. The Swátís are Yúsafzai Patháns of the Akozai clan, and are divided into five sections, one of which is known as Ránízai.

(*b*) **Sam Ránízai.**—A small tract between the Pesháwar border and the hills is occupied by the Sam Ránízais, who were formerly servants and tenants of the Ránízais, but are now independent.

(*c*) **Utmán Khel.**—The country of the Utmán Khels begins where the Pesháwar boundary turns to the south. This tribe occupies the tract on both sides of the Swát river to the west of Swát and Sam Ránízai. On the south-west the Swát river divides the Utmán Khels from the Mohmands. Their country is very barren, but a good many of them cultivate land in the Pesháwar district. The Utmán Khels are quite independent of the surrounding tribes and have been troublesome neighbours to ourselves.

(*d*) **Bajaur.**—Bajaur is a very mountainous tract lying to the north-west of the Utmán Khel country and between it and the Durand line. It includes four valleys, through which flow the Rud river and its affluents with the exception of that known as Jandol. The valley of the last is now included in Dir. The Rud, also known as the Bajaur, is a tributary of the Panjkora. The people consist mainly of Mamunds and other sections of the Tarkanrí clan, which is related to the Yúsafzais. They own a very nominal allegiance to the Khán of

Nawagai, who is recognised as the hereditary head of the Tarkanrís. They manage their affairs in quasi-republican fashion through a council consisting of the particular party which for the time being has got the upper hand.

(*e*) **Dir.**—Dir is the mountainous country drained by the Panjkora and its tributaries, to the north of its junction with the Rud river in Bajaur. It is separated from Chitrál by the Uchiri Range, which forms the watershed of the Panjkora and Kunar rivers. The military road to Kila Drosh crosses this chain by the Lowari Pass at a height of 10,200 feet. The people of Dir are mostly Yúsafzais, relations of the Swátís, whom they much resemble in character. They pay one-tenth of their produce to their overlord, the Khán of Dir, when he is strong enough to take it. The higher parts of the country have a good climate and contain fine *deodár* forests. The Khán derives much of his income from the export of timber, which is floated down the Panjkora and Swát rivers.

(*f*) **Chitrál.**—The Pathán country ends at the Lowari Pass. Beyond, right up to the main axis of the Hindu Kush, is Chitrál. It comprises the basin of the Yárkhun or Chitrál river from its distant source in the Shawar Shur glacier to Arnawai, where it receives from the west the waters of the Bashgul, and is thenceforth known as the Kunar. Its western boundary is the Durand line, which follows a lofty chain sometimes called the Káfiristán range. Another great spur of the Hindu Kush known as the Shandur range divides Chitrál on the east from the basin of the Yasín river and the territories included in the Gilgit Agency (see Chapter XXVIII). Chitrál is a fine country with a few fertile valleys, good forests below 11,000 feet and splendid, if desolate, mountains in the higher ranges. The Chitrális are a quiet pleasure-loving people, fond of children and of dancing, hawking, and polo. They are no cowards and no fanatics, but have little regard for truth or good faith. The common language is Khowár (see page 112). The chief, known as the Mehtar, has his headquarters at Chitrál, a large village on the river of the same name. It is dominated at a distance by the great snow peak of Tirach Mír (see page 22). The British garrison is stationed at Kila Drosh on the river bank about halfway between Chitrál and the Lowari Pass[1].

**Mohmands and Mallagorís.**—South of the Utmán Khel

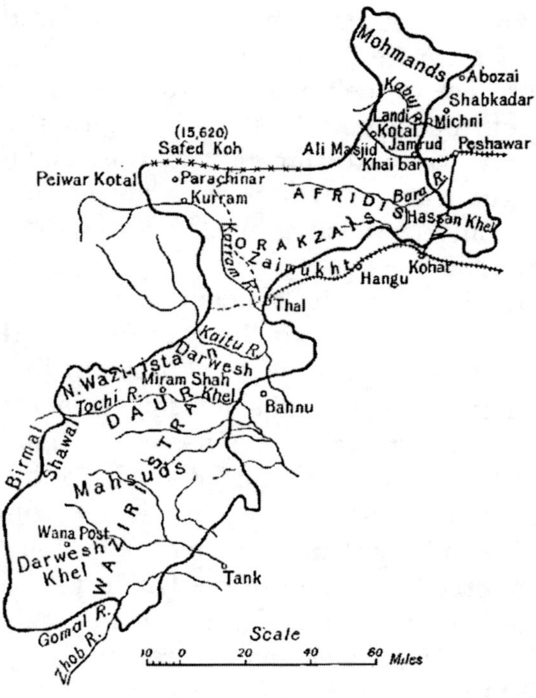


Fig. 135.

country and north of the Khaibar are the rugged and barren hills held by that part of the Mohmand tribe

[1] For recent history see page 196.

which lives inside the Durand line. The clan can muster about 20,000 fighting men and is as convenient a neighbour as a nest of hornets. The southern edge of the tract, where it abuts on the Khaibar, is held by the little Mallagorí tribe, which is independent of the Mohmands. Their country is important strategically because a route passes through it by which the Khaibar can be outflanked. It is included in the charge of the Political Agent for the Khaibar.

**Afrídís.**—The pass and the tract lying to the south of it including the Bazár valley and part of Tirah are the home of the six sections of the Pass Afrídís, the most important being the Zakha Khel, whose winter home is in the Khaibar and the Bazár valley, a barren glen hemmed in by barren hills, the entrance to which is not far from Ali Masjid. Its elevation is 3000 to 4000 feet. The valleys in Tirah proper, where the Pass Afrídís for the most part spend the summer, are two or three thousand feet higher. When the snow melts there is excellent pasturage. The climate is pleasant in summer, but bitterly cold in winter. The Bára river with its affluents drains the glens of Tirah. The Aka Khel Afrídís, who have no share in the Pass allowances, own a good deal of land in the lower Bára valley and winter in the adjoining hills. The fighting strength of the above seven sections may be put at 21,000. When they have been able to unite they have shown themselves formidable enemies, for they are a strong and manly race, and they inhabit a very difficult country[1]. But the Afrídí clan is torn by dissensions. Blood feuds divide house from house, and the sections are constantly at feud one with another. Apart from other causes of quarrel there is the standing division into two great factions, Gar and Samil, which prevails among Afrídís and Orakzais. Afrídís enlist

[1] See page 196.

freely in our regiments and in the Khaibar Rifles, and have proved themselves excellent soldiers. The eighth section of the Afrídís, the Adam Khel, who hold the Kohát Pass and the adjoining hills, have very little connection with

Fig. 136. Khaibar Rifles.

the rest of the clan. The Jowákís, against whom an expedition had to be sent in the cold weather of 1877–78, are a sub-section of the Adam Khel.

**Orakzais, Chamkannís, and Zaimukhts.**—The Orakzais, who in numbers are even stronger than the Pass and Aka Khel Afrídís, occupy the south of Tirah, the Samáná Range on the border of Kohát, and the valley of the Khánkí river. The tribal territory extends westwards as far as the Khurmana, a tributary of the Kurram. The Orakzais do some trade and Sikh *banias* and artizans are to be found in some of their villages. The clan is honey-combed with feuds. North-west of the Orakzais beyond the Khurmana are the Chamkannís, and on the south is a small tribe of vigorous mountaineers called Zaimukhts. One of these Zaimukhts, Sarwar Khán, nicknamed Chikai, was a notorious frontier robber, and a person of considerable importance on the border till his death in 1903.

**The Kurram Valley.**—The Kurram Valley, which is drained by the Kurram river and its affluents, lies to the south of the lofty Safed Koh range, and reaches from Thal in Kohát to the Peiwar Kotal on the borders of Afghán Khost. It has an area of nearly 1300 square miles and in 1911 the population was estimated at 60,941 souls. Though under British administration, it does not form a part of any British district. The people are Patháns of various clans, the predominant element being the Turís, who are Shias by religion and probably of Turkish origin. It was at their request that the valley was annexed in 1892. The political agent has his headquarters at Parachinár in Upper Kurram, which is divided from Lower Kurram by a spur of the Khost hills, through which the river has cut a passage. Such part of the Indian penal law as is suitable has been introduced, and civil rights are governed by the customary law of the Turís. A complete record of rights in land and water has been framed, and the land revenue demand is 88,000 rupees (£5889). Upper Kurram is a wide and fertile valley set in a frame of pine-clad hills. It is not fully cultivated, but has great possibilities, especially in the matter of fruit growing. The snowfall is heavy in winter, but the summer climate is excellent. Lower Kurram is a poor and narrow glen unpleasantly hot and cold according to the season of the year.

Parachinár is connected with the railhead at Thal by a good *tonga* road.

**Wazíristán.**—The country of the Darwesh Khel and Mahsud Wazírs extends from the Kurram valley to the Gomal river. It is divided into the North Wazíristán (2300 square miles) and the South Wazíristán (2700 square miles) Agencies. North Wazíristán consists of four valleys and some barren plateaux. The principal valley is that of Daur (700 square miles) drained by the Tochí. In 1894 the Dauris sought refuge from Darwesh Khel inroads by asking for British administration. In the eyes of the Darwesh Khel they are a race of clodhoppers. Their sole virtue consists in patient spade industry in the stiff rich soil of their valley, their vices are gross, and their fanaticism is extreme. The political agent's headquarters are at Miram Shah. South Wazíristán is the home of the troublesome Mahsuds, who can muster 11,000 fighting men. But parts of the country, e.g. the Wána plain, are held by the Darwesh Khel. Much of South Wazíristán consists of bare hills and valleys and stony plains scored with torrents, which are dry most of the year. The streams are salt. Part of the hinterland is however a more inviting tract with grassy uplands and hills clad with oak, pine, and *deodár*. Wána, where the political agent has his headquarters, was occupied on the invitation of the Darwesh Khel in 1894.

**Sheránís.**—The Sherání country stretches along the Dera Ismail Khán border from the Gomal to the Vihoa torrent. The Lárgha or lower part has been under direct administration since 1899, the Upper part belongs to the Biluchistán Agency.

**Tribal Militias.**—In the greater part of India beyond the border there is no British administration. Respect for our authority and the peace of the roads are upheld, and raiding on British territory is restrained, by irregular forces raised from among the tribesmen. There are Hunza and Nagar levies, Chitrál and Dir levies, Khaibar Rifles, Samána Rifles, and Kurram, North Wazíristán, and South Wazíristán militias.

Fig. 137. North Wazíristán Militia and Border Post.

# CHAPTER XXVIII

## KASHMÍR AND JAMMU

**Kashmír.**—Some account has already been given of the topography and scenery of the wide territory, covering an area about equal to that of the Panjáb less the Ambála division, ruled by the Maháraja of Kashmír and Jammu. The population, races, languages, and religions have been referred to in Chapters IX and X.

**Modern history.**—Some mention has been made of the early history of Kashmír (pages 165, 166, 172, 173). Even the hard Sikh rule was a relief to a country which had felt the tyranny of the Duráni governors who succeeded the Moghals. Under the latter small kingships had survived in the Jammu hills, but the Jammuwál Rajas met at Ranjít Singh's hands the same fate as the Kángra Rájas. Three cadets of the Jammu royal house, the brothers Dhián Singh, Suchet Singh, and Guláb Singh, were great men at his court. In 1820 he made the last Rája of Jammu. Guláb Singh was a man fit for large designs. In 20 years he had made himself master of Bhadráwah, Kishtwár, Ladákh, and Báltistán, and held the casket which enclosed the jewel of Kashmír. He acquired the jewel itself for 75 lakhs by treaty with the British at the close of the first Sikh war.

Excluding a large but little-known and almost uninhabited tract beyond the Muztagh and Karakoram mountains, the drainage of which is northwards into Central Asia, the country consists of the valleys of the

Fig 138. Mahárája of Kashmír.

Chenáb, Jhelam, and Indus, that of the last amounting to three-fourths of the whole. There is a trifling area to the west of Jammu, which contains the head-waters of small streams which find their way into the Ráví.

**Divisions.**—The following broad divisions may be recognised:

1. Chenáb Valley (*a*) Plain and Kandí or Low Hills.
   (*b*) Uplands of Kishtwár and Bhadráwah.
2. Jhelam Valley (*a*) Vale of Kashmír with adjoining glens and hills.
   (*b*) Gorge below Báramúla and Kishnganga Valley.

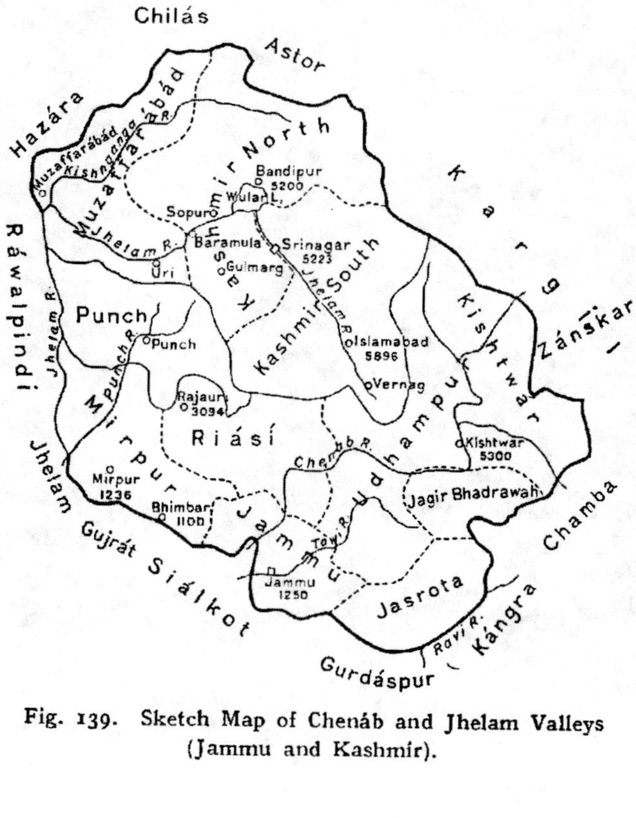


**Fig. 139. Sketch Map of Chenáb and Jhelam Valleys (Jammu and Kashmír).**

3. Indus Valley (*a*) Ladákh including Zánskar and Rupshu.
(*b*) Báltistán.
(*c*) Astor and Gilgit.

**Chenáb Valley.**—(*a*) *Plain and Kandí.* This tract extends from Mírpur on the Jhelam to Kathua near the Rávi and close to the head-works of the Upper Bárí Doáb Canal at Mádhopur. It is coterminous with the Panjáb districts of Jhelam, Gujrát, Siálkot, and Gurdáspur, and comprises four of the five districts of the Jammu Province, Mírpur, .Riásí, Jammu, and Jasrota, and a part of the fifth, Udhampur. The plain is moist and unhealthy. The rough country behind with a stony and thirsty red soil covered in its natural state with *garna* (Carissa spinarum), *sanatan* (Dodonaea viscosa), and *bhekar* (Adhatoda vasica) does not suffer in this respect. The chief crops of the Kandí are wheat, barley, and rape in the spring, and maize and *bájra* in the autumn, harvest. Behind the Kandí is a higher and better tract, including Naoshera, with wide valleys, in which maize replaces *bájra*.

(*b*) *Uplands.* The greater part of the Upper Chenáb Valley is occupied by Kishtwár and *Jagír* Bhadráwah. The rainfall is heavy and there is copious irrigation from *kuhls* (page 142), but elevation and rapid drainage make the climate healthy. In the upper parts snow and cold winds sometimes prevent the ripening of the crops. The poppy is grown in Kishtwár and Bhadráwah. Kishtwár is a part of the Udhampur district.

**Jhelam Valley.**—(*a*) *Vale of Kashmír with adjoining glens and mountains.* This first division of the Jhelam Valley extends from the source above Vernág to Báramúla, and embraces not only the Vale of Kashmír, over 80 miles long and from 20 to 25 miles in breadth, but the glens which drain into it and the mountains that surround it. It therefore includes cultivation of all sorts from rich irrigated rice fields to narrow plots terraced up mountain slopes on which buckwheat and the beardless Tibetan barley are grown. The administrative divisions are the *wazárat* or district of South Kashmír and the southern

Fig. 140. Takht i Sulimán in Winter.

part of North Kashmír. The central valley has an elevation of 6000 feet. It was undoubtedly once a lake bed. Shelving fan-shaped "*karewas*" spread out into it from the bases of the hills. The object of the Kashmírí is to raise as much rice as he possibly can on the alluvium of his valley and on the rich soil deposited on the banks of mountain streams. Manure and facilities for irrigation exist in abundance, and full use is made of them in the cultivation of the favourite crop. *Kangni* takes the place of rice in many fields if there is any deficiency of water. On reclaimed swamps near the Jhelam heavy crops of maize are raised. The tillage for wheat and barley is as careless as that for rice is careful. The cultivation of saffron (Crccus sativus) on *karewas* is famous, but the area is now limited, as the starving people ate up the bulbs in the great famine of 1877 and recovery is slow. Saffron is used as a pigment for the sectarian marks on the forehead of the orthodox Hindu and also as a condiment. The little floating vegetable gardens on the Dal lake are a very curious feature. The "*demb*" lands on the borders of the same lake are a rich field for the market gardener's art. He fences a bit of land with willows, and deposits on it weeds and mud from the lake bed. He is of the boatman or Hanz caste, whose reputation is by no means high, and can himself convey by water his vegetables and fruits to the Srínagar market. The production of fruit in Kashmír is very large, and the extension of the railway to Srínagar should lead to much improvement in the quality and in the extent of the trade. It may also improve the prospects of sericulture.

(*b*) *Jhelam Gorge and Valley of Kishnganga.* The Jhelam gorge below Báramúla is narrow and the cultivation is usually terraced. The Kishnganga joins the Jhelam near Muzaffarábád. The Muzaffarábád district includes the Jhelam gorge and the lower part of the valley of the Kishnganga. The upper part is in the Uttarmachhipura *tahsíl* of the district of North Kashmír.

**Indus Valley.**—(*a*) *Ladákh including Zánskar and Rupshu.* Some description of Ladákh and its scenery has already been given in Chapter II. It may be divided into Rupshu, Zánskar, and Ladákh proper with Leh as its centre. Rupshu in the south-east is a country of great brackish lakes in no part less than 13,500 feet above sea level. At such a height cultivation must be very difficult, but a little beardless Tibetan barley is raised. The scanty population consists mainly of nomad shepherds. In

Ladákh the people are divided into shepherds or *champas*, who roam over the Alpine pastures, and Ladákhís, who

Fig. 141. Ladákh Hills.

till laboriously every available patch of culturable land in the river valleys. Though both are Buddhists they rarely intermarry. Zánskar to the N.W. of Rupshu is drained by the river of the same name, which flows northwards to join the Indus below Leh. It forms part of the Kargil *tahsíl*. Zánskar is a bleak inaccessible region where the people and cattle remain indoors for six months of the year. Its breed of ponies is famous. In Ladákh proper cultivation ranges from 9000 to 15,000 feet. The sandy soil must be manured and irrigated, and is often refreshed by top-dressings of fresh earth from the hill sides. The crops are wheat and barley, rape, lucerne, peas and beans, in spring, and buckwheat, millets, and turnips, in autumn. There is a great lack of wood for building and for fuel, and the deficiency in the latter case has to be supplied by cow-dung cakes. Notwithstanding their hard life the people are cheerful and fairly well off, for polyandry has prevented overcrowding.

(*b*) *Báltistán.* In Báltistán, which lies to the N.W. of Ladákh, they are Muhammadans and there is much more pressure on the soil. They are a cheery race and very fond of polo. To support their families the men have to work as carriers on the roads to Leh and Gilgit. They tend the cattle in the pastures, keep the irrigation channels and the walls of the terraced fields in repair, and do the ploughing. The rest of the work of cultivation is left to the women. The climate is very severe and most of the rivers are frozen in winter. On the other hand near the Indus on the Skardo plain (7250 feet) and in the Rondu gorge further west, the heat is intense in July and August. The dreary treeless stony Deosai Plains on the road to Kashmír have an elevation of 13,000 feet. The cultivation and crops are much the same as in Ladákh. Excellent fruit is grown, and there is a considerable export of apricots. Gold washing is carried on with profit.

Ladákh and Báltistán together form the Ladákh *wazárat*, divided into the three *tahsíls* of Ladákh, Kargil, and Skardo.

(*c*) *Astor and Gilgit.*—Where the Gilgit road from Kashmír descends from the Burzil pass (13,500 feet) the country of Astor is reached. It is drained by the Astor river, which joins the Indus to the south of Bunjí. The bridge which crosses it at Ramghát is only 3800 feet above sea level. The village of Astor itself is at a height of 7853 feet. The cultivation is of the same description as that in Báltistán. The aspect of the country is bleak till the Indus is crossed, and Gilgit (4890 feet) is reached. Here there is a fertile well-watered oasis from which on every side great mountain peaks are visible. The lands are heavily manured. Rice, maize, millet, buckwheat, cotton, wheat, barley, rape, and lucerne are grown. There

Fig. 142. Zojilá Pass (page 12).

is a second and easier road to Gilgit from India over the Bábusar pass at the top of the Kágan Glen in Hazára. But the posts are sent by the Kashmír road. The Astorís and Gilgitís are a simple easy-going folk, and, like the Báltís, very fond of polo. A British Political Agent is stationed at Gilgit. He is responsible to the Government of India for the administration of Hunza, Nagar, and Yasín, and of the little republics in the neighbourhood of Chilás). Hunza and Nagar lie to the north of Gilgit near the junction of the Muztagh and Hindu Kush ranges, and Yasín far to the west about the upper waters of the Gilgit river.

In Astor and Gilgit also Guláb Singh's Dogras replaced the Sikh troops. But across the Indus Guláb Singh was never strong, and after 1852 that river was his boundary. He died in 1857, having proved himself a hard and unscrupulous, but a capable and successful ruler. His son, Randhír Singh, was a better man, but a worse king. A good Hindu, tolerant, and a friend of learning, he had not the force of character to control the corrupt official class, and the people suffered much in consequence. He was a loyal ally in the Mutiny. In 1860 his forces recovered Gilgit, a conquest which for years after was a fruitful source of suffering to his Cis-Indus subjects. The present Maháraja, Sir Pratáp Singh, G.C.S.I., succeeded in 1885. While he lived his brother, Rája Amar Singh, played a very important part in Kashmír affairs. From 1887 to 1905 the administration was managed by a small council, of which after 1891 the Maháraja was President and Rája Amar Singh Vice-President. It was abolished in 1905. There are now under the Maháraja a chief minister and ministers in charge of the home and revenue departments. Judicial business is controlled by the Judge of the High Court. Death sentences must be confirmed by the Maháraja. The highest executive officers are the governors of Jammu and Kashmír, and the *Wazírs Wazárat* of Ladákh and Gilgit. In Jammu and Kashmír each of the eight districts is in charge of a *Wazír Wazárat.* In connection with the land revenue settlement, forests, etc., the services of British officers have been lent to the State. The Government of India is represented at Srínagar by a Resident, and a political agent at Gilgit exercises a general supervision over the *Wazír Wazárat.*

During the reign of the present Mahárája great reforms have been effected. The construction of the Gilgit road has done away with the blood tax, which the conveyance of supplies to that remote post formerly involved. The land revenue settlement has largely substituted cash for kind payments and done away with many abuses. Official corruption and oppression have been scotched, but would speedily revive if vigilance were relaxed. The different peoples ruled by the Mahárája are easily governed if properly treated, and violent crime is rare.

*Note.* In the map appended to Dr Arthur Neve's *Thirty Years in Kashmír* the heights of Gasherbrum and Masherbrum (see page 21) are given respectively as 26,360 and 25,560 feet, and that of Hidden Peak, S.E. of Gasherbrum, as 26,470 feet. These with $K^2$ are the highest mountains round the Baltoro Glacier. Further east is the Siachen, "the greatest glacier in Asia," which feeds the Nubra river (page 36). N.E. of the Siachen is the Teram Kangrí mountain, the height of which does not probably exceed 25,000 feet. The actual height of the Nun Kun (page 12) is 23,447 feet. Dr Neve gives that of the Karakoram Pass as 18,110 feet, not 18,550 as stated on page 20.

# CHAPTER XXIX

## CITIES

**Delhi** (28.38 N., 77.13 E.).—Of imperial cities the most interesting are those which have felt the tragedies as well as enjoyed the glories of Empire. From this point of view Delhi, notwithstanding its small extent and modern foundation, may be grouped with Rome, Constantinople, and Paris. In the matter of size it is in the same class as Edinburgh. The present Delhi or Sháhjahánábád is a creation of the middle of the seventeenth century, and the oldest of the Delhis in the neighbourhood goes back only to the fourth century of our era. The latter endured for six or seven centuries. It was the capital of the Tunwar and Chauhán Rájas, and takes its second name of Rai Pithora's Kila' or Fort from the last Hindu King of Delhi, the famous Prithví Rája. The early Muhammadan kings occupied it and adorned it with splendid buildings. Firoz Sháh Tughlak's city of Firozábád occupied part of the present Delhi and the country lying immediately to the south of it. The other so-called towns Sirí, Tughlakábád, and Indarpat or Puráná Kila' (Old Fort) were fortified royal residences round which other dwelling-houses and shops sprang up.

The visitor to Delhi will be repaid if he can devote a week to the City and the neighbourhood. It is impossible here to give any adequate account of the objects of historic and architectural interest. No visitor should be without

Mr H. C. Fanshawe's *Delhi Past and Present*, a work of great interest. The value of the text is enhanced by good maps and excellent illustrations. In the Civil Station, which lies to the north of the City and east of the Ridge, is Ludlow Castle, from the roof of which General Wilson and his Staff watched the assault on 14th September, 1857, when Delhi was retaken. Ludlow Castle is now the Delhi Club. Between it and the northern rampart of the City, a defence against the Mahrattas built by British officers fifty years earlier, grim fighting took place on that historic day when the little British and Indian force, till then rather besieged than besiegers, was at last strong enough to attack. Here are the sites of the four batteries which breached that rampart, and here are the grave of John Nicholson and the statue recently erected in his honour (page 190). The Ridge to which the little army had clung obstinately from May to September in scorching heat and drenching rain, undismayed by repeated assaults and the ravages of cholera, starts about half-a-mile to the west of the Morí bastion, at the north-west corner of the city wall, and runs north by east to Wazírábád on an old bed of the Jamna. Ascending to the Flagstaff Tower one looks down to-day on the Circuit House and the site of the principal camps at the great *darbár* of 1911. Here was the old Cantonment and its parade ground, on which the main encampment of the British force stood in 1857. The position was strong, being defended by the ridge on the east and the Najafgarh Canal on the west. It is open to the south, where are the Savzí Mandí (Vegetable Market), now the site of factories, and the Roshanára Gardens. It was on this side that the mutineers made their most dangerous attacks. The road along the Ridge from the Flagstaff Tower passes the Chauburjí Mosque and Hindu Rao's house, which was the principal target of the City batteries and was gallantly held by Major Reid with his Sirmúr Gurkhas, the Guides, and the 60th Rifles. Beyond Hindu Rao's house is one of the stone pillars of Aṣoka, which Firoz Sháh Tughlak transported to Delhi. Still further south is the Mutiny Memorial. As one reads the tale of the losses of the different regiments one realizes in some measure the horrors and the heroism of which the Ridge was witness.

'In memory of the officers and soldiers, British and native, of the Delhi Field Force who were killed in action or died of wounds or disease between the 30th May and 20th September 1857.'

'This monument has been erected by the comrades who lament their loss and by the Govmt: they served so well.'

Fig. 143. Delhi Mutiny Monument.

**The City.**—When visiting the City from the Civil Lines it is well to follow the road, which passing the Kudsia Gardens leads straight to the Kashmír Gate, one of two places in India (the Lucknow Residency is the other) which must stir with grateful pride the heart of the most phlegmatic of Englishmen. The road from the Gate to the Fort and the Jama Masjid is rich in memories of the Mutiny. It has on its left S. James' Church, with memorial tablets within and outside the shot-riddled globe which once surmounted its dome. Further on are the obelisk to the telegraph officers who stuck to their posts on the fatal 11th of May, and on a gateway of the Old Magazine a record of the heroism of the nine devoted men, who blew it up, losing five of their number in the explosion. Passing under the railway bridge one comes out on the open space in front of Sháhjahán's palace fort, which was finished about 1648 A.D. To the beautiful buildings erected by his father Aurangzeb added the little Motí Masjid or Pearl Mosque. But he never lived at Delhi after 1682. The palace is therefore associated with the tragedies and squalor of the decline and fall of the Moghal Empire rather than with its glories. In 1739 it was robbed of the Kohinur and the Peacock throne by Nádir Shah, in 1788 it saw the descendants of Akbar tortured and the aged Emperor blinded by the hateful Ghulám Kádir, and on 16th May, 1857 the mutineers massacred fifty Christians captive within its walls. When viewing the public and private halls of audience, known as the Diwán i 'Ám and the Diwán i Kháss, it is however natural to think rather of scenes of splendour such as Bernier described when Aurangzeb sat in royal apparel on the Peacock throne with a king's ransom in the aigrette of his turban and the rope of pearls which hung from his neck. On such an occasion, the pillars of the Diwán i 'Ám were hung with gold brocades and the floors covered with rich silken carpets. Half the court outside was occupied by a magnificent tent and the arcade galleries surrounding it were decked with brocades and covered with costly carpets. The marble Diwán i Kháss with its lovely pillars decorated with gold and precious stones is surely the most splendid withdrawing room that a monarch ever possessed. There is nothing in the Moorish palace at Granada which can for a moment be compared with these two halls. For a description of them and of the

Fig. 144. Kashmír Gate.

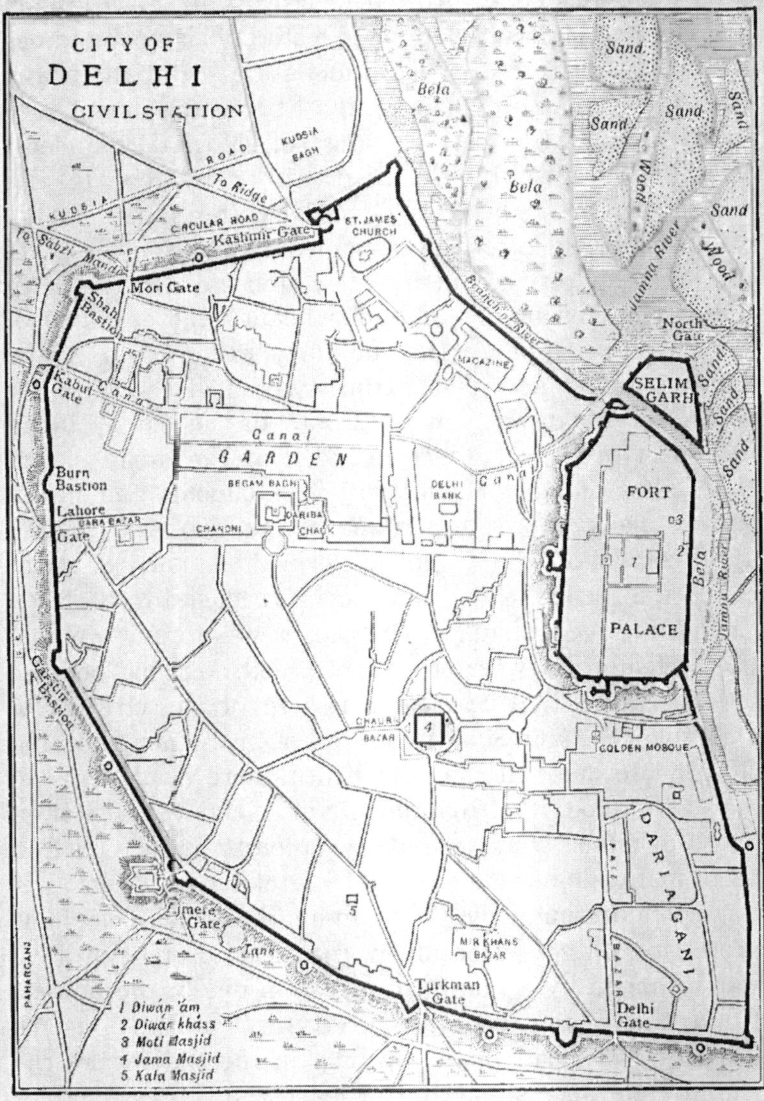


Fig. 145. Map of Delhi City.

other buildings in the Fort the reader must refer to Mr Fanshawe's book. In the Viceroyalty of Lord Curzon and since much has been done to restore their surroundings to some semblance of their former state. But the heavy British barracks occupied by the little garrison are very incongruous with the remains of Moghal grandeur. Leaving the Fort by the Southern or Delhi Gate and turning to the right one is faced by the Jama Masjid, another monument of the taste of Sháhjahán. The gateway and the lofty ascent into this House of God are very fine. The mosque in the regular beauty and grandeur of its lines, appealing to the sublimity rather than to the mystery of religion, is a fitting symbol of the faith for whose service it was raised. South of the Jama Masjid in a part of the city once included in Firozábád stands the Kalán or Kála Masjid with low cupolas and heavy square black pillars, a striking example of the sombre architecture of the Tughlak period. A narrow street called the Daríba leads from the Jama Masjid to the wide Chándní (Silver) Chauk. The Daríba was formerly closed by the Khúní Darwáza or Gate of Blood, so called because here occurred that terrible massacre of the citizens of Delhi which Nádir Shah witnessed from the neighbouring Golden Mosque. Besides its width there is nothing remarkable about the Chándní Chauk. But the visitor in quest of silver work, jewellery, or embroidery will find there many shopkeepers ready to cater for his wants. It was while passing down the Chándní Chauk in an elephant procession on 23rd December, 1912, that Lord Hardinge was wounded by a bomb thrown from one of the houses. From the Chauk one may pass through the Queen's Gardens and Road to the opening in the wall where the Kábul Gate once stood and so leave the City. A tablet in the vicinity marks the spot where John Nicholson fell.

When visiting the old Delhis it is a good plan to drive

again through the City and to leave it by the Delhi Gate. Humáyun's tomb, an early and simple, but striking, specimen of Moghal architecture, is reached at a distance of four miles along the Mathra road. Outside the City the road first leaves on the left side the ruined citadel of Firoz Sháh containing the second Aşoka pillar. North and south of this citadel the town of Firozábád once lay. It ended where the Puráná Kila' or Old Fort, the work of Sher Sháh and Humáyun, now stands, a conspicuous object from the road about three miles from Delhi. The red sandstone gateway very narrow in proportion to its height is a noble structure, and within the walls is Sher Sháh's mosque. The fort and mosque are the last important works of the second or Tughlak period. Hindus call the site of the Old Fort, Indarpat. If any part of Delhi has a claim to antiquity it is this, for it is alleged to be one of the five "pats" or towns over which the war celebrated in the Mahábhárata was waged. A recent cleaning of part of the interior of the fort brought to light bricks belonging to the Gupta period. From Humáyun's tomb a cross road leads to the Gurgáon road and the Kutb. But the visitor who has seen enough of buildings for the day may proceed further down the Mathra road and reach the headworks of the Agra Canal at Okhla by a side road. The view looking back to Delhi up the Jamna is fine.

**The Kutb Minár.**—Starting for the Kutb from Humáyun's tomb (page 207) the Dargáh of the great Chistí saint and political intriguer, Nizám ud dín Aulia, is passed on the left. He died in 1324 A.D. Just at the point where the cross road meets the Gurgáon road is the tomb of Safdar Jang, the second of the Nawáb Wazírs of Oudh. He died after the middle of the eighteenth century, and the building is wonderfully good considering that it is one of the latest important monuments of the Moghal period. Six miles to the south of Safdar Jang's tomb the entrance to the Kutb Minár enclosure is reached. The great Kuwwat ul Islám mosque of Kutbuddín Aibak (page 204) was constructed out of the materials of a Jain temple which stood on the site. Evidence of this is to be found in the imperfectly defaced sculptures on the pillars. An iron pillar nearly 24 feet in height dating back probably to the sixth century stands in the court. The splendid column known as the Kutb Minár (page 205), begun by Kutbuddín and completed by his successor Shams ud dín Altamsh, was the minaret of the mosque from which the *mu'azzin* called the faithful to prayer. The disappointment that may be felt when it is seen from a distance is impossible on a nearer view. Its height is now 238 feet, but it was formerly surmounted "by a majestic cupola of red granite." Close by is the Alai Darwaza, a magnificent gateway built by Alá ud dín Tughlak in 1310, about 90 years after the Minár was finished. Five miles east of the Kutb are the cyclopean ruins of Tughlakábád (page 206).

**Delhi past and present.**—The Delhi of Aurangzeb was as much a camp as a city. When the Emperor moved to Agra or Kashmír the town was emptied of a large part of its inhabitants. It contained one or two fine *bazárs*, and nobles and rich merchants and shopkeepers had good houses, set sometimes in pleasant gardens. But the crowds of servants and followers occupied mud huts, whose thatched roofs led to frequent and widespread fires. In that insanitary age these may have been blessings in disguise. "In Delhi," wrote Bernier, "there is no middle state. A man must either be of the highest rank or live miserably....For two or three who wear decent apparel there may always be reckoned seven or eight poor, ragged, and miserable beings." The ordinary street architecture of modern Delhi is mean enough, and posterity will not open an eyelid to look at the public buildings which its present rulers have erected in the city. But at least the common folk of Delhi are better housed, fed, and clad than ever before. It is now a clean well-managed town with a good water supply, and it has become an important railway centre and a thriving place of trade. Since 1881 the population has steadily increased from 173,393 to 232,837 in 1911. In 1911–12 the imports into Delhi City from places outside the Panjáb amounted to 9,172,302 maunds. There are some fifteen cotton ginning, spinning, and weaving mills, besides flour mills, iron foundries, two biscuit manufactories, and a brewery. The city is well supplied with hospitals including two for women only. Higher education has been fostered by S. Stephen's College in charge of the Cambridge Missionary brotherhood. The Hindu college has not been very successful. Delhi has had famous "hakíms," practising the Yúnáni or Arabic system of medicine, which is taught in a flourishing school known as the Madrasa i Tibbiya.

**Imperial Darbárs.**—In this generation the plain to the north of the Ridge has been the scene of three splendid *darbárs*. When on 1st January, 1877, Queen Victoria assumed the title of Empress of India (*Kaisar i Hind*) it seemed fitting that the proclamation of the fact to the princes and peoples of India should be made by Lord Lytton at the old seat of imperial power. On 1st January, 1903, Lord Curzon held a *darbár* on the same spot to proclaim the coronation of King Edward the VIIth. Both these splendid ceremonies were surpassed by the *darbár* of 12th December, 1911, when King George and Queen Mary were present in person, and the Emperor received the homage of the ruling chiefs, the great officials, and the leading men of the different provinces. The King and Queen entered Delhi on 7th December, and in the week that followed the craving of the Indian peoples for "*darshan*" or a sight of their sovereign was abundantly gratified. None who saw the spectacles of that historic week will ever forget them.

**New Imperial Capital.**—The turn of Fortune's Wheel has again made Delhi an imperial city. The transfer of the seat of government from Calcutta announced by the

Fig. 146. Darbár Medal.

King Emperor at the *darbár*, is now being carried out. The site will probably extend from Safdar Jang's tomb to a point lying to the west of Firoz Sháh's citadel.

**Lahore** (31.34 N., 74.21 E.). The capital of the Panjáb lies on the east bank of the Rávi, which once flowed close to the Fort, but has moved a mile or two to the west. In high floods the waters still spread over the lowlands between the Rávi and the Fort. Lahore lies nearly half-way between Delhi and Peshávar, being nearer to the latter than to the former.

**Early History.**—Practically we know nothing of its history till Mahmúd conquered the Panjáb and put a garrison in a fort at Lahore. Henceforth its history was intimately connected with Muhammadan rule in India. Whether north-western India was ruled from Ghazní or from Delhi, the chief provincial governor had his head-quarters at Lahore. In the best days of Moghal rule

Agra and Lahore were the two capitals of the Empire. Lahore lay on the route to Kábul and Kashmír, and it was essential both to the power and to the pleasures of the Emperors that it should be strongly held and united to Delhi and Agra by a Royal or *Bádsháhí* Road. The City and the Suburbs in the reign of Sháhjahán probably covered three or four times the area occupied by the town in the days of Sikh rule. All round the city are evidences of its former greatness in ruined walls and domes.

**The Civil Station.**—The Anárkalí gardens and the buildings near them mark the site of the first Civil Station. John Lawrence's house, now owned by the Rája of Punch, is beyond the Chauburjí on the Multán Road. The Civil Lines have stretched far to the south-east in the direction of the Cantonment, which till lately took its name from the tomb of Mian Mír, Jahangír's spiritual master. The soil is poor and arid. Formerly the roads were lined with dusty tamarisks. But of late better trees have been planted, and the Mall is now quite a fine thoroughfare. The Lawrence Hall Gardens and the grounds of Government House show what can be done to produce beauty out of a bad soil when there is no lack of water. There is little to praise in the architecture or statuary of modern Lahore. The marble canopy over Queen Victoria's statue is however a good piece of work. Of the two cathedrals the Roman Catholic is the better building. The Montgomery Hall with the smaller Lawrence Hall attached, a fine structure in a good position in the public gardens, is the centre of European social life in Lahore. Government House is close by, on the opposite side of the Mall. Its core, now a unique and beautiful dining-room with domed roof and modern oriental decoration, is the tomb of Muhammad Kásim Khán, a cousin of Akbar. Jamadár Khushál Singh, a well-known man in Ranjít Singh's reign, built a house round the tomb. After annexation, Henry

Lawrence occupied it for a time, and Sir Robert Montgomery adopted it as Government House. It is now much transformed. Beyond Government House on the road to the Cantonment are the Club and the Panjáb Chiefs' College, the only successful attempt in Lahore to adapt oriental design to modern conditions.

**The Indian City.**—In its streets and *bazárs* Lahore is a truly eastern city, and far more interesting than Delhi, so far as private buildings are concerned. In public

Fig. 147 Street in Lahore.

edifices it possesses some fine examples of Moghal architecture. Every visitor should drive through the town to the Fort past Wazír Khán's mosque. Under British rule the height of the city wall has been reduced by one-half and the moat filled in and converted into a garden. Wazír Khán's mosque founded in 1634 by a Panjábí minister of Sháhjahán, is a noble building profusely adorned with glazed tiles and painted panels. The Golden Mosque was constructed 120 years later about the same time as Safdar Jang's tomb at Delhi. The palace fort, built originally by Akbar, contains also the work of his three successors. The Shísh Mahal or Hall of Mirrors, which witnessed the cession of the Panjáb to the Queen of England, was begun by Sháhjahán and finished by Aurangzeb. The armoury contains a curious collection of weapons. The Bádsháhí Mosque opposite with its beautiful marble domes and four lofty minarets of red sandstone was founded in 1673 in the reign of Aurangzeb. The cupolas were so shaken by an earthquake in 1840 that they had to be removed. Mahárája Ranjít Singh used the mosque as a magazine. In the space between it and the Fort he laid out the pretty orange garden known as the Huzúrí Bágh and set in it the marble *báradarí* which still adorns it. Close by are his own tomb and that of Arjan Dás, the fifth Guru.

**Buildings outside Lahore.**—The best example of Moghal architecture is not at Lahore itself, but at Shahdara across the Rávi. Here in a fine garden is the Mausoleum of Jahángír with its noble front and four splendid towers. It enshrines an exquisite sarcophagus, which was probably once in accordance with the Emperor's wish open to the sunlight and the showers. Near by are the remains of the tombs of his beautiful and imperious consort, Nur Jahán, and of her brother Asaf Khán, father of the lady of the Táj. Another building associated with Jahángír is Anárkali's tomb beside the Civil Secretariat. The white marble sarcophagus is a beautiful piece of work placed now in most inappropriate surroundings. The tomb was reared by the Emperor to commemorate the unhappy object of his youthful love. Half-a-mile off on the Multán road is the Chauburjí, once the gateway of the Garden of Zebunnissa, a learned daughter of Aurangzeb. The garden has disappeared, but the gateway, decorated with

Fig. 148. Sháhdara.

blue and green tiles, though partially ruined, is still a beautiful object. On the other side of Lahore on the road to Amritsar are the Shalimár Gardens laid out by Sháhjahán for the ladies of his court. When the paved channels are full and the fountains are playing, and the lights of earthen lamps are reflected in the water, Shalimár is still a pleasant resort.

The Museum in Anárkalí contains much of interest to Indians and Europeans. The "house of wonders" is very popular with the former. It includes a very valuable collection of Buddhist sculptures. Opposite the museum is the famous Zamzama gun (page 187).

**Growth of Lahore.** As the headquarters of an important Government and of a great railway system

Lahore has prospered. Owing to the influx of workers the population has risen rapidly from 157,287 in 1881 to 228,687 in 1911. The railway alone affords support to 30,000 people, of whom 8000 are employed in the workshops.

**Amritsar** (31.38 N., 74.53 E.) is a modern town founded in the last quarter of the sixteenth century by the fourth Guru, Rám Dás, on a site granted to him by Akbar. Here he dug the Amrita Saras or Pool of Immortality, leaving a small platform in the middle as the site of that Har Mandar, which rebuilt is to-day, under the name of the Darbár Sáhib, the centre of Sikh devotion. The fifth Guru, Arjan Dás, completed the Har Mandar. Early in the eighteenth century Amritsar became without any rival the Mecca of the Sikhs, who had now assumed an attitude of warlike resistance to their Muhammadan rulers. Once and again they were driven out, but after the victory at Sirhind in 1763 they established themselves securely in Amritsar, and rebuilt the temple which Ahmad Sháh had burned. Ranjít Singh covered the Darbár Sáhib with a copper gilt roof, whence Englishmen commonly call it the Golden Temple. He laid out the Rám Bágh, still a beautiful garden, and constructed the strong fort of Govindgarh outside the walls.

**Trade and Manufactures.**—Amritsar lies in a hollow close to a branch of the Upper Bárí Doáb Canal. Water-logging is a great evil and accounts for the terrible epidemics of fever, which have occurred from time to time. The population has fluctuated violently, and at the last census was 152,756, or little larger than in 1881. Long before annexation the shawl industry was famous. The caprice of fashion a good many years ago decreed its ruin, but carpet weaving, for which Amritsar is still famous, fortunately did something to fill the gap. Amritsar has also been an entrepôt of trade with other Asiatic countries.

It has imported raw silk from Bokhára, and later from China, and woven it into cloth. It has dealt in China tea, but that is a decreasing trade, in opium from Afghánistán, and in *charas* from Central Asia. There is a considerable export of foreign piece goods to Kashmír and the N. W. F. Province.

**Multán** (30.1 N., 71.3 E.), though now the smallest of the four great towns of the Panjáb, is probably the most ancient. It is very doubtful whether it is the fortress of the Malloi, in storming which Alexander was wounded. But when Hiuen Tsang visited it in 741 A.D. it was a well-known place with a famous temple of the Sun God. Muhammad Kásim conquered it in 712 A.D. (page 166). It was not till the savage Karmatian heretics seized Multán towards the end of the tenth century that the temple, which stood in the fort, was destroyed. It was afterwards rebuilt, but was finally demolished by order of Aurangzeb, who set up in its place a mosque. Under the Moghals Multán was an important town, through which the trade with Persia passed. Its later history has already been noticed (pages 183 and 186).

**The Fort** contains the celebrated Prahládpurí temple, much damaged during the siege in 1848, but since rebuilt. Its proximity to the tomb of Baháwal Hakk, a very holy place in the eyes of the Muhammadans of the S.W. Panjáb and Sindh, has at times been a cause of anxiety to the authorities. Baháwal Hakk and Bába Faríd, the two great saints of the S.W. Panjáb, were contemporaries and friends. They flourished in the thirteenth century, and it probably would be true to ascribe largely to their influence the conversion of the south-west Panjáb to Islám, which was so complete and of which we know so little. The tomb of Baháwal Hakk was much injured during the siege, but afterwards repaired. Outside is a small monument marking the resting place of the brave old Nawáb Muzaffar

Khán. Another conspicuous object is the tomb of Rukn ud dín 'Alam, grandson of Baháwal Hakk. An obelisk in the fort commemorates the deaths of the two British officers who were murdered on the outbreak of the revolt. A simpler epitaph would have befitted men who died in the execution of their duty.

**Trade and Manufactures.**—Though heat and dust make the climate of Multán trying, it is a very healthy place. The population rose steadily from 68,674 in 1881 to 99,243 in 1911. The chief local industries are silk and cotton weaving and the making of shoes. Multán has also some reputation for carpets, glazed pottery and enamel, and of late for tin boxes. A special feature of its commerce is the exchange of piece goods, shoes, and sugar for the raw silk, fruits, spices, and drugs brought in by Afghán traders. The Civil Lines lie to the south of the city and connect it with the Cantonment, which is an important military station.

**Pesháwar** (34.1 N., 71.35 E.) is 276 miles from Lahore and 190 from Kábul. There is little doubt that the old name was Purushapura, the town of Purusha, though Abu Rihan (Albiruni), a famous Arab geographer, who lived in the early part of the eleventh century, calls it Parsháwar, which Akbar corrupted into Pesháwar, or the frontier fort. As the capital of King Kanishka it was in the second century of the Christian era a great centre of Buddhism (page 164). Its possession of Buddha's alms bowl and of yet more precious relics of the Master deposited by Kanishka in a great *stupa* (page 203) made it the first place to be visited by the Chinese pilgrims who came to India between 400 and 630 A.D. Hiuen Tsang tells us the town covered 40 li or 6¾ miles. Its position on the road to Kábul made it a place of importance under the Moghal Empire. On its decline Pesháwar became part of the dominions of the Duráni rulers of

Kábul, and finally fell into the hands of Ranjít Singh. His Italian general Avitabile ruled it with an iron rod. In 1901 it became the capital of the new N. W. F. Province.

**The Town** lies near the Bára stream in a canal-irrigated tract. On the north-west it is commanded by the Bála Hissár, a fort outside the walls. The suburbs with famous fruit gardens are on the south side, and the military and civil stations to the west. The people to be seen in the *bazárs* of Pesháwar are more interesting than any of its buildings. The Gor Khatrí, part of which is now the *tahsíl*, from which a bird's-eye view of the town can be obtained, was successively the site of a Buddhist monastery, a Hindu temple, a rest-house built by Jahángír's Queen, Nur Jahán, and the residence of Avitabile. The most noteworthy Muhammadan building is Muhabbat Khán's mosque. Avitabile used to hang people from its minarets. The Hindu merchants live in the quarter known as Andar Shahr, the scene of destructive fires in 1898 and 1913. Pesháwar is now a well-drained town with a good water supply. It is an entrepôt of trade with Kábul and Bokhára. From the former come raw silk and fruit, and from the latter gold and silver thread and lace *en route* to Kashmír. The Kábulí and Bokháran traders carry back silk cloth, cotton piece goods, sugar, tea, salt, and Kashmír shawls.

**Simla** (31.6 N., 77.1 E.) lies on a spur of the Central Himálaya at a mean height exceeding 7000 feet. A fine hill, Jakko, rising 1000 feet higher, and clothed with *deodár*, oak, and rhododendron, occupies the east of the station and many of the houses are on its slopes. The other heights are Prospect Hill and Observatory Hill in the western part of the ridge. Viceregal Lodge is a conspicuous object on the latter, and below, between it and the Annandale race-course, is a fine glen, where the visitor in April from the dry and dusty plains can gather yellow primroses (Primula floribunda) from the dripping rocks. The beautiful Elysium Hill is on a small spur

Fig. 149. Trans-border traders in Pesháwar.

running northwards from the main ridge. Simla is 58 miles by cart road from Kálka, at the foot of the hills, and somewhat further by the narrow gauge railway.

**History.**—Part of the site was retained at the close of the Gurkha war in 1816, and the first English house, a wooden cottage with a thatched roof, was built three years later. The first Governor General to spend the summer in Simla was Lord Amherst in 1827. After the annexation of the Panjáb in 1849 Lord Dalhousie went there every year, and from 1864 Simla may be said to have become the summer capital of India. It became the summer headquarters of the Panjáb Government twelve years later. The thirty houses of 1830 have now increased to about 2000. Six miles distant on the beautiful Mahásu Ridge the Viceroy has a "Retreat," and on the same ridge and below it at Mashobra there are a number of European houses. There are excellent hotels in Simla, and the cold weather tourist can pay it a very pleasant visit, provided he avoids the months of January and February.

**Srínagar** (34.5 N., 74.5 E.), the summer capital of the Mahárája of Kashmír, is beautifully situated on both banks of the river Jhelam at a level of 5250 feet above the sea. To the north are the Hariparvat or Hill of Vishnu with a rampart built by Akbar and the beautiful Dal lake. Every visitor must be rowed up its still waters to the Násím Bágh, a grove of plane (*chenâr*) trees, laid out originally in the reign of the same Emperor. Between the lake and the town is the Munshí Bágh, in and near which are the houses of Europeans including the Residency. The splendid plane trees beside the river bank, to which house boats are moored, and the beautiful gardens attached to some of the houses, make this a very charming quarter. The Takht i Sulimán to the west of Srínagar is crowned by a little temple, whose lower walls are of great age. The town itself is intersected by evil-smelling canals and consists in the main of a jumble of wooden houses with thatched roofs. Sanitary abominations have been cleansed from time to time by great fires and punished

Fig. 150 Mosque of the Sháh Hamadán.

by severe outbreaks of cholera. The larger part of the existing city is on the left side. The visitor may be content to view the parts of the town to be seen as he is rowed down the broad waterway from the Munshí Bágh passing under picturesque wooden bridges, and beside temples with shining metal roofs and the beautiful mosque of Sháh Hamadán. On the left bank below the first bridge is the Shergarhí with the Mahárája's houses and the Government Offices. Opposite is a fine *ghát* or bathing place with stone steps. Between the third and fourth bridges on the right bank is Sháh Hamadán's mosque, a carved cedar house with Buddhist features, totally unlike the ordinary Indian mosque. The stone mosque close by on the opposite side, built by Mir Jahán, was seemingly rejected by Muhammadans as founded by a woman, and is now a State granary. The Jama Masjid is on the north side, but not on the river bank. The tomb of the great king, Zain ul Ábidín, is below the fourth bridge, which bears his name. In the same quarter are the storehouses of the dealers in carpets and art wares and the Mission School. The last should be visited by anyone who wishes to see what a manly education can make of material in some respects unpromising.

# CHAPTER XXX

## OTHER PLACES OF NOTE

### I. PANJÁB.

### (a) *Ambála Division.*

**Ambála,** 30·2 N.–76·4 E. Population 80,131, of which 54,223 in Cantonments. A creation of British rule. It became the headquarters of the Political Agent for the Cis-Sutlej States in 1823, and the Cantonment was established in 1843. The Native City and the Civil Lines lie some miles to the N.W. of the Cantonment. Headquarters of district and division.

**Bhiwání (Hissár),** 28·5 N.–76·8 E. Headquarters of *tahsíl* in Hissár. Population 31,100. On Rewárí—Ferozepore branch of Rájputána—Málwa Railway. Has a brisk trade with Rájputána.

**Hánsí (Hissár),** 29·7 N.–75·6 E. Headquarters of *tahsíl.* Population 14,576. A very ancient town. In centre of canal tract of Hissár, and a local centre of the cotton trade.

**Hissár,** 29·1 N.–75·4 E. Headquarters of district. Population 17,162. Founded by the Emperor Firoz Sháh Tughlak, who supplied it with water by a canal taken from the Jamna. This was the origin of the present Western Jamna Canal. Is now a place of small importance.

**Jagádhrí (Ambála),** 30·1 N.–77·2 E. Headquarters of *tahsíl.* Population 12,045. Connected with the N.W. Railway by a light railway. The iron and brass ware of Jagádhrí are well known.

**Kaithal (Karnál),** 29·5 N.–76·2 E. Headquarters of subdivision and *tahsíl.* Population 12,912. A town of great antiquity. Kaithal is a corruption of Kapisthala—the monkey town, a name still appropriate. Timúr halted here on his march to Delhi. Was the headquarters of the Bhais of Kaithal, who held high rank among the Cis-Sutlej Sikh chiefs. Kaithal lapsed in 1843.

**Karnál**, 29·4 N.–76·6 E. Headquarters of district. Population 21,961. On Delhi—Kálka Railway. Till the Western Jamna Canal was realigned it was most unhealthy, and the Cantonment was given up in 1841 on this account. The health of the town is still unsatisfactory. Trade unimportant.

**Kasaulí (Ambála)**, 30·5 N.–76·6 E. Small hill station overlooking Kálka. Height 6000 feet. The Pasteur Institute for the treatment of rabies is at Kasaulí, and the Lawrence Military School at Sanáwar, three miles off.

**Pánipat (Karnál)**, 29·2 N.–76·6 E. Headquarters of *tahsíl*. Population 26,342. On Delhi—Kálka Railway. An important place in Hindu and Muhammadan times (pages 172 and 179). Local manufactures, brass vessels, cutlery, and glass.

**Pihowa (Karnál)**, 29·6 N.–76·3 E. A very sacred place on the holy stream Sarustí.

**Rewárí (Gurgáon)**, 28·1 N.–76·4 E. Headquarters of *tahsíl*. Population 24,780. Junction of main line and Rewárí—Bhatinda branch of Rájputána—Málwa Railway. Trade in grain and sugar with Rájputána.

**Rúpar (Ambála)**, 30·6 N.–76·3 E. Headquarters of subdivision and *tahsíl*. Population 6935. Exchange market for products of Hills and Plains. Headworks of Sirhind Canal are at Rúpar.

**Sirsa (Hissár)**, 29·3 N.–75·2 E. Headquarters of subdivision and *tahsíl*. Population 14,629. Sirsa or Sarsútí was an important place in Muhammadan times. Deserted in the great famine of 1783 it was refounded in 1838. On the Rewárí—Bhatinda Branch of the Rájputána—Málwa Railway. Has a brisk trade with Rájputána.

**Thanesar (Karnál)**, 29·6 N.–76·5 E. See pages 165 and 168. Noted place of pilgrimage. Headquarters of a *tahsíl*. Population 4719. The old Hindu temples were utterly destroyed apparently when Thanesar was sacked by Mahmúd in 1014. There is a fine tomb of a Muhammadan Saint, Shekḥ Chillí.

## (*b*) *Jalandhar Division.*

**Aliwál**, 30·6 N.–75·4 E. Scene of Sir Harry Smith's victory over the Sikhs on 28th January, 1846.

**Dharmsála (Kángra)**, 32·1 N.–76·1 E. Headquarters of district. On a spur of the Dhauladhár Range. A Gurkha regiment is stationed here. The highest part of Dharmsála is over 7000 feet, and the scenery is very fine, but the place is spoiled as a hill station by the excessive rainfall, which averages over 120 inches. In the earthquake of 1905, 1625 persons, including 25 Europeans, perished.

**Fázilka (Ferozepore)**, 30·3 N.–74·3 E. Headquarters of subdivision and *tahsíl*. Population 10,985. Terminus of Fázilka extension of Rájputána—Málwa Railway, and connected with Ludhiána by a line which joins the Southern Panjáb Railway at Macleodganj. A grain mart.

**Ferozepore**, 30·6 N.–74·4 E. Headquarters of district. Population 50,836 including 26,158 in Cantonment. (See page 245.)

**Ferozesháh (Ferozepore)**, 30·5 N.–74·5 E. The real name is Pherushahr. Sir Hugh Gough defeated the Sikhs here after two days' hard fighting on Dec. 21–22, 1845.

**Jalandhar**, 31·2 N.–75·3 E. Headquarters of district. Population 69,318, including 13,964 in Cantonment. The Cantonment lies four miles to the S.E. of the native town and three miles from the Civil Lines. (See page 241.)

**Jawála Mukhí (Kángra)**, 31·5 N.–76·2 E. Celebrated place of Hindu pilgrimage with a famous temple of the goddess Jawálamukhí, built over some jets of combustible gas.

**Kángra**, 30·5 N.–76·2 E. Headquarters of *tahsíl*. Ancient name Nagarkot. The celebrated temple and the fort of the Katoch kings of Kángra were destroyed in the earthquake of 1905. (See pages 168, 171, 183.)

**Ludhiána**, 30·6 N.–75·5 E. Headquarters of district. Population 44,170. The manufacture of *pashmína* shawls was introduced in 1833 by Kashmírís. Ludhiána is well known for its cotton fabrics and turbans (p. 152).

**Mudkí (Ferozepore)**, 30·5 N.–74·5 E. The opening battle of the 1st Sikh War was fought here on 18th December, 1845.

## (c) *Lahore Division.*

**Batála (Gurdáspur)**, 30·5 N.–75·1 E. Headquarters of *tahsíl*. Population 26,430. Chief town in Gurdáspur district on the Amritsar—Pathánkot Railway. Cotton, silk, leathern goods, and soap are manufactured, and there is a large trade in grain and sugar. The Baring Anglo-Vernacular High School for Christian boys is a well-known institution.

**Dalhousie** (Gurdáspur), 33·3 N.–75·6 E. A well-known hill station at height of 7687 feet, 51 miles N.W. of Pathánkot, from which it is reached by tonga. The Commissioner of Lahore and the Deputy Commissioner of Gurdáspur spend part of the hot weather at Dalhousie. It is a very pretty and healthy place, with the fine Kálatop Forest in Chamba close by, and is deservedly popular as a summer resort.

**Gujránwála**, 32·9 N.–74·1 E. Headquarters of district. Population 29,472. An active trade centre. Ranjít Singh was born, and the tomb of his father, Mahán Singh is, at Gujránwála.

**Kasúr** (**Lahore**), 31·8 N.–74·3 E. Headquarters of *tahsíl* in Lahore. Population 24,783. Between Raiwind and Ferozepore on N.W. Railway, and has direct railway communication with Amritsar. A very ancient place and now an active local trade centre.

**Nankána-Sáhib** (**Gujránwala**), 31·6 N.–73·8 E. In south of Gujránwála district on Chichoki—Shorkot Railway. Venerated by Sikhs as the early home of Bába Nának.

**Siálkot**, 32·3 N.–74·3 E. Headquarters of district. Population 64,869, of which 16,274 in Cantonment. A very old place connected with the legendary history of Raja Sáliváhan and his two sons Púran and Rája Rasálu. (See also page 165.) The Cantonment is about a mile and a half from the town. Siálkot is an active trade centre. Its hand-made paper was once well known, but the demand has declined. Tents, tin boxes, cricket and tennis bats, and hockey sticks, are manufactured.

**Tarn Táran** (Amritsar), 31·3 N.–74·6 E. Headquarters of *tahsíl*. Population 4260. On Amritsar—Kasúr Railway. The tank is said to have been dug by Guru Arjan and it and the temple beside it are held in great reverence by the Sikhs. The water is supposed to cure leprosy. The leper asylum at Tarn Táran in charge of the Rev. E. Guilford of the Church Missionary Society is an admirable institution. Clay figures of this popular missionary can be bought in the *bazár*.

### (*d*) *Ráwalpindí Division.*

**Attock** (**Atak**), 32·5 N.–72·1 E. The fort was built by Akbar to protect the passage of the Indus. In the river gorge below is a whirlpool between two jutting slate rocks, called Kamália and Jamália after two heretics who were flung into the river in

Akbar's reign. The bridge which carries the railway across the Indus still makes Attock a position of military importance. Population 630.

**Bhera** (**Sháhpur**), 32·3 N.–72·6 E. Headquarters of *tahsíl.* Population 15,202. A very ancient town which was sacked by Mahmúd and two centuries later by Chingiz Khán. Has an active trade. The wood-carvers of Bhera are skilful workmen. Woollen felts are manufactured.

**Chilianwála** (**Chelianwála**) (**Gujrát**), 32·7 N.–73·6 E. Famous battlefield (page 187).

**Gujrát**, 32·3 N.–74·5 E. Headquarters of district. Population 19,090. An old place, famous in recent history for the great battle on 22 February, 1849 (page 187). Has a brisk local trade.

**Hasn Abdál** (**Attock**), 33·5 N.–72·4 E. On N.W. Railway. Shrine of Bába Walí Kandahárí on hill above village. Below is the Sikh shrine of the Panja Sáhib, the rock in which bears the imprint of Bába Nának's five fingers (*panja*).

**Jhelam**, 32·6 N.–73·5 E. Headquarters of district and an important cantonment. Population 19,678, of which 7380 in cantonment. Has only become a place of any importance under British rule. Is an important depot for Kashmír timber trade.

**Kálabágh** (**Mianwálí**), 32·6 N.–71 3 E. Population 6654. Picturesquely situated below hills which are remarkable for the fantastic shapes assumed by salt exposed on the surface. The Kálabágh salt is in favour from its great purity. The Malik of Kálabágh is the leading man in the Awán tribe.

**Katás** (**Jhelam**), 32·4 N.–72·6 E. A sacred pool in the Salt Range and a place of Hindu pilgrimage. The tears of Şiva weeping for the loss of his wife Satí formed the Katáksha pool in the Salt Range and Pushkar at Ajmer.

**Khewra** (**Jhelam**), 32·4 N.–73·3 E. In Salt Range five and a half miles N.E. of Pinddádankhán. The famous Mayo Salt Mine is here.

**Malot** (**Jhelam**), 32·4 N.–72·5 E. Nine miles W. of Katás (see above). Fort and temple on a spur of the Salt Range. Temple in early Kashmír style (*Archaeological Survey Reports*, Vol. v. pp. 85–90).

**Mankiála** (**Manikyála**) (**Ráwalpindí**), 33·3 N.–74·2 E. A little village close to which are the remains of a great Buddhist *stúpa* and of a number of monasteries (page 202).

**Murree** (**Marrí**) (**Ráwalpindí**), 33·5 N.–73·2 E. Hill Station near Kashmír road on a spur of the Himálaya—height 7517 feet—39 miles from Ráwalpindí, from which visitors are conveyed by tonga. The views from Murree are magnificent and the neighbourhood of the Hazára Galís is an attraction. But the climate is not really bracing. The summer headquarters of the Northern Army are at Murree, and before 1876 the Panjáb Government spent the hot weather there. The Commissioner and Deputy Commissioner of Ráwalpindí take their work there for several months.

**Murtí** (Jhelam), 32·4 N.–72·6 E. In Gandhála valley on bank of Katás stream. Remains of a Buddhist *stúpa* and of a Jain temple. (*Archaeological Survey Reports*, Vol. II. pp. 88 and 90.)

**Ráwalpindí,** 33·4 N.–73·7 E. Headquarters of district and division, and the most important cantonment in Northern India. Population 86,483, of which 39,841 in Cantonment. It owes its importance entirely to British rule. Large carrying trade with Kashmír. Contains the N.W. Railway Locomotive and Carriage works and several private factories, also a branch of the Murree brewery. There is an important arsenal. The Park, left fortunately mainly in its natural state, is an attractive feature of the cantonment.

**Rohtás** (Jhelam), 32·6 N.–73·5 E. Ten miles N.W. of Jhelam on the far side of the gorge where the Kahá torrent breaks through a spur of the Tilla Range. Fine remains of a very large fort built by the Emperor Sher Sháh Surí.

**Sakesar** (Sháhpur), 31·3 N.–71·6 E. Highest point of Salt Range, 5010 feet above sea level. The Deputy Commissioners of Sháhpur, Mianwálí, and Attock spend part of the hot weather at Sakesar.

**Sháhdherí** (Ráwalpindí), 33·2 N.–72·5 E. On the Hazára border and near the Margalla Pass. Site of the famous city of Táxila (Takshasilá). See pages 161, 165, and 204. Excavation is now being carried out with interesting results.

**Táxila.** See Sháhdherí.

### (*e*) *Multán Division.*

**Chiniot** (Jhang), 31·4 N.–73·0 E. Headquarters of *tahsíl*. Population 14,085. A very old town near the left bank of the Chenáb. Famous for brasswork and wood-carving. The Muhammadan Khoja traders have large business connections with Calcutta, Bombay, and Karáchí. Fine mosque of the time of Sháhjahán.

**Kamália (Lyallpur),** 30·4 N.–72·4 E. Population 8237. An old town. Cotton printing with hand blocks is a local industry. The town should now prosper as it is a station on the Chichoki—Shorkot Road Railway and irrigation from the Lower Chenáb Canal has reached its neighbourhood.

**Lyallpur,** 31·3 N.–73·9 E. Fine new Colony town. Headquarters of district. Population 19,578. Large wheat trade with Karáchí, and has a number of cotton ginning and pressing factories.

**Montgomery,** 30·4 N.–73·8 E. Headquarters of district. Population 8129. May become a place of some importance with the opening of the Lower Bárí Doáb Canal. Hitherto one of the hottest and dreariest stations in the Panjáb, but healthy.

**Pákpattan,** 30·2 N.–73·2 E. Headquarters of *tahsíl*. Population 7912. On Sutlej Valley Railway. Anciently known as Ajodhan and was a place of importance. Contains shrine of the great Saint Faríd ul Hakk wa ud Dín Shakarganj (1173–1265). Visited by Timúr in 1398. There is a great annual festival attracting crowds of pilgrims, who come even from Afghánistán. There is great competition to win eternal bliss by getting first through the gate at the entrance to the shrine.

## II. Panjáb Native States.

**Baháwalpur,** 29·2 N.–71·5 E. Capital of State on N.W. Railway 65 miles south of Multán. Population 18,414. There is a large palace built by Nawáb Muhammad Sadík Muhammad Khán IV in 1882.

**Barnála (Patiála),** 32·2 N.–75·4 E. Headquarters of Anahadgarh Nizámat on Rájpura—Bhatinda branch of N.W. Railway. Population 5341. For the famous battle see page 179.

**Bhatinda (Patiála),** 30·1 N.–75·0 E. Also called Govindgarh. Old names are Vikramagarh and Bhatrinda. Historically a place of great interest (page 167). Fell into decay in later Muhammadan times. Is now a great railway junction and a flourishing grain mart. The large fort is a conspicuous object for many miles round. Population 15,037.

**Brahmaur,** 32·3 N.–76·4 E. The old capital of Chamba, now a small village. Has three old temples. One of Lakshana Deví has an inscription of Meru Varma, who ruled Chamba in the seventh century.

**Chamba**, 32·3 N.–76·1 E. Capital of State picturesquely situated on a plateau above right bank of Rávi. Population 5523. The white palace is a conspicuous object. There is an excellent hospital and an interesting museum. The group of temples near the palace is noteworthy (page 201). That of Lakshmí Naráyan perhaps dates from the tenth century. The Rávi is spanned at Chamba by a fine bridge.

**Chíní** (Bashahr), 31·3 N.–78·2 E. Headquarters of Kanáwar near the right bank of Sutlej. Elevation 9085 feet. Was a favourite residence of Lord Dalhousie. There is a Moravian Mission Station at Chíní.

**Kapúrthala**, 31·2 N.–75·2 E. Capital of State. Contains Mahárája's palace. Population 16,367.

**Malerkotla**, 30·3 N.–75·6 E. Capital of State. Population 23,880.

**Mandí**, 31·4 N.–76·6 E. Capital of State. Population 7896. On the Biás, 131 miles from Pathánkot, with which it is connected by the Pathánkot—Palampur—Baijnáth road. There is a fine iron bridge spanning the Biás. It is a mart for trade with Ladákh and Yárkand.

**Nábha**, 30·2 N.–76·1 E. Capital of State. Population 13,620, as compared with 18,468 in 1901. Founded in 1755 by Hamír Singh (page 277). Since irrigation from the Sirhind Canal has been introduced the environs have become waterlogged and the town is therefore unhealthy.

**Náhan**, 30·3 N.–77·2 E. Capital of Sirmúr State. Elevation 3207 feet. Population 6341. There is a good iron foundry at Náhan.

**Patiála**, 30·2 N.–76·3 E. Capital of State. Population 46,974. On Rájpura—Bhatinda Branch of N.W. Railway. Contains fine gardens and modern buildings. The old palace is in the centre of the town. Patiála is a busy mart for local trade.

**Pattan Munára** (**Baháwalpur**), 28·1 N.–70·2 E. There are the ruins here of a large city and of a Buddhist monastery. They are situated in the south of the State five miles east of Rahím Yár Khán Station.

**Sangrúr** (Jínd), 30·1 N.–75·6 E. Became the capital of Jínd State in 1827. Population 9041. On Ludhiána—Dhurí—Jakhal Railway.

**Sirhind** (Patiála), 30·4 N.–76·3 E. Properly Sahrind. On N.W. Railway. Population 3843. The idea that the name is

Sir-Hind = head of India is a mistake. An old town of great importance in Muhammadan period (pages 177 and 180). The ruins extend for several miles. There are two fine tombs known as those of the Master and his Disciple dating probably from the fourteenth century.

**Suí Vehar** (**Baháwalpur**), 29·2 N.–71·3 E. Six miles from Samasata. Site of a ruined Buddhist *stúpa*. An inscription found at Suí Vehár belongs to the reign of Kanishka (page 164).

**Uch** (**Baháwalpur**), 29·1 N.–71·4 E. On the Sutlej near the point where it joins the Chenáb. Consists now of three villages. But it was in early Muhammadan times a place of great importance, and a centre of learning. It is still very sacred in the eyes of Musalmáns.

## III. North West Frontier Province.

### (*a*) *Districts.*

**Abbottábád**, 34·9 N.–73·1 E. Headquarters of district and a cantonment with four battalions of Gurkhas. Population 11,506. At south end of Orash Plain 4120 feet above sea level. Appropriately named after Captain James Abbott (page 299).

**Bannu.** See Edwardesábád.

**Cherát** (**Peshávar**), 33·5 N.–71·5 E. Small hill sanitarium in Peshávar near Kohát border, 4500 feet above sea level.

**Dera Ismail Khán**, 31·5 N.–70·6 E. Headquarters of district and a cantonment. Population 35,131, including 5730 in cantonment. The Powinda caravans pass through Dera Ismail Khán on their march to and from India.

**Dungagalí** (**Hazára**), 34·6 N.–73·2 E. Small sanitarium, elevation 7800 feet, in Hazára Galis, two miles from Nathiagalí. Moshpurí rises above it to a height of 9232 feet.

**Edwardesábád** (**Bannu**), 33·0 N.–70·4 E. Headquarters of Bannu district and a cantonment. Founded by Lieutenant (afterwards Sir Herbert) Edwardes in 1848. Population 16,865. It is unhealthy owing to the heavy irrigation in the neighbourhood.

**Fort Lockhart** (**Kohát**), 33·3 N.–70·6 E. Important military outpost on Samána Range, elevation 6743 feet. Saragarhí, heroically defended by twenty-one Sikhs in 1897 against several thousand Orakzais, is in the neighbourhood.

**Kohát,** 33·3 N.–71·3 E. Headquarters of district and a cantonment. Population 22,654, including 5957 in Cantonment. On Khushálgarh—Thal Branch of N.W. Railway.

**Mansehra (Hazára),** 34·2 N.–73·1 E. Headquarters of *tahsíl*. The two rock edicts of Aşoka are in the neighbourhood (pages 163 and 202).

**Nathiagalí (Hazára),** 34·5 N.–73·6 E. Summer headquarters of Chief Commissioner of N.W.F. Province in Hazára Galís. Elevation 8200 feet. It is a beautiful little hill station. Míran Jáni (9793 feet) is close by, and on a clear day Nanga Parvat can be seen in the far distance.

**Naushahra (Peshávar),** 34 N.–72 E. Population 25,498, including 14,543 in cantonment. On railway 27 miles east of Pesháwar. Risálpura, a new cavalry cantonment, is in the neighbourhood.

**Shekhbudín,** 32·2 N.–70·5 E. Small hill station on Níla Koh on border of Dera Ismail Khán and Bannu districts. Elevation 4516 feet. It is on a bare limestone rock with very scanty vegetation and is hot in summer in the daytime. Water is scarce. The Deputy Commissioners of Bannu and Dera Ismail Khán spend part of the hot weather at Shekhbudín.

**Thal (Kohát),** 33·2 N.–70·3 E. Important military outpost at entrance of Kurram Valley. Terminus of Khushálgarh—Thal branch of N.W. Railway.

**Thandiání (Hazára),** 34·1 N.–73·2 E. Small hill station in Galís sixteen miles N.E. of Abbottábád. Elevation about 8800 feet A beautifully situated place chiefly resorted to by residents of Abbottábád and Missionaries.

## (*b*) *Agencies and Independent Territory.*

**Ali Masjid (Khaibar),** 34·2 N.–71·5 E. Village and fort in Khaibar, 10½ miles from Jamrúd. Elevation 2433 feet.

**Ambela (Indep. Territory),** 34·2 N.–72·4 E. Pass in Buner, which gave its name to the Ambela campaign of 1863 (page 191).

**Chakdarra (Dir, Swát, and Chitrál),** 34·4 N.–72·8 E. Military post to N.E. of Malakand Pass on south bank of Swát River.

**Chitrál,** 35·5 N.–71·5 E. A group of villages forming capital of Chitrál State. There is a small *bazár*.

**Jamrúd (Khaibar),** 34 N.–71·2 E. Just beyond Pesháwar boundary at mouth of Khaibar. Terminus of railway. 10½ miles west of Peshâwar. There is a fort and a large *sarai*. Elevation 1670 feet.

**Landi Kotal (Khaibar)**, 34·6 N.–71·8 E. 20 miles from Jamrúd. Fort garrisoned by Khaibar Rifles at highest point of Khaibar route. Elevation 3373 feet. Afghán frontier 6 miles beyond.

**Malakand (Dír, Swát, and Chitrál)**, 34·3 N.–71·6 E. Pass leading into Swát Valley from Pesháwar district.

**Míram Sháh (N. Wazíristán)**, 33·6 N.–70·7 E. Headquarters of North Wazíristán Agency in Tochí Valley 3050 feet above the sea.

**Parachinár (Kurram)**, 33·5 N.–70·4 E. Headquarters of Kurram Agency and of Kurram Militia. Climate temperate. Population 2354.

**Wána (S. Wazíristán)**, 37·2 N.–69·4 E. Headquarters of South Wazíristán Agency. In a wide valley watered by Wána Toi. There is much irrigation and the place is unhealthy, though the elevation of the Valley is from 4300 to 5800 feet.

## IV. Kashmír and Jammu.

**Báramúla**, 34·1 N.–74·2 E. Situated at the point where the Jhelam gorge ends and the Vale of Kashmír begins. Travellers who intend to go to Srínagar by water board their house boats here. There is an excellent poplar-lined road from Báramúla to Srínagar and a bad road to Gulmarg.

**Chilás**, 35·4 N.–74·2 E. See page 323.

**Gulmarg**, 34·1 N.–74·4 E. S.W. of Srínagar. It is a favourite hot weather resort of Europeans. The Maháraja has a house here. The forest scenery is beautiful, especially on the way to the limit of trees at Khilanmarg. Good golf links on beautiful turf.

**Gurais**, 34·7 N.–74·8 E. A beautiful valley drained by the head waters of the Kishnganga. It lies between Bandipura and the Burzil Pass on the road to Gilgit.

**Hunza**, 36·4 N.–74·7 E. (See page 323.) Hunza is a group of villages. The Rajá's (or Tham's) fort, Baltit castle, at an elevation of 7000 feet is splendidly situated in full view of Rakaposhi, distant 20 miles. It is overhung by the enormous mass of snow peaks said to be called in the language of the country Boiohagburduanasur (the peak of the galloping horse).

**Islámábád**, 33·4 N.–75·1 E. About 40 miles by river from Srínagar, near the point where the Jhelam ceases to be navigable. Achabal and Mártand are easily visited from Islámábád, and it is the starting point for the Liddar Valley and Pahlgam. It is a dirty insanitary place.

**Jammu**, 32·4 N.–74·5 E. Capital of the Jammu province and winter residence of the Mahárája. Connected with Siálkot by rail. Situated above the ravine in which the Tawí flows. At a distance the white-washed temples with gilded pinnacles look striking. The town was once much more prosperous than it is to-day.

**Leh**, 34·2 N.–77·5 E. Capital of Ladákh. On the Indus 11,500 feet above sea-level. The meeting place of caravans from India and Yárkand. The Central Asian caravans arrive in Autumn, when the *bazár*, in a wide street lined with poplars, becomes busy. The Wazír Wazárat has his headquarters here, and there is a small garrison in the mud fort. The old palace of the Gyalpo (King) is a large pile on a ridge overhanging the town. There are Moravian and Roman Catholic missions at Leh.

**Mártand**, 33·4 N.–75·1 E. Remains of a remarkable temple of the Sun god three miles east of Islámábád (pages 166 and 201).

**Payer** (erroneously **Payech**). Nineteen miles from Srínagar containing a beautiful and well-preserved temple of the Sun god, dated variously from the fifth to the thirteenth century (page 202).

**Punch**, 33·4 N.–74·9 E. Capital of the *jágír* of the Rája of Punch, a feudatory of the Kashmír State. 3300 feet above sea level. There is a brisk trade in grain and *ghí*. Decent roads connect Punch with Ráwalpindí and Urí on the Jhelam. Cart Road into Kashmír. Kashmírís call the place Prunts and its old name was Parnotsa.

**Skardo**, 35·3 N.–75·6 E. Old capital of Báltistán. 7250 feet above sea-level. In a sandy basin lying on both sides of the Indus, and about five miles in width. A *tahsíldár* is stationed at Skardo.

TABLE I. *Tribes of Panjáb (including Native States) and N.W.F. Province*[1].

| Landholding etc. | | | Traders | | | Artizans and menials | | | Impure Castes | | |
|---|---|---|---|---|---|---|---|---|---|---|---|
| Tribe | Panjáb p.c. | N.W.F. P. p.c. | Tribe | Panjáb p.c. | N.W.F. P. p.c | Tribe | Panjáb p.c. | N.W.F. P. p.c. | Tribe | Panjáb p.c. | N.W.F. P. p.c. |
| Jats ... ... | 20·5 | 3·9 | Aroras | 2·8 | 3·1 | Lohárs and Tarkháns[2] | 4·0 | 3·3 | Chúhra[8] | 5·1 | |
| Rajputs ... | 6·8 | ·7 | Khatrís | 1·8 | 1·2 | Juláhas[3] | 2·6 | 1·7 | Chamár[9] | 4·7 | |
| Arains and Kambohs ... | 4·8 | — | Banias | 1·7 | — | Jhínwar and Máchhi[4] | 2·6 | — | | | |
| Brahmans ... | 4·2 | ·6 | | | | Kumhár[5] | 2·3 | 1·0 | | | |
| Gujars ... | 2·5 | 5·2 | | | | Nai[6] | 1·4 | 1·1 | | | |
| Biloch ... | 2·2 | 1·2 | | | | Telí[7] | 1·2 | ·3 | | | |
| Awán ... | 1·8 | 12·6 | | | | | | | | | |
| Shekhs including Kureshí | 1·7 | | | | | | | | | | |
| Kanet ... | 1·7 | — | | | | | | | | | |
| Sainís, Málís, and Malliárs | 1·3 | 1·8 | | | | | | | | | |
| Patháns ... | 1·2 | 38·3 | | | | | | | | | |
| Saiyyids ... | 1·0 | 4·4 | | | | | | | | | |

[1] Only tribes amounting in number to 1 p.c. of total population shown.

[2] Blacksmiths and Carpenters. [3] Weavers. [4] Water carriers. [5] Potter.

[6] Barber. [7] Oilman. [8] Scavenger. [9] Leather-worker.

## TABLE II. *Rainfall, Cultivation, Population, and Land Revenue.*

| Zone | District | Rainfall in Inches | No. of Masonry Wells | Cultivated Area Acres 1911–12 | Classes of Cultivation, p.c. Well | Canal | *Abi* | Total Irrd. | Moist | Dry | Total Unirrd. | Population 1911 | Land Revenue in 1911–12 in hundreds of rupees |
|---|---|---|---|---|---|---|---|---|---|---|---|---|---|
| Mountain and Submontane | Kángra ... | 125 | 5 | 587,826 | — | — | 20 | 20 | — | 80 | 80 | 770,386 | 9,267 |
| | Simla ... ... | 68 | — | 9,984 | — | — | 7 | 7 | — | 93 | 93 | 39,320 | 175 |
| | Ambála ... | 35 | 2,154 | 750.515 | 4 | — | 2 | 6 | 4 | 90 | 94 | 689,970 | 11,477 |
| | Hoshyárpur ... | 36 | 6,841 | 722,122 | 5 | 2 | 1 | 8 | — | 92 | 92 | 918,569 | 14,225 |
| | Total British dts. Panjáb ... | — | 9,000 | 2,070,447 | 3 | 1 | 6½ | 10½ | 1½ | 88 | 89½ | 2,418,245 | 35,144 (1.10.0[1]) |
| | Hazára (N.W.F. P.) | 46 | 353 | 430,872 | — | — | 10 | 10 | — | 90 | 90 | 603,028 | 5,129 (1. 3. 1) |
| | Kashmír and Jammu ... | 35[3] | — | 1,750,056 | — | — | — | 32 | — | — | 68 | 2,893,066 | — |
| | Indus Valley[2] | 5[4] | — | 121,952 | — | — | — | — | — | — | 100 | 210,315[5] | — |
| | Total Kashmír | — | — | 1,872,008 | — | — | — | 30 | — | — | 70 | 3,103,381 | — |
| North Central Panjáb Plain (British Districts) | Gujrát ... | 28 | 10,221 | 845,023 | 26 | — | — | 26 | 6 | 68 | 74 | 784,011 | 8,445 |
| | Siálkot ... | 35 | 23,010 | 941,558 | 54 | 1 | 3 | 58 | 9 | 33 | 42 | 979,553 | 14,847 |
| | Gurdáspur ... | 35 | 6,439 | 844,403 | 16 | 11 | — | 27 | 14 | 59 | 73 | 836,771 | 15,410 |
| | Amritsar ... | 24 | 12,386 | 787,229 | 31 | 31 | — | 62 | 4 | 34 | 38 | 880,728 | 12,746 |
| | Jalandhar ... | 28 | 28,289 | 695,571 | 44 | — | — | 44 | 5 | 51 | 56 | 801,920 | 14,871 |
| | Ludhiána ... | 28 | 9,991 | 754,373 | 19 | 7 | — | 26 | 4 | 70 | 74 | 517,192 | 11,103 |
| | Total ... ... | — | 90,336 | 4,868,157 | 32 | 8 | 1 | 41 | 7 | 52 | 59 | 4,800,175 | 77,422 (1. 9. 5) |

| | | | | | | | | | | | | | |
|---|---|---|---|---|---|---|---|---|---|---|---|---|---|
| North-West Area | Ráwalpindí ... | 33 | 947 | 598,371 | ½ | — | ½ | 1 | — | 99 | 99 | 547,827 | 6,754 |
| | Jhelam ... | 26 | 4,103 | 754,585 | 4 | — | — | 4 | 4 | 92 | 96 | 511,175 | 7,576 |
| | Attock ... | 19 | 6,850 | 1,031,962 | 2½ | — | 1 | 3½ | 1 | 96 | 97 | 519,273 | 6,741 |
| | Mianwálí ... | 12 | 7,128 | 748,255 | 17 | 2 | — | 19 | 38½ | 42½ | 81 | 341,377 | 4,866 |
| | Total Panjáb | — | 19,028 | 3,133,173 | 6 | ½ | ½ | 7 | 10 | 83 | 93 | 1,919,652 | 25,937 (o. 13. 3) |
| | Pesháwar ... | 13 | 6,597 | 894,803 | 5 | 33 | ½ | 38½ | 2 | 59½ | 61½ | 865,009 | 11,375 |
| | Kohát ... | 18 | 467 | 327,949 | ½ | — | 12 | 12½ | ½ | 87 | 87½ | 222,690 | 2,755 |
| | Bannu ... | 13 | 11 | 523,688 | — | 24 | — | 24 | — | 76 | 76 | 256,086 | 3,040 |
| | Total N.W.F.P. | — | 7,075 | 1,746,440 | 3 | 24½ | 2½ | 30 | 1 | 69 | 70 | 1,343,785 | 17,170 (o. 15. 8) |
| South-Western Plains | Gujránwála ... | 24 | 10,926 | 1,179,348 | 37 | 40 | — | 77 | 4 | 19 | 23 | 923,419 | 10,497 |
| | Lahore ... | 21 | 13,828 | 1,462,108 | 31 | 43½ | 1 | 75½ | 5 | 19½ | 24½ | 1,036,158 | 11,301 |
| | Sháhpur ... | 14 | 6,403 | 1,267,566 | 14 | 55 | — | 69 | 6 | 25 | 31 | 648,989 | 8,701 |
| | Jhang... ... | 10 | 11,588 | 723,733 | 36 | 46 | — | 82 | 16 | 2 | 18 | 515,526 | 6,429 |
| | Lyallpur ... | 9 | 121 | 1,373,892 | — | 99 | — | 99 | 1 | — | 1 | 857,711 | 12,736 |
| | Montgomery ... | 10 | 10,472 | 815,355 | 27 | 28 | 1 | 56 | 25 | 19 | 44 | 555,219 | 6,225 |
| | Multán ... | 7 | 20,132 | 1,081,030 | 58½ | 26 | 1 | 85½ | 13½ | 1 | 14½ | 814,871 | 15,865 |
| | Muzaffargarh | 6 | 14,053 | 553,643 | 36 | 33 | 4 | 73 | 27 | — | 27 | 569,461 | 7,316 |
| | Dera Ghází Khán | 6 | 9,564 | 1,035,011 | 25½ | 16 | 2½ | 42 | 53½ | 2½ | 56 | 499,860 | 5,752 |
| | Total Panjáb districts | — | 97,087 | 9,491,686 | 28 | 46 | 1 | 75 | 14½ | 10½ | 25 | 6,420,814 | 84,822 (o. 14. 4) |
| | D.I. Khán N.W.F.P. | 8 | 795 | 544,746 | 1 | 17 | 8 | 26 | 11 | 63 | 74 | 256,120 | 3,062 (o. 9. 0) |
| South-Eastern Plains (British Districts) | Karnál ... | 30 | 7,827 | 1,148,876 | 13 | 21 | — | 34 | 10 | 56 | 66 | 799,787 | 10,833 |
| | Delhi[6] ... ... | — | 7,133 | 555,057 | 19 | 18 | — | 37 | 6 | 57 | 63 | 657,604 | 8,563 |
| | Gurgaon ... | 26 | 6,594 | 988,613 | 13 | 10 | 1 | 24 | 3½ | 72½ | 76 | 643,177 | 12,182 |
| | Rohtak ... | 21 | 2,450 | 974,200 | 4½ | 30 | — | 34½ | — | 65½ | 65½ | 541,489 | 9,660 |
| | Hissár ... | 16 | 720 | 2,691,478 | — | 11¼ | — | 11¼ | 2¼ | 86½ | 88¾ | 804,809 | 8,582 |
| | Ferozepore ... | 21 | 7,940 | 2,248,322 | 7 | 40½ | — | 47½ | 2 | 50½ | 52½ | 959,657 | 12,066 |
| | Total Panjáb districts | — | 32,664 | 8,606,546 | 7 | 22½ | — | 29½ | 3½ | 67 | 70½ | 4,306,523 | 61,886 (o. 11. 6) |

[1] Rate per cultivated acre in rupees (Rupee 1 = 16 pence). [2] = Ladákh, Baltistán, Astor, and Gilgit. [3] At Jammu. [4] At Gilgit. Leh 3, Skardo 5. [5] Including Frontier *Ilάka* 264,750. [6] The Delhi district has been broken up, and, with the exception of the area now administered by the Government of India, has been divided between Rohtak and Gurgaon.

## TABLE III. *Diagrams relating to Cultivation.*

### PANJÁB

(*a*) Harvests and Irrigation

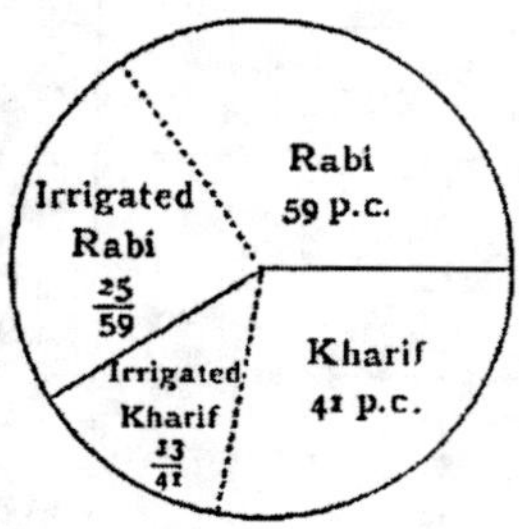


### N.W.F. PROVINCE

(*a*) Harvests

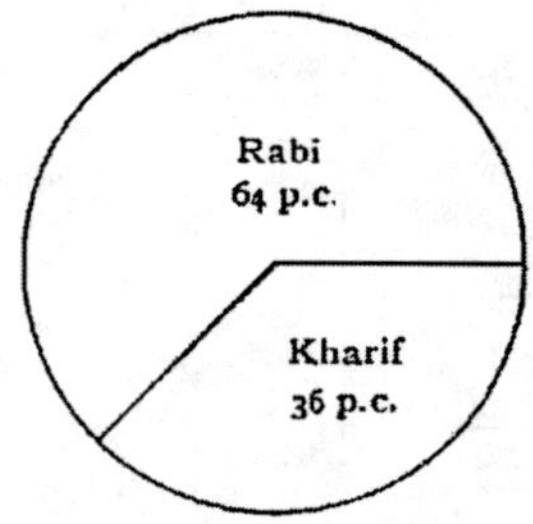


### PANJÁB

(*b*) Classes of Land

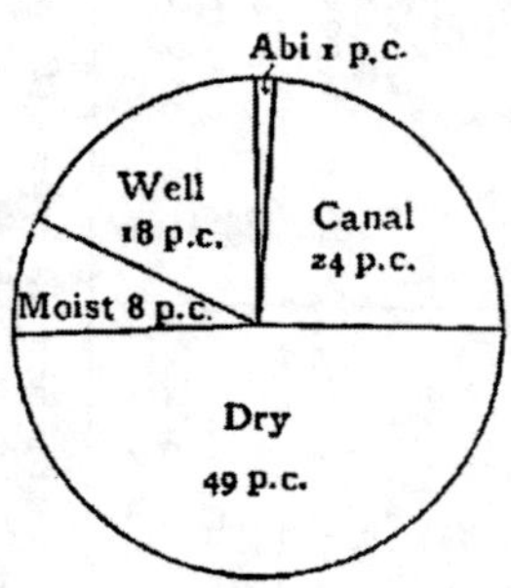


### N.W.F. PROVINCE

(*b*) Classes of Land

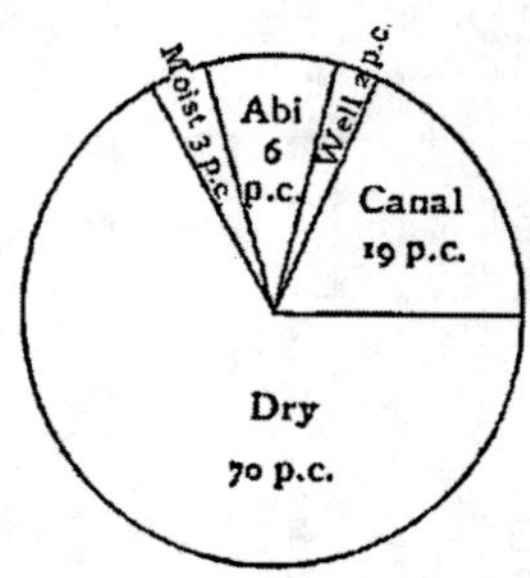

TABLE III (*continued*).

*Diagrams relating to Cultivation.*

PANJÁB

(*c*) Crops

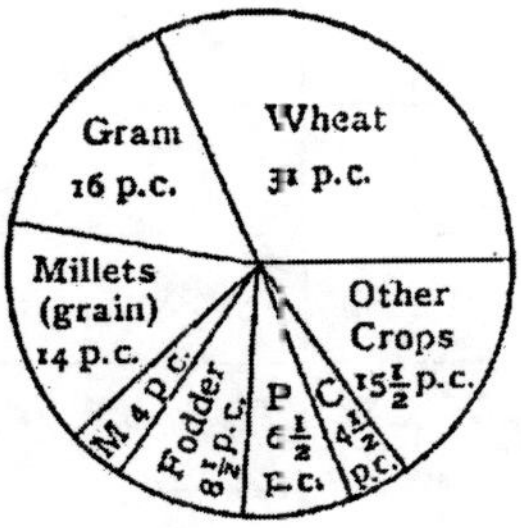


P = Other Pulses

C = Cotton

M = Maize

N.W.F. PROVINCE

(*c*) Crops

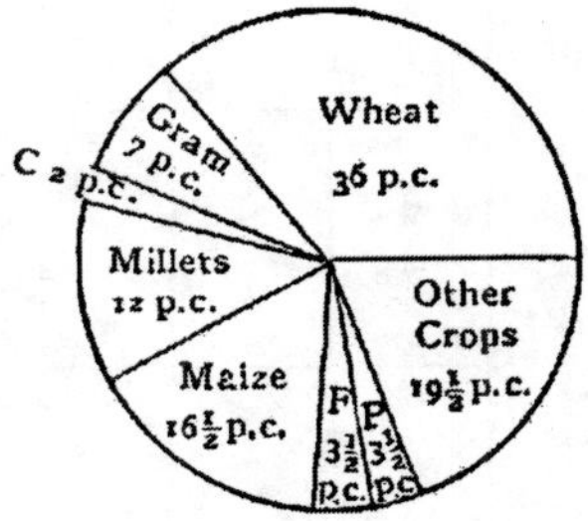


P = Other Pulses

C = Cotton

F = Fodder

## Table IV. *Percentages of Principal Crops*[1].

| Zone | Districts | Wheat | Barley | Rape *Toria* and *Tara mira* | Pulses |  | Fodder (both harvests) | Maize | Millets |  | Rice | Cotton | Cane | Other Crops (both harvests) |
|---|---|---|---|---|---|---|---|---|---|---|---|---|---|---|
|  |  |  |  |  | Gram | Other Pulses (both harvests) |  |  | *Bájra* | *Jowár* |  |  |  |  |
| Mountain and Submontane Zone | Kángra ... ... | 32 | 7 | 1 | 4 | 4 | — | 21 | — | — | 15 | ½ | 1 | 14½ |
|  | Simla ... ... | 31 | 15 | — | — | 3 | — | 13 | — | — | 6 | — | — | 32 |
|  | Ambála ... ... | 26 | 2 | 1 | 17 | 9 | 11 | 10½ | 1½ | 1 | 7 | 6 | 2 | 6 |
|  | Hoshyárpur ... ... | 33 | 1½ | 1 | 17 | 5 | 7 | 17½ | ½ | 1 | 4 | 2 | 3 | 7½ |
|  | Total Panjáb districts | 30 | 3 | 1 | 13 | 6 | 6 | 16 | ½ | ½ | 8 | 3 | 2 | 11 |
|  | Hazára N.W.F.P. ... | 26 | 10 | 1 | — | 10 | 1½ | 43 | 1½ | 1 | 3 | 1 | — | 2 |
|  | Kashmír and Jammu | 21 | 4 | — | 7 |  | — | 38 | — | — | 9 | — | — | 21 |
|  | Indus Valley ... | 29 | 4 | — | 12 |  | — | 7 | — | — | 1 | — | — | 47 |
|  | Total Kashmír ... | 23 | 4 | — | 8 |  | — | 35½ | — | — | 8 | — | — | 21½ |
| North Central Panjáb Plain (British districts) | Gujrát ... ... | 42 | 4 | 1 | 8 | 7 | 8 | 2½ | 15 | 6 | 1 | 1½ | 1 | 1 |
|  | Siálkot ... ... | 43 | 6 | 1 | 3 | 5 | 15 | 8 | 1½ | 1½ | 6½ | 2 | 4 | 3½ |
|  | Gurdáspur ... ... | 36 | 4 | 1 | 7 | 13 | 11 | 8 | ½ | ½ | 6½ | 1 | 7 | 4½ |
|  | Amritsar ... ... | 36 | 2 | 3 | 16 | 3 | 20 | 5 | — | — | 4½ | 4 | 3 | 3½ |
|  | Jalandhar ... ... | 33 | 1 | — | 15 | 7 | 23 | 10 | — | — | — | 3½ | 3½ | 4 |
|  | Ludhiána ... ... | 28 | 2 | 2 | 3 | 8 | 11 | 7 | ½ | 3 | — | 2 | 2 | 12 |
|  | Total ... ... | 37 | 3 | 1 | 11 | 8 | 14 | 7 | 3 | 2 | 3 | 2½ | 3½ | 4½ |

| | | | | | | | | | | | | | | |
|---|---|---|---|---|---|---|---|---|---|---|---|---|---|---|
| North-West Area | Rawalpindí ... ... | 41 | 2 | 1 | 1 | 19 | 2½ | 8 | 17 | 4 | — | 1 | — | 3½ |
| | Jhelam ... ... | 47 | 2 | 2 | 3 | 10 | 5 | 1 | 21 | 2 | — | 2 | — | 5 |
| | Attock ... ... | 50 | 2 | 2 | 9 | 7½ | 2½ | 2½ | 19 | 2½ | — | 2 | — | 1 |
| | Mianwálí ... ... | 34 | 4 | 3 | 19 | 10 | 2 | — | 19 | 4 | — | ½ | — | 4½ |
| | Total Panjáb districts | 43 | 2 | 2 | 7 | 11 | 3½ | 3 | 19 | 3 | — | 1½ | — | 5 |
| | Pesháwar ... ... | 36½ | 16 | 1 | 1 | 3 | 7 | 18½ | 1 | 4½ | 1½ | 4 | 3 | 3 |
| | Kohát ... ... | 43 | 2½ | 1 | 5 | 4 | 2 | 8 | 27½ | 2 | 1 | 1 | — | 3 |
| | Bannu ... ... | 49 | 4 | — | 24 | ½ | 4 | 8 | 3 | 1¼ | ½ | ½ | 1¼ | 4 |
| | Total N.W.F. P. ... | 41 | 10 | 1 | 8½ | 2½ | 5 | 13½ | 6 | 3 | 1 | 2½ | 2 | 4 |
| South-Western Plains | Gujránwála ... ... | 40 | 3 | 4 | 15½ | 3 | 12 | 2½ | 2½ | 3 | 5 | 5 | 2½ | 2 |
| | Lahore ... ... | 37 | 1 | 6 | 16 | 1 | 15 | 4½ | 1 | 1 | 2½ | 9 | 1 | 5 |
| | Shahpur ... ... | 44 | 1 | 7 | 7 | 3 | 10 | 2 | 10 | 3½ | 1 | 8 | ½ | 3 |
| | Jhang ... ... | 47 | 1 | 2 | 4½ | 4 | 10 | 2 | 2 | 8 | ½ | 5½ | — | 13½ |
| | Lyallpur ... ... | 42½ | ½ | 13 | 8 | 2½ | 5 | 4½ | ½ | 1 | — | 9 | 2½ | 11 |
| | Montgomery ... | 41 | 1½ | 2 | 13 | 4½ | 17 | 3 | 1 | 2 | 3 | 5 | — | 7 |
| | Multán ... ... | 41 | 1 | 2 | 4 | 6 | 13 | ½ | 4 | 8 | 3 | 9 | — | 8½ |
| | Muzaffargarh ... | 44½ | 3 | 2 | 8 | 10 | 7 | — | 3 | 2 | 7 | 6 | 1 | 6½ |
| | Dera Ghází Khán ... | 27 | 1 | 10 | 3½ | 5½ | 5 | — | 9 | 23 | 8 | 6 | — | 2 |
| | Total Panjáb districts | 40½ | 1½ | 6 | 9 | 4 | 10 | 2 | 3½ | 4 | 3 | 7 | 1 | 8½ |
| | D.I. Khán N.W.F. P. | 31 | 2 | 13 | 8 | 3 | ½ | — | 22 | 9 | — | 2 | — | 9½ |
| South-Eastern Plains (British Districts) | Karnál ... ... | 21 | 2 | 5 | 26½ | 4½ | 6½ | 5½ | 5 | 11½ | 4 | 6 | 2 | ½ |
| | Rohtak ... ... | 8 | 2½ | 1 | 34½ | 7 | 2 | — | 21 | 14 | — | 6½ | 2 | 1½ |
| | Gurgáon ... ... | 8 | 13 | 1½ | 20 | 12 | 4 | — | 25 | 5 | — | 8 | ½ | 3 |
| | Hissar ... ... | 4 | 7 | 4 | 28 | 8 | 4 | — | 26 | 6½ | — | 3 | — | 9½ |
| | Ferozepore ... ... | 28 | 7 | 4 | 31½ | 4 | 8 | 2½ | 3 | 6 | — | — | — | 6 |
| | Total Panjáb districts | 14 | 6 | 3 | 28½ | 7 | 5 | 1½ | 15 | 8 | ½ | 3½ | ½ | 7½ |
| | Grand total Panjáb | 31 | 3½ | 4 | 16 | 6½ | 8½ | 4 | 9 | 5 | 2½ | 4½ | 1½ | 4 |
| | „ N.W.F. P. | 36 | 8½ | 3 | 7 | 3½ | 3½ | 16½ | 8 | 4 | 1 | 2 | 1 | 6 |

[1] In case of Panjáb districts figures relate to *Kharif* 1910 and *Rabi* 1911.

## TABLE V. *Revenue and Expenditure*, 1911–12.

| Heads | Income | | | Expenditure | | |
|---|---|---|---|---|---|---|
| | Total in Rs. 000 | Provincial | | Total in Rs. 000 | Provincial | |
| | | Share | Amount in Rs. 000 | | Share | Amount in Rs. 000 |
| Land Revenue ... | 3,47,92 | Half | 1,73,96 | 47,76 | Whole | 47,76 |
| Salt ... ... | 38,16 | Nil | — | 4,82 | Nil | — |
| Stamps ... ... | 52,57 | Half | 26,29 | 1,77 | Half | 89 |
| Excise ... ... | 64,00 | Half | 32,00 | 1,71 | Half | 86 |
| Income-tax .... | 16,22 | Half | 8,11 | 11 | Half | 5 |
| Forests ... ... | 13,10 | Whole | 13,10 | 7,64 | Whole | 7,65 |
| Registration ... | 3,16 | Whole | 3,16 | 1,20 | Whole | 1,20 |
| General Administration ... | — | — | — | 18,33 | Various | 13,65 |
| Law and Justice —Courts ... | 4,35 | Whole | 4,35 | 42,18 | Whole | 42,18 |
| Law and Justice —Jails ... | 3,41 | Whole | 3,41 | 12,24 | Whole | 12,24 |
| Police ... ... | 1,80 | Whole | 1,80 | 58,57 | Whole | 58,57 |
| Education ... | 3,64 | Whole | 3,64 | 23,27 | Whole | 23,27 |
| Irrigation— Major Works | 2,13,08 | Half | 1,06,54 | 1,36,42 | Half | 68,21 |
| Irrigation— Minor Works | 7,99 | Various | 56 | 11,17 | Various | 1,07 |
| Civil Works ... | 6,93 | Various | 6,20 | 67,90 | Various | 62,70 |
| Medical ... ... | — | — | — | 21,20 | Whole | 21,20 |
| All other heads[1] | 27,60 | Nil and various | 15,21 | 56,96 | Whole, various, and nil | 41,29 |
| Total ... ... | 8,03,93 | — | 3,99,33 | 5,13,25 | — | 4,02,79 |

[1] Under Income "Salt," "Tribute," "Interest," "Miscellaneous," and "All other heads." Under Expenditure "Political," "Scientific," "Pensions," "Stationery," "All other items."

**Note.** More complete and accurate details of mountains and glaciers of Muztagh-Karakoram Range will be found in the sketch map appended to Dr Arthur Neve's *Thirty Years in Kashmir*, published in 1913.

Cambridge University Press

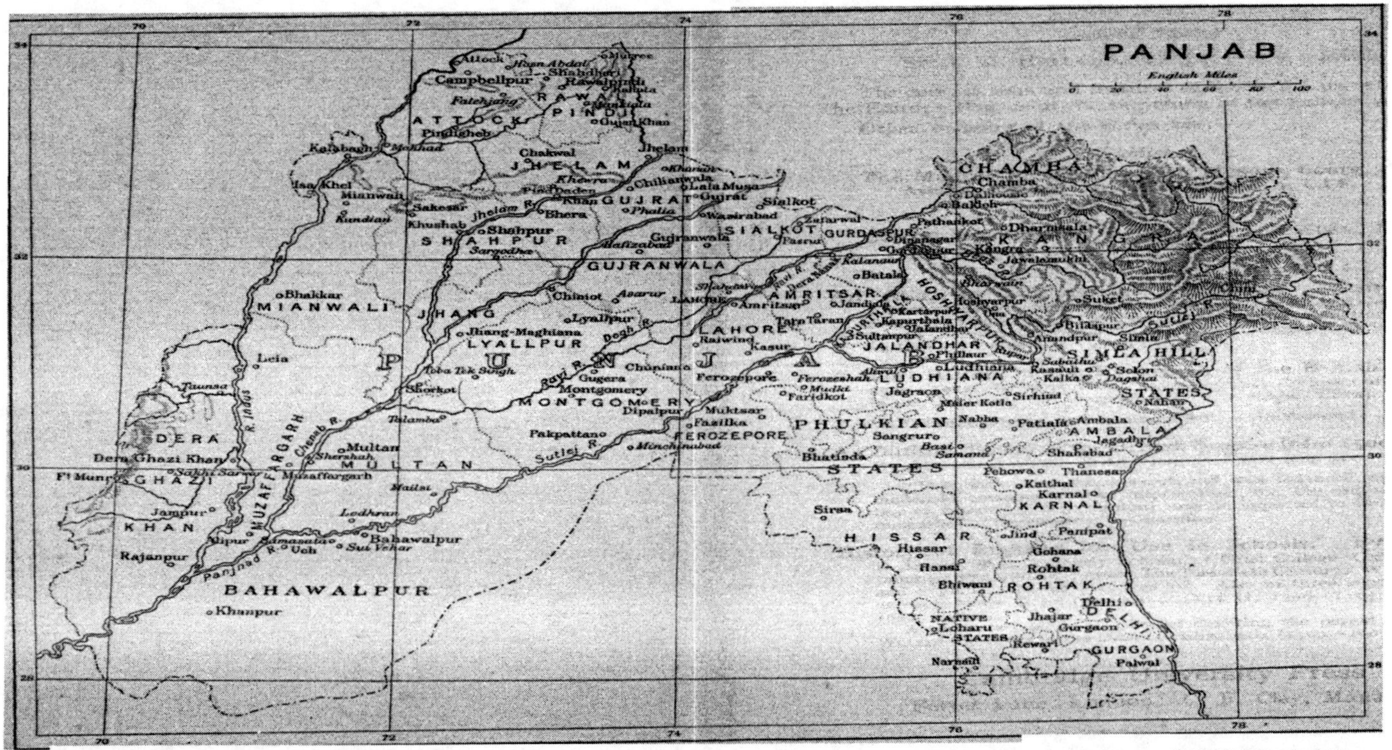


Cambridge University Press

# INDEX

IN PREPARATION

# THE CAMBRIDGE HISTORY OF INDIA

In six volumes, royal 8vo, of between 500 and 600 pages each. With maps (inserted in the text), and abundantly illustrated. Bound in Buckram. Price 15s net per volume.

## THE EARLY HINDU PERIOD,

under the editorship of Professor E. J. RAPSON, M.A.

Vol. I. Ancient India, from the earliest historical times to about the beginning of the Christian era.

Vol. II. Medieval India, from about the beginning of the Christian era to the Muhammadan conquests in the 11th century A.D.

## THE MUHAMMADAN PERIOD,

under the editorship of Lieut.-Col. T. W. HAIG, C.M.G.

Vol. III. Turks and Afghans, from the end of the 10th century A.D. to the conquest of Northern India by Bābar, A.D. 1525.

Vol. IV. The Mughal Empire, from A.D. 1525 to 1757.

## BRITISH INDIA,

under the editorship of Sir THEODORE MORISON, K.C.I.E.

Vol. V. The Honourable East India Company.

Vol. VI. India under the Crown.

*Terms to subscribers*

The subscription price for the whole work will be £3 12s net; payable in six instalments of 12s net each, one instalment becoming due on publication of each of the volumes.

**Cambridge University Press**

Fetter Lane, London: C. F. Clay, Manager